MULTIPROCESSORS AND PARALLEL PROCESSING

Multiprocessors and Parallel Processing

COMTRE CORPORATION   Philip H. Enslow, Jr., *Editor*

A WILEY-INTERSCIENCE PUBLICATION

JOHN WILEY & SONS, New York • London • Sydney • Toronto

Library of Congress Cataloging in Publication Data:

Comtre Corporation.
  Multiprocessors and parallel processing.

  "A Wiley-Interscience publication."
  1. Parallel processing (Electronic computers)
I. Enslow, Philip H., 1933–   ed.
II. Title.

QA76.6.C64   1974   001.6′4   73-18147
ISBN 0-471-16735-5

Printed in the United States of America

10 9 8 7 6 5 4 3 2 1

PREFACE

With the growing importance and availability of multiprocessor digital computer systems, the computer professional who has not actually been working with one or more of these systems finds himself at a distinct disadvantage in understanding their overall significance as well as the significance of specific details of individual systems as they are presented in the normal sales-oriented literature. There is no question of the important role that multiprocessors will play in the future of digital computer systems of all sizes and capabilities. The goal of this book is to prepare the reader for the "age of the multiprocessor." That is not meant to be a claim or even a prediction that multiprocessors will take over the entire market for new systems or even that they will necessarily become the dominant factor in it; however, as contrasted with the past when multiprocessors were something of a unique curiosity, they will become commonplace in the future for both their performance and cost-effectiveness characteristics as well as other features such as reliability and availability.

The U.S. Air Force has long been a developer and user of multiprocessor systems. Much of the earliest work in this field was financed by the U.S. Air Force to develop the machines required for their highly critical command and control systems. Some of these early projects were the Ramo-Wooldridge RW-400 (the "Polymorphic Computer"), the SAGE system, the Strategic Air Command Control System, and the Burroughs D 825. These were all large, immobile systems; however, the U.S. Air Force, recognizing the size and capability trends in digital hardware, would like to utilize multiprocessor systems at lower levels of command that are mobile but still require the reliability and availability provided by the multiprocessor system. Several projects have been directed at automating the Tactical Air Control Center. One of these, "Development of Selection and Evaluation Criteria for a Multiprocessor as the Post-1985 TACC Central Com-

v

puter System" was performed by the COMTRE Corporation (Contract F19628-70-C-0370). The final reports were published on April 30, 1971, in "Technical Report—Derivation of Selection Criteria and Comparative Analysis," TR-5700-03 (2 volumes) and "Technical Report—Multiprocessor Test Requirements," TR-5700-04. Although the main thrust of the study work performed was toward the specific application of multiprocessors to the TACC, the comparative analyses presented in the appendix to the COMTRE report were extensive in nature and covered both commercial and military systems as examples of the state-of-the-art. These comparative analyses formed the basis for the appendix to this book as well as the motivation for the preparation of this monograph.

This text has several unusual unique features.

- It is the only work devoted entirely to a discussion of multiprocessors.
- It is the only source providing a complete treatment of multiprocessor system organization covering both hardware and software.
- It illustrates how the multiprocessor is a logical result of the efforts to increase computer performance by the use and exploitation of concurrency and parallelism in both program execution and in hardware.
- It provides a succinct discussion of most of the major multiprocessor systems now in production.

PHILIP H. ENSLOW, JR.
Editor

London, England
January 1974

ACKNOWLEDGMENT

The coverage of a subject area as broad as multiprocessors would be impossible without a large amount of assistance. All of the manufacturers involved have participated in the review of the descriptions of their own systems. However, many other individuals have provided substantive input to the main portion of the text. I would like to thank specifically Elmer Branyan, Harvey Cragon, Ken G. Day, A. U. Elser, Jr., John W. Esch, Robert A. Mosier, E. Rudofsky, John E. Schier, R. Stoke, Joe Watson, and Jay Wolf for their greatly appreciated assistance.

PHILIP H. ENSLOW, JR.
Editor

I acknowledge the considerable efforts of those staff members of The Comtre Corporation who participated in the various post 1985 Multiprocessor system studies leading to this book. Special thanks are due to Harry C. Collins for his great contribution, to Steve Tatusko for his cooperation, to Thomas G. Shack, Jr. for his counsel, and Jane Otto and Lana Hutton for their unending secretarial support, without whom this book could have not been possible. In addition, I thank the Editor, Dr. Philip H. Enslow, Jr., for his dedicated and effective work on this project. Lastly, an expression of gratitude to TeleDynamics Inc. for their valuable assistance. This book is dedicated to individuals in search of tomorrow's visions who synthesize today's applications.

M. JAMES ERRICO
President, The Comtre Corporation

CONTENTS

CHAPTER 1
MOTIVATION FOR MULTI-PROCESSOR AND PARALLEL PROCESSING SYSTEMS

IMPROVING SYSTEM PERFORMANCE

In response to the ever-increasing requirements for digital computer systems that can handle larger problems in less time with higher reliability, the design of the systems has been advanced in several distinct but interrelated areas:

- *Devices and circuits.* New or improved devices that can be used in faster and more reliable circuits that provide the fundamental building blocks for the logic designer.
- *Systems architecture.* Algorithms for executing the basic functions such as the arithmetic and logic operations.
- *Systems organization.* The topology of the interconnection of the major assemblies such as the control unit, memory modules, input/output controllers, and arithmetic and logic unit; also the specification of the rules governing the flow of data and control signals between these units and the possibility of allowing multiple simultaneous paths.
- *System software.* The control and support programs required for maximum utilization of the hardware capabilities inherent in the system.

This book focuses on one technique used in improving system organization, the integration of multiple functional units into a multiprocessing or parallel processing system. Although it will be necessary to amplify the

1

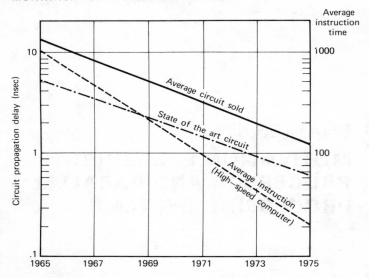

Figure 1-1 Improvements in performance factors. (Based on data from Quantum Science Corp.)

definition later, for the time being, a multiprocessor or parallel processor can be sufficiently defined as a unified system containing more than one processing element capable of simultaneous operation. Although the emphasis of this book is on the physical organization of these systems, it is impossible to consider that topic in a vacuum. There must also be some discussion of architecture and software where appropriate. The complete treatment of these last two topics, however, would consume much more space than desirable, and the reader is asked to bear in mind that this text is primarily an exposition on system organization.

PERFORMANCE TRENDS

Major advances in circuit performance have been made on a regular rate for the past 20 years. The improvement has been recorded as a factor of 10 per decade. However, utilizing improvements in basic architecture (better algorithms and higher speed implementations), the increase in speed in executing the basic functions, that is, the average instruction speed, has been improving at a rate three times as high in large-scale high-speed computers. Figure 1–1 illustrates these two factors as well as the improvement of state-of-the-art circuits which are not reflected in production units for 4 to 5 years. Note that the state-of-the-art improvements are less than those for "average circuits sold." It is in recognition of this prospect for the future that more emphasis is being placed on algorithms that will exploit concurrency in operation to maintain the overall rate of improvement in average instruction execution time.

In 1944, the Mark I, a relay computer, required 333 msec to complete one addition. In 7 years this was improved by a factor of more than a thousand; the UNIVAC I in 1951 required 282 μsec for an addition. Another thousandfold improvement was demonstrated by the CDC 6600 in 1964 which reduced the add time to 300 nsec. Can this thousandfold improvement be repeated to produce a machine with an add time of 300 pisec? That is very unlikely, since the maximum velocity at which electrical signals can propagate will intervene. An electrical signal will travel only a little less than 12 in./nsec. Then 300 pisec will allow the signal to travel less than 4 in. during the entire instruction execution time. This might be achieved within the adder alone, but consideration must also be given to the time that it takes for the signal to get from the memory to the adder, for 4 in. would certainly not permit a very large storage unit. There must be other solutions rather than circuit execution time. The most likely candidates for further major increases in affective operating speeds are simultaneous or concurrent operations.

CONCURRENCY* *Introduction*

Because, at any point in time, device and circuit technology is fixed with respect to speed and reliability, the immediate goal of systems architecture, organization, and software is to create a system which allows the parallel, concurrent, or simultaneous execution of tasks and then exploits this capability. This goal is common to the development of all large-scale systems, not just multiprocessors.

Concurrency is desirable, and attainable in varying degrees, in all types of operations that the system must perform:

- Concurrent execution of several different user programs (multiprogramming).
- Input/output operations simultaneous with execution of user programs (overlapped input/output, spooling).
- Multiple input/output operations to include data communications being executed simultaneously.

---

* Two terms that create some confusion in their use are concurrent and simultaneous. Concurrent events occur during the *same interval* of time; simultaneous events occur at the *same instant* of time.

- Concurrency of central processor operations in general.

The two approaches that have been used in attaining the latter goal have been:

- Parallelism where functional units are replicated and operated concurrently on different problems (the basis of multiprocessing).
- Pipelining where each instruction is broken down into its elemental parts and an operation on a stream of data is executed incrementally as each operand passes a station in the pipeline.

Concurrency is an extremely cost-effective means to improve system performance. It is not unusual for all modern systems, even minicomputers, to have simultaneous or overlapped input/out capabilities. Other forms of concurrency, originally developed and implemented in large systems, will also spread to the smaller ones as the user demands increased performance by the smaller machines. ⎤ End of Introduction

IMPROVING RELIABILITY AND AVAILABILITY

The requirement for high reliability, or more specifically high availability, of the minimum configuration required to perform the essential workload, has been the motivation for much of the work done in the area of multi-processors—development, equipment, system organization, application program control, and system software. The system designs that have resulted from work focused specifically on this requirement have been known as "fault-tolerant."

The requirements for high reliability and availability for the on-board computers in the manned space vehicles have certainly been the prime motivation for the NASA research programs in multiprocessors. The NASA work was centered at the former NASA Electronics Research Center in Cambridge, Mass., and at the Charles Stark Draper Laboratory (Instrumentation Laboratory) of the Massachusetts Institute of Technology [Filene et al., Hopkins, and Miller et al.] In this work, the increased throughput attainable from multiprocessor systems was not exploited, since the separate units were utilized primarily to check the performance of one another. Some of the general system organizations developed under this program are described below in the discussion of various hardware system organizations.

There are two general approaches to obtaining high reliability and the resultant high availability for the entire system or a major portion of it. These two methods are best described as reconfigurable systems or duplexed systems. Nearly all of the multiprocessor system organizations discussed in Chapter 2 provide or implement the first method only. This technique utilizes several identical units or components of each type organized and interconnected so that each of them can execute different programs. The resulting system then "gracefully degrades" in performance or throughput capability, as it is reconfigured and the workload redistributed as individual functional units fail. Of course, to identify a failure, each hardware or software unit must include complete error detection capabilities. The other approach known as duplexing is to operate two or more of each functional unit or complete system in parallel on the same problem and data. Any disagreement in the answers obtained by the separate units will be the first indication of a failure. Complete checks can then be made, and the malfunctioning unit removed from operation to be serviced if possible. The throughput is not degraded, since the duplicate unit is still capable of performing the entire workload (although there is now a reduced error checking capability). The duplicate or parallel functional units utilized in the duplexing method may be interconnected in a manner very similar to that of other multiprocessors; however, to protect against failures in the interconnection means, special organizations have been developed and are described below following a discussion of the more common arrangements.

In addition to the high-reliability and availability requirements of manned space flight, similar requirements are placed on the systems installed by the Federal Aviation Administration for Air Traffic Control (FAA–ATC) [Dancy]. However, in ATC the requirement for fault-tolerance is coupled with a requirement for very large capacities which are not applicable at the present time to on-board computers. Since physical size constraints are not as critical in the ground environment, and delivery time and cost-effectiveness are more important factors, the FAA has utilized existing or only slightly modified standard equipment. These factors have resulted in system designs for ATC that provide only a small amount of excess or redundant capability that can be utilized to maintain capacity while the failed unit is repaired. The use of 100% backup which is common in space computers is not normally utilized in this area.

Military command and control systems have requirements similar to the ATC system. The early military systems that were involved in critical applications such as SAGE and BMEWS utilized completely duplexed systems; however, the trend is toward multiprocessors because they offer more cost-effective solutions.

The uniprocessor is basically unreliable because of its single-thread organization. As a minimum, duplex operation is necessary to achieve high reliability and availability. This is often a wasteful approach, since the added equipment does not add to the productivity of the overall system. The multiprocessor organization overcomes this inefficiency factor by providing that all of its functional units work on different programs until something fails. Then the system can execute the most essential tasks by reconfiguring even though its total capabilities have been decreased. In instances where it is critical to maintain the same operational capabilities, there will be one or two spares for each type of functional unit that can be utilized when others fail.

SINGLE-COMPUTER SYSTEMS

To understand the functional characteristics and capabilities of multiprocessors, the reader must have a firm understanding of single-computer system architecture. It is amazing how many practioners of the art of programming, and even of hardware, do not have such knowledge. Before reading the discussion of multicomputer systems, it is strongly recommended that the reader review these concepts and implementations as they have been developed to produced third-generation single-computer systems.

The early systems performed all of their input and output operations primarily by reading cards and preparing printed output and punched cards. There are two characteristics of these types of operations that greatly affect the performance of the overall system. The first, and most commonly thought of, are the slow transfer rates possible with card equipment and printers. Even *today's* best high-speed equipment restricts transfer rates to the following:

- *Card readers*. 800 to 1400 80-column cards/min or 1400 characters/sec (1050 cpm).
- *Card punches*. 300 to 600/cpm or 700 characters/sec (525 cpm).
- *Line printers*. 1000 to 2000, 120 to 132 character lines/min or 3600 charcters/sec (1500 lpm).*

However, very stringent timing constraints in presenting the output to the punch or printer usually limits performance to a rate much lower than those shown. In any event, the rates are very slow, and the processor was often idle waiting for input or outputting of results.

Even the earliest magnetic tape driver attached to large-scale systems had

---

* Omitted from this list is computer output microfilm equipment (COM). Such equipment does provide much higher output rates for special applications; however, it is not yet in general use.

transfer rates of 15,000 characters/sec and higher. The logical path was then followed. A separate, special-purpose, off-line unit was built that would read the 80-column card and write it on the tape in a direct image, an 80-character block. This tape could then be used as the input to the large system in lieu of cards. Similar, but separate and unique devices were also built to convert output tapes to punched cards or printed copy. The transfer rate problem had been alleviated; however, one old problem still remained and a new one was created.

The original problem was still unsolved. The format of the data on the input and output tapes coming from and going to the converters still had the characteristics of data going directly to and from unit record equipment (cards and printers). It was all in relatively small blocks, and a lot of time was spent in moving the tape past interblock gaps. The utilization of even low-performance tape was only about 20% which reduced the transfer rate to 3000 characters/sec. (For the present high-performance units in use today, the rate would be down to 6%.) These special converters did not have the capability to create multicard (multirecord) blocks or to break them down on output.

The new problem was the cost of the three special converters which often were not utilized very much but which were essential to this type of operation.

Though a gross oversimplification, it is reasonable to say that one of the primary motivating factors behind the development of all multicomputer systems was that of relieving the unit-record I/O load from the main processor. Before discussing multicomputer systems, it is important to review the progression or advances in the organization of single or uniprocessor systems. The discussion thus far has focused on the peripherals and their effects on the system performance. This discussion is now expanded to include the central processor as well.

The Basic Five-Unit Computer—The Von Neumann Machine

The simplest organization is the basic five-unit single computer or uniprocessor system shown in Figure 1–2. The earliest stored program machines all followed this fundamental structure, and numerous commercial systems of this type were placed in use. The major weakness in this design is the routing of all I/O operations through the Arithmetic and Logic Unit. This was done to share the use of costly buffer registers and other hardware. The problem is that all processing stops while any input/output is in progress.

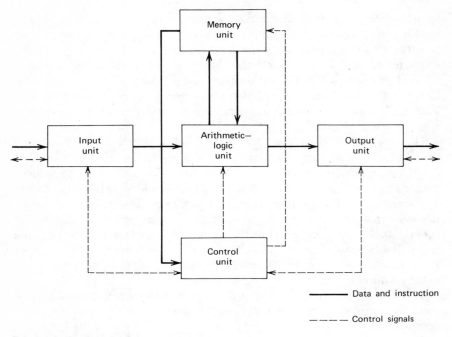

Figure 1-2 The basic Von Neuman machine.

This system organization was prevalent until 1958. However, even as late as the mid-1960s, the Control Data 3600 passed all messages to and from the operator's console typewriter through the accumulator.

Direct Memory Access

In the mid-1950s the flow paths were altered to provide direct access to the memory for input and output for data transfer (see Figure 1–3). This released the hardware in the Arithmetic and Logic Unit; however, the Control Unit was still responsible for the detailed control of I/O operations and processor performance was still degraded during I/O.

The Input/Output Channel

In the mid-1950s, the independent I/O channel was introduced. Although earlier examples of semi-independent or buffered I/O operations are available, the channel is more common in current systems. The channel, shown in Figure 1–4, provided a separate access path to and from the

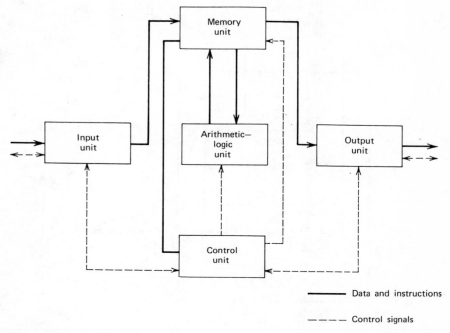

Figure 1-3 Direct memory access.

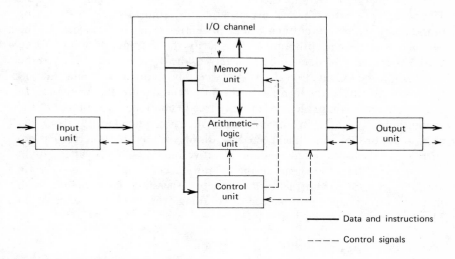

Figure 1-4 Introduction of I/O channel.

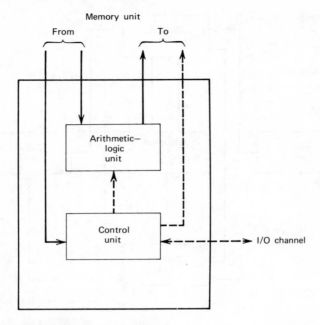

Figure 1-5 The processor unit.

memory plus a separate control for the I/O operations. The channel is actually a small computer itself. It has very limited capabilities; however, it is able to operate in parallel (i.e., simultaneously) with the main processor. The programs for the channel are generated by control software executing in the main processor and then placed in central memory for access by the channel. The channel program must specify the memory locations to be used, the quantity of data to be transferred, the device to be used, and the operation to be executed on the I/O device. The main control unit then informs the channel of the location of this program and directs the channel to execute it. The main processor is totally free to continue operation until the channel interrupts it to indicate that it has completed the assigned program(s) or that some unexpected condition such as an I/O error has occurred. It should be noted that the effective operating speed of the main processor will be lowered due to the memory accesses devoted to servicing the I/O operations. (For a more complete discussion of the channel with specifics on its operation and programming, the reader is referred to Flores, *Computer Organization*.)

The Processor Unit

In the paragraph above the term processor unit was used, which is an abbreviated term referring to the combination of the control unit and the arithmetic and logic unit (see Figure 1–5). This notation is used extensively in the other discussions of organization. Also, the only interconnections between units that are shown are those for data flow unless there is something unusual or significant about the routing of control.

MULTICOMPUTER SYSTEMS

Multicomputer systems are almost as old as modern digital computers. The earliest versions were two identical, or almost identical, systems, each executing the same program independently on the same input data and comparing intermediate as well as final results to verify the operational status of the equipment. These systems were assembled from vacuum-tube computer components and duplicate verifying units were used at all levels from the subassembly to complete computers. The best-known complete duplicate system was the Semi-Automatic Ground Environment (SAGE) Air Defense System. The AN/FSQ-7, a vacuum-tube system, was a duplex machine. One complete computer was designated the "active" system and the other was the "standby." The two systems could exchange roles under a more or less automatic arrangement. They did not duplicate the processing of the incoming data. Rather the active machine periodically transmitted a subset of the data base to the standby by means of a drum accessible to both systems. In the event of a switchover, the new active computer would commence a startover procedure utilizing the subset of the data base that had been transferred. The standby program merely received the data base information and stored it in the standby tables. The AN/FSQ-7 was used at the Direction Centers; the Q-8 was a similar duplexed system that was used at the Combat Control Centers. Except for slightly dovetailed I/O, these systems cannot be called multiprocessors; however, duplexed systems such as these did contribute to the development of multiprocessors, for they were an example of one method of obtaining more reliability, or at least confidence in the answers that were obtained. Other than that, they contributed little else, since there was no interaction except the comparisons.

The multicomputer systems discussed below all did interact with one another during the execution of a program or series of programs; however, the interaction was at the data set level. Another characteristic common to all of the systems described below that distinguishes them as multicomputer systems rather than multiprocessors, regardless of the shared hardware in-

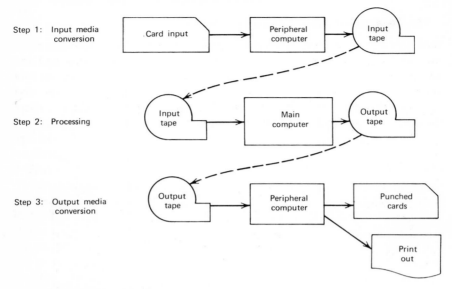

Figure 1-6   Peripheral, stand-alone processor system.

terface, is the fact that each sees and treats the other as an I/O channel or device.

The primary characteristic differentiating the four multicomputer system organizations discussed below is the actual means used to interconnect the various separate computers. Each organization in turn is more closely coupled both physically and logically. The name used for each was selected as that being most descriptive of the system. Unfortunately, as in almost every aspect of computer terminology, there is some variety in the use of these names. However, with one exception, the ones here are those commonly used to refer to each specific system. The one exception is the term "satellite computer."

Satellite Computers

When they were first introduced, stand-alone peripheral systems were referred to as satellites. Then later, when coupling (i.e., physical or electrical connection between two systems) was introduced, "satellite" was reserved for the next level past stand-alone—obviously an unfortunate use of the same term. Perhaps the best thing to do is to fall back on the standard dictionary definition of satellite, "an attendant upon a person of importance," and realize that all of the systems below contain a "satellite computer."

Peripheral Stand-Alone Computer Systems

With the introduction of the IBM 1401, a very popular small computer specifically designed for character-oriented applications such as payroll and billing, a solution was seen to the dual problems of slow unit record I/O and the cost of special devices. A 1401 with reader, punch, printer, and tapes cost less than the aggregate cost of the three special converters. Also, the performance of the I/O devices on the 1401 was better (although the converters would certainly have been up-graded if the 1401 had not appeared). The real advantage came from the ability of the 1401 to perform error checking, data editing, and blocking and deblocking as necessary. Not only was the workload on the main processor reduced, but also the effective transfer rates of the input and output tapes were greatly increased.

It was soon found that use of this system still required the handling of each job individually, necessitating a lot of tape changing and other work. To accompany this new hardware, which was capable of having an intelligent I/O converter, the system software was developed to support the processing of a "batch" of jobs of the same type sequentially without breaks or manual restarts except for error conditions. A complete discussion of this aspect of the problem properly belongs in a text on operating systems and not in a discussion of hardware systems organization.

Stand-alone systems were designed to provide off-line I/O support to the main processor. There was no direct physical connection between the peripheral processor and the main system. Nor was there any "shared" hardware resource such as there is in the other systems discussed below. The motivation was concurrency and economics—a small, inexpensive system for time-consuming I/O operations (i.e., cards and printing), and a main system which executed high-speed operations such as tape and disk only (Figure 1-6).

One of the earliest examples of the peripheral, stand-alone system organization was the IBM 1401 system used with a 709 or 7090.* This combination was assembled because of the complementary nature of the characteristics of each component system:

EQUIPMENT CHARACTERISTICS

   IBM 1401

- A character oriented machine.

---

* This use of the 1401 as a peripheral processor should not be confused with some other very special applications of the 1401 as an on-line I/O channel for a large computer such as the USAF AN/FSQ-31, -32, and others.

- Very cost effective on I/O, editing, blocking, and so on.
- Weak on computation (when compared to the 7090).

IBM 709 or 7090

- A binary, word-oriented machine.
- Extremely powerful on computation in comparison to the 1401.

OPERATING SEQUENCE

- Convert cards to magnetic tape on the peripheral system.
- Switch the tape to the main computer after a "batch" of jobs had been collected.

   First, this was done by manually moving the tape from a peripheral system tape transport to one connected to the main processor.

   Later, a switch was added to the tape transport to electrically transfer the entire transport.

- Computation by the main system.
- Output tape switched to peripheral system.
- Output printed by the peripheral system.

OUTCOME

Overall installation performance was affected greatly by this mode of operation.

- There was increased through-put. More jobs were completed, and the main system was better utilized, since the central processing unit did not sit idle waiting for the channel to execute unit-record input/output operations.
- However, there was an increase in the turn-around time for all users, since jobs were collected into batches and there was the time delay incurred on both input and output while *all* jobs were converted.

Coupled Systems—General

Coupled systems are connected electrically or, more commonly, they concurrently share a common hardware resource. The two processors are usually quite asymmetrical in both capacity and operating characteristics. Combinations that are good for peripheral processor systems are usually good for coupled systems if they can be interfaced electrically.

The two processors in a coupled system may execute two programs with total autonomy or in cooperation with each other. More commonly, one system acts as an I/O or communications processor for the other. The interaction between the two processors is still at the data set level, and the main processor still sees the other as an I/O unit.

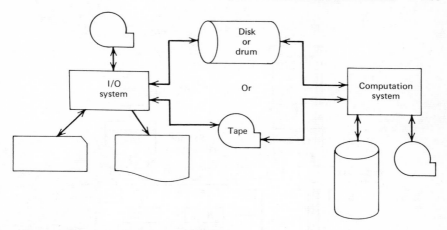

Figure 1-7 Indirectly or loosely coupled system.

Coupled Systems—Indirectly or Loosely Coupled

Indirectly coupled systems share a piece of I/O equipment such as a disk or tape (see Figure 1-7).

In an indirectly coupled system there can be no interaction between the programs being executed in each system except at the data set level. One system deposits a data set on the common device in a "mailbox" fashion. The other system does not know of its existence unless it "looks" in the mailbox, or it may be possible for the first system to "ring a doorbell" indicating to the second that there is something in the mailbox.

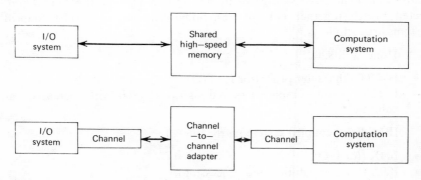

Figure 1-8 Directly coupled systems.

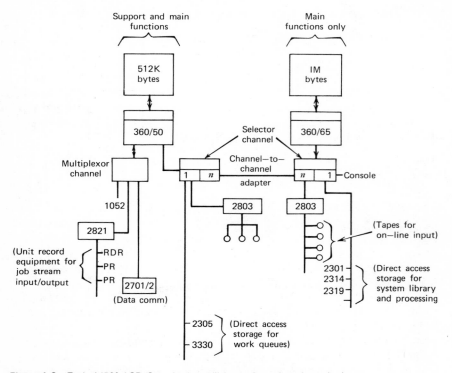

Figure 1-9   Typical IBM ASP. Organization utilizing a channel-to-channel adapter.

Coupled Systems—Directly Coupled

Directly coupled systems have closer electrical connection either by sharing addressable high-speed storage or by having two high-speed channels connected directly together, (Figure 1-8). Some examples of directly coupled systems are as follows:

Honeywell 8200

- H-4200 (character processor for I/O).
- H-1800 (main computer) (a redesigned H-1800 with increased capabilities).

IBM direct coupled system (early 1960's)

- 704X (for I/O).
- 709X (for computation and processing).

The large Control Data Corporation systems

- CDC 6400 (with 10 peripheral processor units).
- CDC 6600 (with 10 PPU's).
- CDC 7600 (with 20 PPU's).

The distinction between a directly coupled system and a multiprocessing system described below is in the nature or degree of interaction between the two computers at the software or program level. Even with direct coupling, the interaction is still primarily at the data set level.

Coupled Systems—Attached Support Processor

The term "attached support processor" refers to a indirectly coupled configuration of up to four IBM computers. One system supervises overall installation scheduling. All systems may do job processing. The primary objective of the organization is a division of labor with the smaller, less powerful system doing the I/O and other support roles.* (A single system version called local ASP (LASP) is also provided.)

The ASP concept was originally an outgrowth of the 7040/7090 direct-coupled system. It is a loose association of processors utilizing a channel-to-channel adapter. An example of a S/360 ASP System is shown in Figure 1-9. There is no sharing of main memory, although peripheral devices can be shared through two-channel switches.

As contrasted to most other forms of transfer over I/O paths, the communication of one processor with the other through the channel-to-channel adapter requires collaboration and positive action by both. The requestor utilizes the adapter to notify the other system of its desire either to transfer data to, or to obtain data from, the other processor's memory. Both computers must then initiate the proper READ and WRITE channel programs before the channel-to-channel adapter (CTC) will allow the transfer to take place.

To each of the channels to which it is connected, the adapter appears to be a control unit. It is selected and responds in the same fashion as any control unit, and, in essentially the same manner as a control unit, it accepts and decodes commands from the channel. The adapter, however, differs from a control unit in that it does not use these commands to operate and control input/output devices; instead, it uses them to open a path between the two channels it connects and then synchronizes the operations performed between the two channels.

---

* This includes reading jobs into the system, maintaining data submitted with the jobs, and handling time-sharing users and all output from local batch jobs.

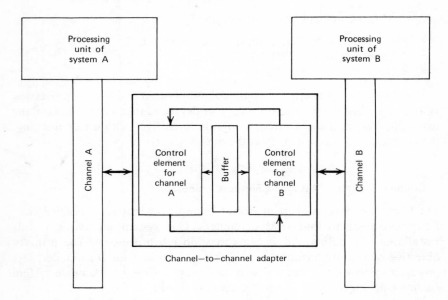

Figure 1-10 Data flow through a channel-to-channel adapter in an IBM multisystem.

The adapter functionally consists of two control elements connected to and communicating with each other by means of a common, one-byte buffer register and several signal lines. One of the two control elements serves one channel and the other control element the other channel. IBM System/360 Special Feature, Channel-to-Channel Adapter," IBM Form GA 22-6892-1. (See Figure 1-10).

The advantages claimed by IBM for the ASP are as follows:

1. A "single system" image is presented to users. Multiple computers appear as one computer to programmers and operations personnel. ASP will balance the use of each system in the complex. Provision is also made for users to specify which system should run a job to allow processors with unlike characteristics to be included in the complex. This option is used when, for example, one processor has an emulator or other special feature that must be used to process a job. As well as providing system coupling through channel connectors, ASP also allows connection of systems via communication lines.

2. The elimination of concurrent use of (central processor) time on the main processors for processing support functions (such as printing). Because the clerical functions are assigned to the support processor, the main processors no longer share central processor time between the support func-

tions and the application programs. Therefore, the application has the opportunity to use all the resources of the main processor to full capacity.

3. An algorithm for efficient management of the devices for system I/O data sets. The algorithm was designed specifically to accommodate the data demands, the data set characteristics, and the available devices. I/O routines always know the position of the access mechanisms, thereby ensuring minimum seek time when data are transferred to the devices. This job scheduling function improves I/O and CPU overlap and the resulting equipment utilization.

Bell and Newell [p. 506] take exception to some of these claims, stating:

Ideally, a multiprogrammed single-processor or multiprocessor structure would easily provide all the above advantages without the overhead of having large [processor memories] on two computers (both of which hold nearly the same operating system).

BASIC MULTIPROCESSORS

Now that several multi-computer systems that are not multiprocessors have been defined and discussed, it is easier to discuss specifics on defining multiprocessors. The ANSI definition of multiprocessor is not too helpful although it does contain some key points:

"A computer employing two or more processing units under integrated control [Vocabulary for Information Processing," American National Standard X3. 12-1970].

Definition of a Multiprocessor System

A more complete definition is based on both the hardware and system software characteristics of the system:

- There are two or more central processing units.
  Some qualify further the definition that these must be of approximately equal capability (i.e., symmetric CPU's).
  Others allow asymmetric systems to be included as long as they meet all other conditions.

- Main processor memory must be shared and accessible by all processors.
  Some require that *all* memory be common; however, examples are given later where some private memory is highly advantageous.

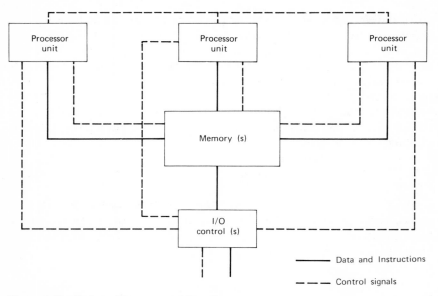

Figure 1-11   Basic multiprocessor configuration.

Total sharing may complicate some of the system software problems, and most definitions do allow some private memory for each processor.

• I/O access must be sharable to include channels, control units, and devices as appropriate.
• There must be a *single* integrated operating system in overall control of all hardware and software.
• There must be intimate interaction possible at both hardware and software operating levels.
   At the system software level in the execution of system tasks.
   At the program level for the execution of portions of the same program by several processors in turn and the execution of an independent task of a program on a processor other than the one executing the main task (the ability to move a job).
   At the data set level.
   At the hardware interrupt level.

It is possible to illustrate the basic hardware interconnection relationships as shown in Figure 1-11. However, it should be noted that the hardware and software interactions depend on the systems software and operating procedures as well as the interaction configuration.

A multiprocessor then is a system with

- Two or more processing units.
- Shared memory.
- Shared I/O.
- Single integrated operating system.
- Hardware and software interaction at all levels.

Multiprocessor Development and Its Objectives

In all of the multicomputer systems discussed in the preceeding section, a common thread focused or guided their development. The objective for all of those systems was to remove the I/O workload from the main processor, usually a large and powerful source of computation, and place it on a smaller more appropriately matched unit. This is not the situation with multiprocessors. Some of the results may appear similar, but the motivations were quite different.

The first real use or research in the area of multiprocessors was in military command and control systems. At the beginning, the primary objective was the high system availability that could be obtained by having a group of identical units, each capable of performing the same tasks and being reconfigured into an operational system, even if it were only a portion of the original. It is only after that point had been passed that the designers of general-purpose machines began to capitalize on the fact that the multiprocessors could also improve system performance. The objectives were to do the following:

Provide high availability by utilizing.

- Reliability improvement attained through multiple units.
- Ability to reconfigure the system.

Improve system performance by:

- Ability to exploit parallel execution of independent tasks.
- Improved performance and system balance.
- Providing for more economic handling of exceptional jobs or peaks loads.
- Attaining higher overall "effective resource utilization" without developing new architecture.

HISTORICAL EVOLUTION OF CONCURRENT PROCESSORS

As with many of our digital computers concepts, including the original stored program machine, the impetus, motivation, and money for the research, development, and production came from special military requirements. Specifically, it was the need of the U.S. Air Force for more reliable processors for their command and control system that really started concrete projects in this area. Some of these were unsuccessful or proved too costly, but several, primarily the various models of the D825, were outstanding successes and provided the models and knowledge base for commercial exploitation.

Unfortunately, widespread acceptance and use of system organizations embodying concurrent or parallel processing have taken much longer than one would have anticipated. There are two possible explanations for this delay. The fact that the many of the better designers in the commercial fields were busy developing the next generation of standard computers may explain part of the delay. There were only a few multiprocessor projects being pursued outside of the military both in the universities and in the manufacturers' laboratories. However, the experience gained was enough to show that the main problem with multiprocessors was the system software, the operating system. More research was needed in that area before a suitable multiprocessor operating system could be produced. In fact, many feel that this is still the "Achille's" heel of the implementation of the concept. A long list of existing multiprocessors and parallel processors is given in Chapter 4, and the Appendix contains descriptions of over 20 of them. It is not surprising to note that nearly all of them were delivered initially with no operating system whatsoever, and many of them still have none leaving that task to the user. Many of them have fallen back on the simplest type of multiprocessor operating system, the "master-slave" mode of operation, and the attainment of good performance for the overall system has often been a slow and arduous task for the manufacturers and the users.

It seems fitting to close this introductory chapter with a summary of the actual developments in this field. These are best given in the form of a brief chronology which is depicted in Table 1-1.

Optional

TABLE 1-1   A   BRIEF   CHRONOLOGY   OF   MULTIPROCESSOR   AND PARALLEL SYSTEMS 11

Date	System Manufacturer and Model Number	Remarks
1958	National Bureau of Standards PILOT	Three independently operating computers that could work in cooperation.
1958 (circa)	IBM, AN/FSQ-31 and 32	Solid-state SAGE computer; not multi-processors; merely duplexed systems.
1960	Ramo Wooldridge TRW-400	"Polymorphic system"; for USAF command and control. Some construction done, not completed. Important for early concepts.
May 1960	UNIVAC LARC	One I/O processor and one computational processor capable of operating in parallel. One delivered to Livermore AEC Laboratories. Not a "true" multi-processor.
May 1961	IBM Stretch(7030)	Original design called for separate character-oriented processor and binary arithmetic processor. These were dropped from final design; therefore, final product was not a multiprocessor. It did contain look-ahead. Only seven delivered.
Nov. 1962	Burroughs, D-825 (This system carried various military model designations depending on the major system of which it was part.)	First modular system with identical processors. Total memory shared by all processors. Up to four processors, 16 memory modules, 10 I/O controllers, and 64 devices. Important feature was one of the earliest examples of a modern operating system—the Automatic Operating and Scheduling Program (ASOP).
Feb. 1963	Burroughs B-5000	One or two processors. Up to eight memory modules. Programs independent of addresses. Supervisor was the Master Control Program (MCP). Utilized virtual memory concepts and hardware. Machine code based on Polish notation. Users programmed only in ALGO or COBOL. Became the B-5500 in Nov. 1964.

23

TABLE 1-1 *(Continued)*

Date	System Manufacturer and Model Number	Remarks
1963	IBM 704X/709X (7040 or 44 and 7090 or 94)	"Direct Coupled System"
1963	Bendix G-21 (later CDC)	A multiprocessor version of the G-20 developed for Carnegie Institute of Technology. A crossbar system.
Sep. 1964	CDC 6600	Contained multiple arithmetic and logic units each of which can execute only a small fraction of the total instruction repetoire. Ten peripheral processors were an integral part of the system. (Number of PPU's increased to 20 in 1969.) The PPU's do constitute a multiprocessor system. Overall system an example of an asymmetric multiprocessor.
Nov. 1964	Burroughs B-5500	An upgrade of the B-5000 (see Feb. 1963).
1964	GE 645 (now Honeywell)	Ordered by Project MAC at MIT.
May 1965	GE 645 (now HIS-645)	Delivered to Project MAC at MIT. Hardware not a standard product; however MULTICS operating system is being released.
Ded. 1965	UNIVAC 1108	
1965	SOLOMON I	Design only. First large-scale array processor.
Mar. 1966	IBM S/360 Model 67	Special dual-processor time-sharing system.
Apr. 1966	CDC 6500	Dual 6400's
Dec. 1966	XDS Sigma 7	
1966	SOLOMON II	Design only.
Jun. 1967	CDC 6700	Dual CDC 6600's
Aug. 1967	XDS Sigma 5	
1968	CDC 7600	Very similar to 6600, but higher speed and included hierarchy of main memory as standard feature.
Apr. 1969	IBM S/360 Model 65 MP	Dual-processor version of standard model 65. A true multiprocessor.
Jun. 1970	XDS Sigma 6	

TABLE 1-1 *(Continued)*

Date	System Manufacturer and Model Number	Remarks
Oct. 1970	Burroughs B-5700	Similar to B-5500 with capability for increased memory. Capability for four B-5700 systems to share disk storage.
Feb. 1971	Honeywell 6050, 6060, 6080	
Jun. 1971	Burroughs B-6700	
Sep. 1971	Digital Equipment System 10/1055, 10/1077	
Sep. 1971	XDS Sigma 8, 9	
Nov. 1971	UNIVAC 1110	
1971	SDC, PEPE (Parallel Element Processing Ensemble)	Prototype for processing of radar data for ballistic missile defense system.
Jan. 1972	Honeywell 2088	
Sep. 1972	ILLIAC IV	Array processor. 64 processor elements. Driven by a conventional multiprocessor used as a front-end control processor.
Feb. 1972	Burroughs B-7700	
1972	CDC, Cyber 72, 73, 74, 76	
1972	Goodyear STARAN	Parallel associative system.
1972	Texas Instruments ASC (Advanced Scientific Computer)	Embodies both multiprocessing and pipelining.
1973	CDC STAR-100	Pipeline system.
1974	IBM S/370, Models 158 MP & 168 MP	Shared real and virtual storage

CHAPTER 2
SYSTEMS HARDWARE

BASIC REQUIREMENTS

Using as a basis the fundamental definition of a multiprocessor system it is relatively easy to enumerate the capabilities that must be provided by the hardware: A multiprocessor computer is a system containing two or more processor units of approximately comparable capabilities.

- All having access to shared common memory.
- All having common access to at least a portion of the I/O devices.
- All being controlled by one operating system that provides interaction between the processors and the programs they are executing at the job, task, step, data set, data element, and hardware levels.

The most obvious results of the definition above are in the major characteristics of the topology of the connection network between the various functional units. There must be several groups of multiple paths, either paths present physically at all times or logical paths created by the connection network on an "as needed basis." These paths then provide the following capabilities:

- Any processor can control and transfer data to and from any location in memory (although it may be convenient for each processor to have a *small* amount of private store as discussed below).
- Any processor can pass control commands to any I/O channel controller.
- Any I/O channel can transfer data to and from any location in memory.
- Any I/O channel can control and transfer data between the central memory and any of its appropriate I/O devices.

These interconnections will provide the full requirement for total resource sharing. The other hardware capabilities that must be provided are more in direct support of the general control function rather than sharing.

If the operating system controlling the complete system is to function effectively and reliably, several hardware features should be present. Depending on the specifics of the functioning of the operating systems, some of these are essential and others optional.

- To ensure the integrity of tables or data sets while being accessed by one processor, there should be a hardware "lock" that can be set to prevent entry by another. (The specific features of this lock and the reasons for having it are discussed in Chapter 3.)
- There must be a capability for variable logical address or names of processor channels, memories, and devices rather than fixed physical addresses.
- Often one processor must have the capability to signal or interrupt another to request that it perform a certain function or to determine if the other processor is still functioning. This may be accomplished with an interrupt or a mailbox and polling message passing procedure (a "soft-interrupt").
- If a processor has failed, another processor detecting this and wishing to reschedule the work in progress on the down machine must be able to access all of the information necessary to do this even if some of that data are within the processor itself.
- Finally, it may be necessary to have the ability for one processor to start or restart another no matter what state the latter may be in as long as it is still operational.

As stated in the introduction, only the data transfer paths are shown in the systems depicted below. This is quite appropriate, since the primary function of any system can be visualized as the flow of data through it; however, the reader should realize that the latter group of hardware capabilities enumerated above are primarily the transfer of control signals that are not depicted in the figures given in the remainder of this chapter.

SYSTEM ORGANIZATIONS

Focusing on the flow of data and the parallelism or concurrency that can be obtained with a multiprocessor, it is indeed the topology and mode of operation of the network that interconnects the functional units that becomes of paramount importance. The material below covers all of the general forms of configuration that have been used for "true" multiprocessors as well as several other system organizations that are included for completeness, since they are often grouped with multiprocessors although they may not comply with all four points given in the definition at the beginning of this chapter. The system organizations to be covered and the discussion to be presented on each assume that the entire system is at one physical location within distances so that unit to unit transfers can be made at full machine speed. This provision excludes systems consisting of units connected by communications lines. None of these that have yet been developed or proposed meet all four of the criteria in the definition; however, with the work now in progress on very high-speed distributed control communications networks such as ARPANET, loops, rings, and other configurations, the day may not be too far away when the functional units of a "true" multiprocessor are separated by hundreds or thousands of miles.

There is no particular rationale for the order of presentation. The discussion of the first three types of system organizations builds on the preceding ones. After the first three configurations, all of which can be used to produce "true" multiprocessors, four other types of quasi-multiprocessors are discussed. The seven system organizations discussed are:

- Time-shared or common-bus.
- Crossbar.
- Multiple-bus/multiport.
- Asymmetrical or nonhomogeneous (some implementations of this configuration are very close to being "true" multiprocessors).
- Array or vector processor.
- Pipeline processors.
- Fault-tolerant systems (some implementations are multiprocessors, but the primary objective is fault or failure tolerance).

Time-Shared or Common-Bus Systems

The time-shared or common-bus system is one of the simpler and cheaper organizations to implement. It is also quite simple to depict (see Figure 2–1). There are no continuous connections between functional units. Control of transfers between the memory modules and other units is accomplished using time-sharing or multiplexing techniques.

In addition to the fact that each unit has only a single interface point, lower costs are also achieved by the fact that all memory is shared. However, since there is only one transfer path for *all* transfers, delays will be greater than in the multipath systems described below. A strong argument in favor of this organization is the flexibility and ease of adding or removing modules or functional units.

All modules are connected in parallel to the bus which may be a full word wide or only one byte wide, or may be able to handle only a single bit at a time. As the bus becomes narrower, the control functions become more complex.

The processor and peripheral units may be connected to a single bidirectional bus as shown in Figure 2–1 or unidirectional buses may be used as shown in Figure 2–2. In the latter case the transfer path is completed through the unit on the far left, the bus modifier. The trade-offs here are primarily in the implementation of a single bidirectional interface as opposed to two unidirectional ones. The control logic of the latter is simpler; however, the former has the advantage of utilizing a single buffer register in the interface and less cabling.

It is also possible to have more than one time-shared bus as shown in Figure 2–3. This is approaching the topology of the next system configuration to be discussed, the crossbar system. The distinguishing feature of the time-shared bus is that even if there were an equal number of processors and memories, they could not all be active at the same time because of the time-sharing property of the transfer path(s).

Each packet that is placed on a bus must contain the data that are to be transferred and the address of the unit to which they are directed. There is no problem with conflicts between multiple packets arriving at a unit simultaneously, since only one packet is on the bus at a time and a transmitter has to wait until the bus is free to place its packet on the line. Even though conflict resolution is automatic and not a severe problem, the conflicts still exist and slow the operation of the ensemble considerably. Each unit on the bus must contain the circuitry necessary to recognize its address in a packet and respond accordingly.

As a "simple" example of a single bus system, consider the Digital Equipment Corporation PDP-11 which exploits fully the flexibility of its

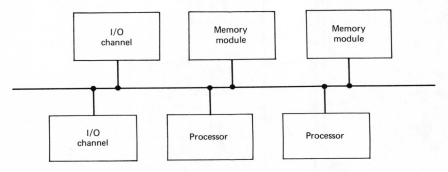

Figure 2-1   Time-shared/common-bus system organization—single bus.

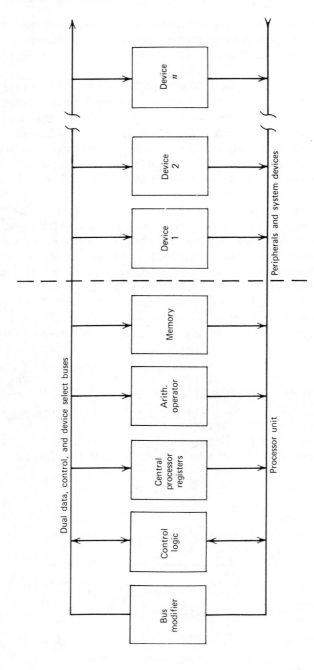

Figure 2-2 Time-shared/common-bus system organization—unidirectional buses. (Based on GRI-99 organization.)

UNIBUS, (see Figure 2-4). The bus has 56 lines, of which only 16 are for the transfer of data (PDP-11 word is 16 bits long). The functions of all the lines in the bus are listed below.

Function	Number of Lines
Data transfer	16
Address (of a unique memory or device register; peripherals normally assigned in block 760000–777777)	18
Control (IN, OUT, PAUSE, BYTE)	2
Master synch (address and control information is present)	1
Slave synch (response to Master)	1
Parity bits	2
Bus request (by peripheral)	4
Bus grant (by processor)	4
Other bus request signals	3
Interrupt	1
Bus busy	1
Miscellaneous control	3
Total	56

The disadvantage of being able to execute only one transfer operation at a time is balanced against the conceptual simplicity of the system and its flexibility for growth. However, this configuration may result in unacceptable long waiting times for the exchange of data packets as the size of the system grows and the traffic becomes heavier. One other benefit of the

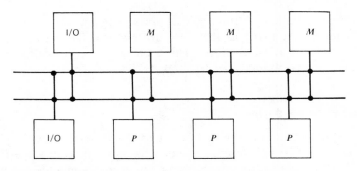

Figure 2-3   Multiple time-shared/common-bus system organization.

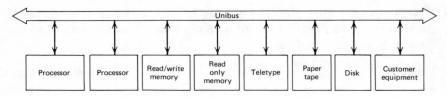

Figure 2-4   PDP-11 system simplied block diagram—UNIBUS system.

common-bus organization is the capability for one processor to execute a complete data-interlock which is easily implemented by having it briefly monopolize the bus. There is no requirement for special software or hardware to accomplish this interlock.

Another disadvantage of this system organization can be a low reliability. There is the danger of a catastrophic failure if the bus contains active components or if there is a single bus control unit. The reliability of the time-shared bus configuration can be improved if the bus is totally passive with no controller (i.e., just a multitapped cable).

Examples of multiprocessor systems using this organization are as follows:

- IBM Stretch.
- UNIVAC LARC.
- CDC 6600 for transfer between main memory and the peripheral processors.
- DIGITAL System 10.
- Data General NOVA message switch (although there is private memory associated with each processor) [Seligman].
- Plessy Laboratories controller for small telephone exchange [Seligman].

One final variation of this type of system architecture is the use of several, but not as many as there are processors, time-shared buses, see Figure 2–3, as described in Curtin. This topology does provide some redundancy and increase in total transfer rates.

Crossbar Switch Systems

Another system configuration that can be used with single access port functional unit is the configuration utilizing a crossbar switch matrix (see Figure 2–5). In this system organization, any memory module can be connected to any processor or any I/O unit. An actual full-time connection is established between the two units for the complete duration of the transfer. In contrast to the time-division switching done on the common-bus system, the technique used here is often referred to as space-division switching. It is very similar to the technique utilized by most telephone central offices.

Although not quite as flexible as the single bus system, it is still relatively easy to add modules to a crossbar system if the switch matrix is large enough. The size of the system is not limited by the access capabilities of the individual functional units, since they all are connected by a single port.

Conflicts in requests for the same memory module are resolved within the switch matrix utilizing one of several techniques possible. Since a fulltime connection does exist, the effective transfer rates can be higher that on a single time-shared bus. Also several paths can be established simultaneously.

The crossbar matrix is totally seperate from the functional units and can also be designed in a modular manner to facilitate expansion. However, because of the complexity of the functions that the switch may have to perform, it can become quite large and complex. The switch matrix and its control circuitry for the maximum configuration of the Hughes H4400 (eight CPU's or IOC's and 16 memory modules) contains as many components as

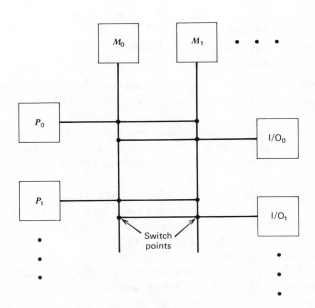

Figure 2-5 Crossbar switch system organization.

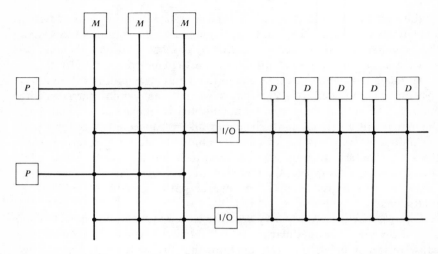

Figure 2-6   Crossbar switch system organization with separate I/O crossbar switch matrix.

2.5 processor units [Miller et al.]. Another example cited by Lehman had the following capabilities:

- 24 processors.
- 32 memory modules.
- 32 data-bit plus four parity-bit words.
- 16 data-bit plus four parity-bit addresses.

The number of circuits required for the switch would be two to three times the number required for the processor of an IBM S/360 Model 75 [Baer, 1972].

In a crossbar system the individual unit interfaces are quite simple, since they have to perform neither conflict resolution nor recognition of which data are directed toward them. These functions are all done by the logic of the switch matrix.

Input-output devices may be attached to the I/O units in the same manner as with uniprocessors, dedicated or shared between channels, or another crossbar switch matrix may be used-on the device side of the IOC's to provide maximum flexibility (Figure 2-6). Most of the Burroughs large systems including both military (D825) and commercial systems (B5500, B6700, and B7700) use this approach.* An interesting variation is proposed for the Burroughs Multi-Interpreter system which will utilize a group of

---

* It should be noted that the switching logic for the D825 system was distributed while the other Burroughs systems have switches which operate in a centralized mode.

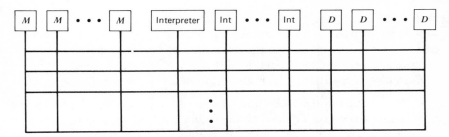

Figure 2-7 Burroughs multiinterpreter system organization.

identical microprogrammed processors [Davis et al.]. In this system the same units are utilized as central processors or as I/O controllers by reloading the writable microprogram memory. This capability thus allows all the devices to be attached to the same switch matrix as the memories and processors (Figure 2–7).

Another variation of the crossbar configuration was found in one of the earliest multiprocessors, the Thompson-Ramo-Wooldridge TRW–400. The TRW–400, or as it was also called, the "Polymorphic Computer," had only one switch matrix, just as the design proposed for the Multi-Interpreter; however, the units attached to the matrix in the TRW–400 were devices and complete computers each with its own memory (see Figure 2–8). The

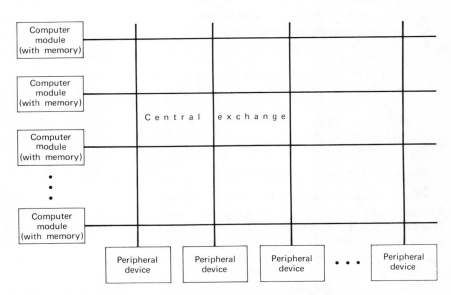

Figure 2-8 Ramo-Wooldridge, RW-400 system—the "Polymorphic Computer."

processor and memory units were not attached as separate entities. There were some provisions for interprocessor communications and the cross-accessing of memory by closing the proper set of two cross-points; however, the awkwardness and inefficiencies of this procedure are obvious.

Examples of crossbar systems are as follows:

- Ramo-Wooldridge, RW–400. A very early system developed for the U.S. Air Force. Of special significance in this system was the fact that there were no seperate memory units; the memory was associated with each processor to create a complete CPU. Also a special control processor is dedicated to controlling the switch matrix. The switch control processor contained a large number of components reducing the overall reliability of the system. Although some of the functional units of the RW–400 were built, a complete system was never assembled.
- Burroughs D825 [AN/GYK–3(V)]. This system along with the RW–400 were the first true multiprocessors developed. The "switch" of the D825 was distributed among the memory modules. The system normally had three computer modules. Each of these was connected to one of the five transfer buses available for each memory module. (The other two memory buses were normally used for I/O.). The memory bus interfaces had the logic circuitry necessary to accomodate and queue simultaneous memory access requests. The computer modules did have relative address registers to facilitate relocation of programs for multiprogramming.
- CDC 6600. For communications between the peripheral processors and I/O channels.
- Hughes H 4400. Eight processors or IOC's and 16 memories.
- PRIME (University of California). The crossbar switch is to be used to control external access [Quatse et al., 1972].
- Burroughs Multi-Interpreter system (microprogrammed) [Davis et al.].

Multibus/Multiport Memory Systems

Another configuration capable of providing more than one simultaneous transfer path is the multibus/multiport memory system organization (Figure 2–9). To implement this organization it is essential that the memory modules have more than one access port, and that there be control circuitry within the memory module to resolve the conflicts that occur if two or more processors or I/O units request access to the same memory module during a single memory cycle.

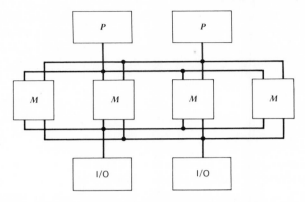

Figure 2-9   Multiport-memory/multibus system organization, basic form.

This system topology is less costly than the crossbar, since there are fewer points at which conflicts have to be resolved. This advantage is offset, however, by the fact that the maximum configuration possible is limited by the number of ports available on the memory module, and this is a basic design and manufacturing decision that is probably made long before full consideration is given to all of the possible system organizations that will be desirable. Port "expanders" or multipliers can be added to increase the number of interconnection points; however, the transfer rate of the total may be restricted to that allowed for the single port. Another characteristic of multiple memory ports is that they often have a priority physically

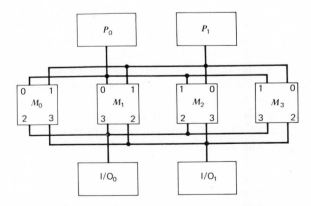

Figure 2-10   Assignment of memory access priorities—multiport system organization.

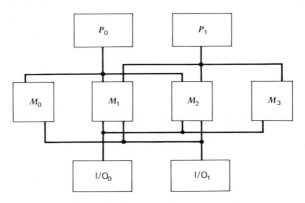

Figure 2-11 Multiport system with private memory.

associated with the connecting point. These priorities can be utilized as the basis for settling conflicts for simultaneous access with each I/O unit and processor being given preference in the access to its "primary" memory module as shown in Figure 2–10.

Just as in the previous organizations, the width of the data transfer path can be any convenient and economical size. If the basic storage unit is a word and the data transfer path is less than one word wide, then special assemble and disassembly registers will have to be included in the interface points as well as special control circuitry so that the transfer path is not preempted and broken when the transfer of a word is only partially complete.

It is not necessary that every memory module be connected to every processor. In fact in some systems it is essential that each processor have some "private memory" in which to store private tables for control functions, recovery, allocation of private resources, and so on (see Figure 2–11). There are reliability and recovery drawbacks, however, to the use of private memory. If a processor fails and the interrupted task must be completed on another processor, it may not be possible for the new processor to access the control information that it requires in order to do so.

Considerable generality is lost if every processor cannot access any memory. Flexibility in relocatability of object programs, as well as in the operating, is lost. The advantages of a single copy of the operating system are obvious. Failure of a memory module as well as of a processor (discussed above) represents a drawback to this organization if it has restrictions on processor to memory access.

In all systems of this configuration, the memory module must recognize and handle requests for access to the specific memory locations that it contains. It is also the responsibility of the memory control unit to resolve conflicts for simultaneous access and to notify the unit requesting access that it can transmit.

Examples of multiport/multibus systems are as follows:

- UNIVAC 1108.   Maximum of four memory banks or modules. Utilizes two multiple module access control units each capable of handling and resolving conflicts between five data paths, two from I/O controllers (high priority), and three from processors.
- HIS 635.
- CDC 3600.
- XDS-Sigma 7.   Six memory ports with fixed priority relationships.
- HIS (GE) 645 (MULTICS System).
- IBM S/360 Model 67.   Multiport memories are used throughout both the IBM S/360 and S/370 systems.
- UNIVAC 1832, AN/UYK-7, and ARTS-III.

Asymmetrical or Nonhomogeneous Systems

Although it has not been specifically stated, a basic assumption underlying all of the system configurations described thus far is a homogeneity within the group of processors and a similar commonality between the memory modules and I/O units. This is not always the situation. In fact, there may be very large differences between various components of the same type. This is usually the result of linking together general-purpose and special-purpose units into a common system or the design of a system utilizing all general-purpose units in which some are dedicated to special purposes. It should be emphasized again that the organizations under consideration all qualify as true multiprocessor systems because they meet the following basic criteria:

- Share or have common access to main memory.
- Operate under a single integrated operating system.
- Have hardware and software interaction at the program/task level as a common mode of operation.

One of the earliest examples of this type of organization was the National Bureau of Standards PILOT system. PILOT had three processors each dedicated to a primary task:

- Arithmetic computation.
- Housekeeping.
- Input/output.

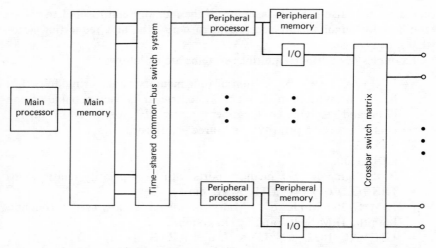

Figure 2-12   Example of asymmetrical/nonhomogeneous system organization—CDC 6600.

Estrin proposed a general design for a nonhomogeneous multiprocessor system consisting of these parts:

- A variable part of special purpose units as required that can be al-itself.
- A variable part in special purpose units as required that can be altered or reconfigured as necessary by the supervisory either electromechanically or mechanically.
- A supervisory system that links together and controls the entire system.

Utilizing the concept above a special-purpose system oriented toward a specific problem or class of problems could be assembled from available "building blocks" as necessary. The entire system was not actually assembled and run; thus it is not clear which interconnection scheme would be followed.

Perhaps the most common asymmetric systems that are actually in use are the CDC 6600 and 7600 (see Figure 2–12). The peripheral processors are significantly smaller than the main processors; they have approximately the computational capability of the CDC 160A, a very small 12-bit machine with a completely different but totally general-purpose instruction repertoire. The peripheral processor memory is fixed at 4K 12-bit words. The PPs are responsible for all housekeeping functions, job set-up and control, and all I/O operations. They each have an apparent path to every I/O device. The PPs actually perform most of the functions found in the I/O controller of other systems.

One of the PPs is usually dedicated to driving the console operator's display system and another acts as the overall master monitor of the entire system assigning tasks to the main processor as well as to the other PPs. An interesting feature of the system software is that interrupts are not used between the processors. All control directives and responses are passed back and forth utilizing a mail-box technique.

There have been several other proposals and experiments for nonhomogeneous systems. One of these is the "intrinsic multiprocessor" proposed by Aschenbrenner, Flynn, and Robinson. The main feature of this design was the type of building blocks available—sequence control units (similar to conventional CPUs without any arithmetic capabilities) and a commonly shared set of arithmetic functional units such as adders and multipliers.

It should also be noted that the Burroughs multiinterpreter system might be considered as falling into this category, since any interpreter can be defined or redefined in real time by changing the firmware (microprogram) so that it is a "standard," "special," or I/O processor as necessary.

Pipeline Systems

Pipeline systems provide yet another method for obtaining concurrency or parallelism of operations and are usually included in any discussion of this topic. Whereas array systems attain concurrency by performing common operations simultaneously on multiple data streams, the pipeline computer performs the same operation repeatedly on several items in a single data stream.

The best example of this type of operation and the pay-offs possible is the floating-point addition of two vectors each with n elements, $\bar{A} + \bar{B} = \bar{C}$.*

A floating-point addition can be broken down into five component steps:

1. Normalization (removal of leading zeros by shifting) of both operands and appropriate adjustment of their exponents.
2. Comparison of exponents.
3. Shifting of characteristic of operand with smaller exponent to agree with larger exponent.
4. Straight addition of characteristics.
5. Normalization of results.

Typical times to execute each step might be:

1. 100 nsec.

---

* For a more complete discussion of the hardware involved in pipelining and the benefits attainable see Thomas G. Hallen and Michael J. Flynn, "Pipelining of Arithmetic Functions," *IEEE Trans. Comput.*, 880–886 (August 1972).

2.   60 nsec.
3. 100 nsec.
4. 120 nsec.
5. 100 nsec.

Therefore, each floating-point addition would require at least 480 nsec. In a pipeline machine, each step would be executed by a separate set of hardware and then moved to the next station. New sets of operands would be inserted in the pipeline as appropriate.

Time

Step 1	a_1, b_1	a_2, b_2	a_3, b_3	a_4, b_4	a_5, b_5	$\ldots$	a_{i+4}, b_{i+4}
Step 2		a_1, b_1	a_2, b_2	a_3, b_3	a_4, b_4	$\ldots$	a_{i+3}, b_{i+3}
Step 3			a_1, b_1	a_2, b_2	a_3, b_3	$\ldots$	a_{i+2}, b_{i+2}
Step 4				c_1	c_2	$\ldots$	c_{i+1}
Step 5					c_1	$\ldots$	c_i

Now it will be necessary to clock each step at 120 nsec to allow sufficient time for step 4 to be completed. The first result will be available in 600 instead of 480; however, each succeeding answer will be available in 120-nsec increments. Obviously, such a technique is of full value only when the computations to be performed lend themselves to pipelining, and the software and hardware provided will exploit automatically this characteristic.

Two examples of how a set of basic arithmetic units can be interconnected in different ways to perform various operations are shown in Figure 2-13, which is based on the pipeline arithmetic unit in the Texas Instruments ASC system.

In Baer's discussion of large-scale systems, he states three questions that have to be answered about the value and usefulness of pipelining a general-purpose arithmetic unit:

- Can two different operations, for example, addition and multiplication, be pipe-lined?
- Can one pipeline the same operation on different data bases, for example, short and long floating-point operations?
- Can one pipeline two operations of same type and same data base but the operands not related in any way by indexing? That is, can the two operations $A = B + C$ and $D = B + C$ be pipelined? (Note that $A = B + C$ and $D = A + E$ will never be pipelined.) [Baer]

Highly partitioned and overlapped instruction execution techniques such as those utilized in the IBM S/360 Model 91 are a form of pipelining;

however, they are distinctly different from the "vector" or "stream" pipelining being discussed here. The major distinction is the fact that in the Texas Instruments ASC and the Control Data STAR-100, pipelining is employed to perform the same arithmetic operation on a series of operands as they progress down the pipeline.

The major job in exploiting the capacities of the pipeline system is to keep the pipeline filled. For most of the systems, this is only moderately critical, since there are not too many stages or steps in the pipeline, and

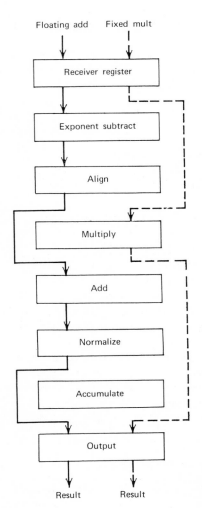

Figure 2-13 Two examples of the pipeline flow for two different instructions. (Based on the Texas Instruments ASC.)

even the basic philosophy and goals of the pipeline in the Model 91 differ totally from those of the CDC STAR.

The STAR is truly a linearized array processor and its performance will be degraded significantly if long strings of identical operations are not being performed on the data streams. The Model 91, on the other hand, does not use as many steps and does not require such long strings. In some systems keeping the pipeline filled is the responsibility of the programmer; in the S/360 Model 91, the hardware attempts to maximize concurrency.

The pay-off of the pipeline concepts obviously increases with the complexity of the operations to which it is applied. Hallin and Flynn cited figures such as 40% improvement in adding obtained by pipelining with a 230% increase in "multiplier efficiency."

A final comment on handling interrupts in a pipeline. Since there are so many operations concurrently being executed with different sets of data, the interrupt identification problem is greatly magnified.

Examples of Pipelined Systems

- IBM S/360 Model 91.   Both of the floating-point units utilize it; however, there are only two steps in the pipeline.
- CDC 7600.   All nine of the functional arithmetic units are pipelined with various step counts in each.
- CDC STAR-100.   In addition to other forms of parallelism such as peripheral service stations that are large enough to be stand-alone systems performing I/O and file management tasks and multiple arithmetic units in the central processor,there are also two pipelines and a stream unit. It is designed as an extremely high-performance, scientific computer optimized for STring ARray (i.e., STAR) processing. The number of stages varies with different operations; there are about thirty, 40-nsec stages for floating-point arithmetic operations.
- Texas Instruments Advanced Scientific Computer (ASC). A pipelined central processor with both vector and scalar instructions. Eight peripheral processes that give the ASC some of the characteristics of an asymmetric multiprocessor. Central processors with 1, 2, 3, or 4 pipelines are available. The basic cycle of the pipeline is 60 nsec.

Parallel Systems—Array or Vector Processor Organizations

All of the configurations discussed above except the pipeline systems achieved concurrency or parallelism by the replication of complete processing units, each capable of autonomous operation on a separate instruction stream utilizing separate data streams also. The major characteristic of array or vector operations is that the same operation is to be performed on a large collection of data elements that are somehow related, and it is often possible for this operation to be executed on all of the data elements at the same time. If this is the situation, then only a single control unit can decode the single instruction stream and issue control signals to a collection or array of processing elements.

The basic configuration of an array processor is shown in Figure 2-14. Since the individual processing elements are not complete CPUs and are not capable of independent operation, the organizations discussed here are parallel systems rather than multiprocessors. The only possible variation in the operation of a processing element in an array is the ability to turn it off and on for specific instructions. These activation signals are also generated and distributed by the control processor.

The first major work in this area was on SOLOMON [Murtha]. SOLOMON I was followed by SOLOMON II and then by ILLIAC IV [Barnes et al.]. The two SOLOMON systems were studies leading up to the

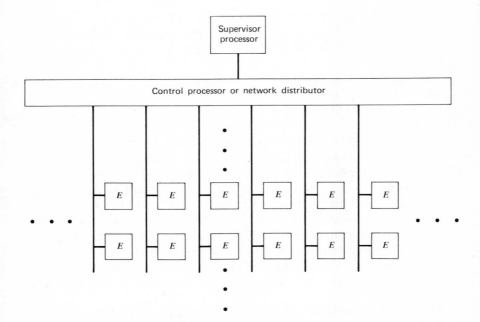

Figure 2-14 Array processor—basic configuration. *Note.* Each *E* is an execution or processing element which has most of the capabilities of a stand-alone CPU plus its own private memory.

design of the ILLIAC IV which has been constructed and is in operation. SOLOMON was a very ambitious design containing 1024 processing or execution elements in one array under the control of a single control processor. Each processing element was not very powerful and had a small private memory of only 4096 bits [see Lorin, p. 300].

SOLOMON consists of a 32 × 32 array of processing elements (PEs) under control of a central control processor. The central control unit contains program storage, has the means to retrieve and interpret the stored instruction, and has the capability, subject to multimodal logic, to cause execution of those instructions within the array. Thus at any given instant, each processing element in the system is capable of performing the same operation on the operands stored in the same memory location of each PE. Because each PE is provided with its own core storage unit, these operands may all be different.

Each processing element may communicate with its four adjacent "neighbors." The "edge" elements, which do not possess a full set of neighbors, use their free connections for I/O. Additionally, the central control may broadcast constants for use by all members of the array.

Each PE in the array has a mode register; commands from the central control to the PE are executed by the PE only when the mode signals from the controller match the mode stored in the PE. [Slotnick, Borck, and McReynolds]

SOLOMON was criticized for both its size and "the relatively awkward mechanism for transferring data from one PE to another and because of the relative inflexibility accruing from fixed local allocation of storage" [Lorin, p. 301].

The major difference between SOLOMON I and II was the technology utilized in the processing elements and their speed.

The successor to SOLOMON was the ILLIAC IV. The basic design of the ILLIAC IV included 256 processing elements, each considerably more powerful than those proposed for SOLOMON. The 256 PEs were arranged in four quadrants of 64 each (8 × 8 array) with a separate control unit for each quadrant. Each PE has a much larger private memory, and 2000 64-bit words, and each PE has direct access to I/O as well as the four-way communication with each neighbor as in SOLOMON. The control processor is a Burroughs B6700 which performs executive programs such as loading and common support such as compiling. One quadrant of the ILLIAC IV, 64 PEs and one B6700, has been assembled thus far and is in operation. Because of the nature of the system organization this portion will probably be quite sufficient to assess the value of parallel array processing.

Although it is estimated that the ILLIAC IV will invert a 700 × 700 matrix in 1sec at an approximate cost of $1.50, the main problem or deterent to the exploitation of this form of multiprocessing will be the preparation of programs that can utilize its capabilities and the development of translators and other support software that will analyze automatically programs and produce code for parallel execution.

The ILLIAC IV is also rather unusual in that it represents a hierarchy of multiprocessors. There is a Control Processor for each quadrant of 64 PE's, and then a Central Control Processor coordinating the four quadrants (see Figure 2-15).

Other examples of parallel processors either already produced or in development are as follows:

- Goodyear Aerospace STARAN.   This system utilizes both array processing organization and associative processing techniques for additional parallelism. It was designed specifically for the processing of multiple radar tracks in air traffic applications, although it can certainly be used in other applications such as data management. Although each processing element in the STARAN is not extremely fast, the associative and array characteristics of the system combined result in quite high throughput for the tracking application. A basic

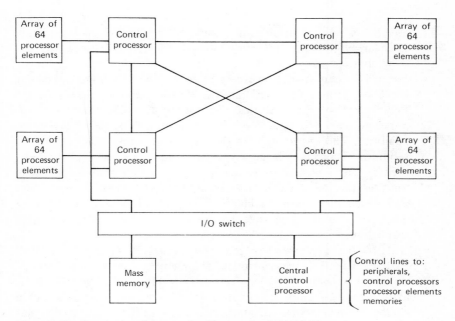

Figure 2-15   Organization of the complete (four-quadrant) ILLIAC IV.

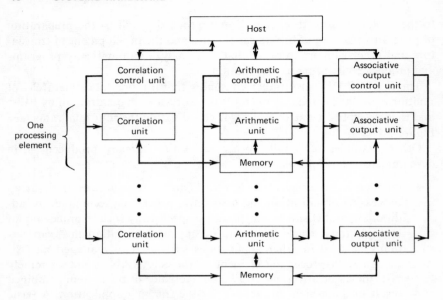

Figure 2-16   PEPE system organization.

STARAN configuration can include up to 32 associative arrays. Each array contains 65K bits (256 × 256) with 256 processing elements in each array.

- Parallel Ensemble of Processing Elements (PEPE). Developed for the U.S. Army Advanced Ballistic Missile Defense Agency by the Bell Telephone Laboratories and the System Development Corporation with Honeywell producing a prototype of reduced capabilities. The overall size of the final configuration is not yet determined. There is a large asymmetric multiprocessor (CDC 7600) used as the control host (see Figure 2-16), with additional special units used as the Correlation Control Unit, Arithmetic Control Unit, and Associative Output Unit. PEPE also utilizes a combination of both array and associative techniques to attain extremely high throughput.

- OMEN-60 Orthogonal Computer by Sanders Associates. A DEC PDP-11 is used as the controller. The memory can be accessed horizontally (as 16-bit words) or vertically in bit slices. The PDP-11 is used as the horizontal arithmetic unit and a special processor is used as the vertical arithmetic unit. An organization such as this has specific applicability to problems in linear algebra, fast Fourier transforms, and so on.

System Organizations Emphasizing Fault-Tolerance

It is in the area of special highly fault-tolerant designs that the "art" of system organization appears. Every multiprocessor possesses a large degree of fault tolerance when compared to a uniprocessor. However, it is possible to give special emphasis to this aspect of system performance by using redundant elements that can be duplexed and reconfigured similarly to multiprocessors as necessary. A definite amount of engineering design analysis is involved in determing the reliability of any given configuration; however, it is usually an unstructured decision that derives the form of the configuration to be examined. A more complete discussion of this topic is given in Miller et al.

One system that is neither a multiprocessor or even a multicomputer is the Massachusetts Institute of Technology, Instrumentation Laboratory, SIRU (part of Strapped-down Inertial Reference Unit) computer* shown in Figure 2-17. Even though it has two processors and what appears to be a multiprocessor interconnection system it is not a "multi-" system at all times; both processors are working on the same problem, executing the same instruction stream and same data stream in synchronization. Only one processor is "active" in that it issues "write" commands. Both

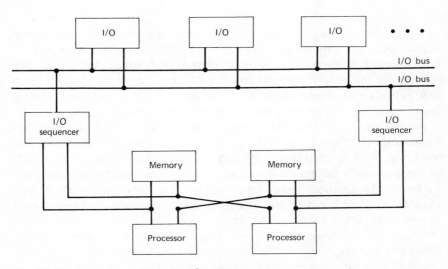

Figure 2-17 Fault-tolerant design—MIT/IL SIRU computer.

* R. Crisp, J. P. Gilmore, and A. L. Hopkins, Jr., "SIRU — A New Inertial System Concept for Inflight Reliability and Maintainability," MIT Instrumentation Laboratory Report E-2407, May 1969.

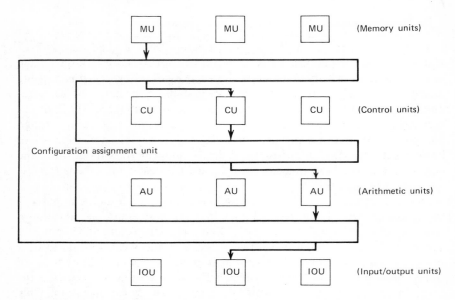

Figure 2-18 Fault-tolerant design—Electronics Research Center, Hamilton Standard modular computer.

memories have identical contents, since they respond to all write commands; however, only the primary one responds to "read" requests. The interconnection system is designed to permit continuous checking of the accuracy of the various modules and immediate reconfiguration to establish new active or primary units as the case may be. Obviously, the primary intent of this system design is high availability with little lost time.

NASA also developed a high availability system at the Electronics Research Center (Figure 2-18) [Wang; Wood, 1968; and Wood, 1969]. The work was done by Hamilton Standard. In this system, there are three sets of components including memory units, control units, arithmetic units, and I/O units. In addition, there was a configuration assignment unit (CAU) capable of interconnecting the functional units to maintain an operational system. The CAU could also connect multiple memory modules to the same processor. However, since *no memory is shared*, the system is certainly not a multiprocessor. It is merely a method to maintain two or three uniprocessors with high availability.

Possible modes of operation include the following:

1. Three computers working on the same problem and voting on their results during a high reliability period such as boost (i.e., comparing the independently obtained results and accepting those that are the same in case of disagreement).

2. Three computers working on independent problems.

3. A method to keep several computers on-line with a minimum of spares.

The system has possibilities but is complex because of the amount of switching hardware needed. It also necessities an infallible CAU to achieve the reliability goals. It seems of dubious value compared to an equivalent multiprocessor. [Miller et al.]

The CAU in this system was basically a crossbar switching matrix and, as such, had all the problems of complexity found in other crossbar systems.

Another fault-tolerant design that uses multiple units but is not a multiprocessor is the Jet Propulsion Laboratory STAR (Self-Testing and Repairing) system [see Avizienis and Avizienis, Mathur, and Rennels]. The multiple modules are used only for fault detection and backup. A failed module is switched out of the system and replaced (Figure 2-19):

STAR is built around a hard-core monitor called the test and repair processor

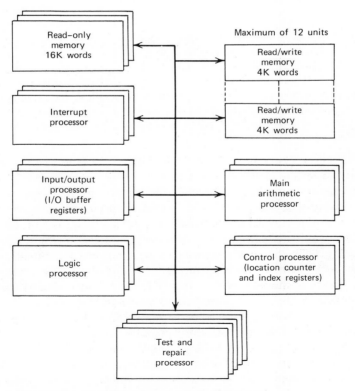

Figure 2-19 JPL STAR system organization [Weitzman].

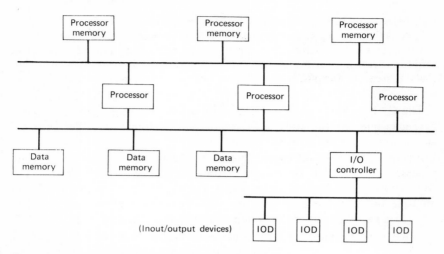

Figure 2-20   Fault-tolerant design—MIT/IL ACGN computer.

(TARP), which rolls back the program to a built-in checkpoint and restarts it if an error is detected. Each 32-bit instruction includes four bits that establish a modulo 15 residue check—each 32-bit word, that is, considered as a binary number, must be divisible by 15. If it is not, the TARP assumes that a transient error has occurred, and rolls back the program. If the error shows up again at the same point, the TARP assumes that the error is permanent, not transient. It shuts off the power to the fault unit and powers up a standby to take over, again from the same checkpoint. [Weitzman]

Every multiprocessor has a limited capability to be fault-tolerant. One of the major problems in standard systems is identifying the occurrence of a fault and determining how to reconfigure the system to overcome its effects. Looking past the Apollo space flight program the instrumentation laboratory of the Massachusetts Institute of Technology has worked on the design of a complete multiprocessor system that is also highly reliable and fault-tolerant. This involves the inclusion of additional functional units to allow work to continue even after failures and voting or other types of error detection mechanisms to identify failures. The layout of the basic system design for the ACGN Computer is shown in Figure 2-20.

A discussion of the reliability of several multiprocessors proposed as candidates for Air Traffic Control processors is presented by Dancy. Some actual numeric projections of system reliability as a function of component reliability and system organization are given. The primary systems discussed are the Parallel Element Processing Ensemble, (PEPE) the Goodyear

STARAN Associative Processor, the IBM 9020, the UNIVAC A\
and the IBM S/370.

Interconnection Paths

After observing the numerous methods for interconnecting the functional units, it is possible to see that there are several considerations in the design of the transfer path itself. The primary conflict arises between speed or total transfer rate possible and the complexity of the interface with the path and its control. The designer of the system should consider all of the following:

- The destination of the transfer must be specified.

  - This requires circuitry at both the source and the sink.
  - The ability to specify a large number of destinations widens the width of the path devoted to control (nonproductive transfer).
  - The destination may have to be specified for each transfer or it may be possible to establish a temporary path available for multiple transfers.
  - The identification of the source may be implied, may not be necessary, or may have to be specified in a similar manner to the destination.

- The width of the path affects directly the overall transfer rate and cost.

  - Wide paths are more complex in terms of circuitry and more costly to switch.
  - The ideal path width is the word size of the normal accessing or processing unit; that is, the number of bits accessed in one memory cycle or the number of bits accessed in one word as operated on by the processor. The decision depends on the cost/performance goal. The path width may be a divisor of the word length for low cost or a multiple for high performance.
  - There are nearly always discrepanicies between the access or processing widths between memory units, processor units, I/O devices, and addresses. In fact, the processor unit width may be variable (i.e., byte, half-word, single-word, and double-word operations are often possible).
  - Any differences between data transfer path width and the width of the accessing or processing unit will require that assemble and disassemble buffer registers be used adding to the cost of the interface at each functional unit where they are required.

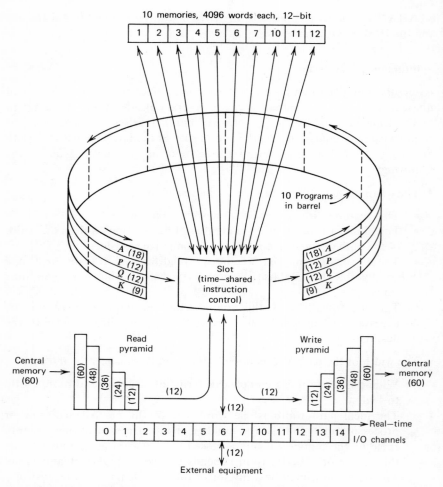

Figure 2-21 CDC 6600 peripheral processors (showing connections to PP and central memory and I/O channels).

- The clock rate of the transfer path also affects directly the overall transfer rate.
  - Transit time has to be allowed.
  - Higher speed circuitry at both the interfaces and switching points will add to the cost, complexity, and maintenance of the system.
- Type of signal being transferred (i.e., control, data, or address).
- Number of separate paths.

Needless to say, these are not all of the factors that must be
however, they do provide some insight into the compromises th
be made in this extremely important part of the system. If the s
not transfer data rapidly enough, then performance will suffer, and the
benefits of configuring a parallel system to obtain concurrency may be
negative.

Virtual Processors

In several systems, what appear to be separate multiple processors are
actually only virtual processors. Each "processor" has its own memory and
control registers, such as accumulator and instruction counter. However,
all of the processors share a single arithmetic and logic unit on a round
robin or other sharing basis. Two examples of this technique are the peripheral processors on both the CDC 6600 and the Texan Instruments Advanced Scientific Computer and the main processors on the Memorex
MRX-40 and 50.

In the CDC 6600, the four control register for the 10 peripheral
processor units are arranged in a logical "barrel" with the "slot," or the
logical location of the arithmetic system, moving around the barrel once
each microsecond spending 100 nsec at each position. These 100 ns are sufficient for the completion of most PPU operations while 1000 ns is the
storage cycle time (see Figure 2-21).

The Texan Instruments ASC has a similar system in its peripheral
processing unit. A complete cycle through all the virtual systems takes 1360
ns with each position receiving a 85-ns slice. The maximum number of virtual processors is eight. The assignment of virtual processors to the 16 time
slots can be changed to allocate more time to a specific processor or to
effectively eliminate one or more completely (see Figure 2-22).

Multiple Arithmetic Units

Thus far all of the system organizations discussed have exhibited a multiplicity of operating elements at the functional unit level (processor,
memory, I/O controller, etc.). Parallelism or concurrency can be carried to
a lower level if desired. One example is the central processor of the CDC
6600. A standard processor makes use of the same arithmetic and logic
building blocks for various operations—there is only one accumulator used
for holding the results of all arithmetic operations, the same accumulator is
used for all logical and shifting operations, there is only one adder, and so
on.

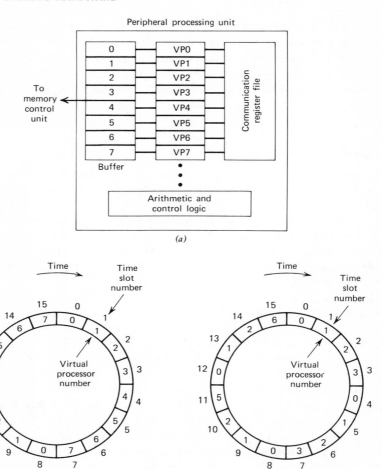

Figure 2-22 Peripheral processors in the T. I. Advanced Scientific Computer. (*a*) Multiple instruction streams in the peripheral processing unit. (*b*) Equal time slot assignments. (*c*) Weighted time slot assignments.

A key description of the operation of the 6600 is "parallel by function." This means that a number of arithmetic functions may be performed simultaneously. There are ten functional units that operate somewhat independently (see Figure 2-23). There are two incrementing units, one add, two multipliers, one divide, one long add, one shift, one bollean, and one branching unit. Of course, the degree of parallelism that is attained is de-

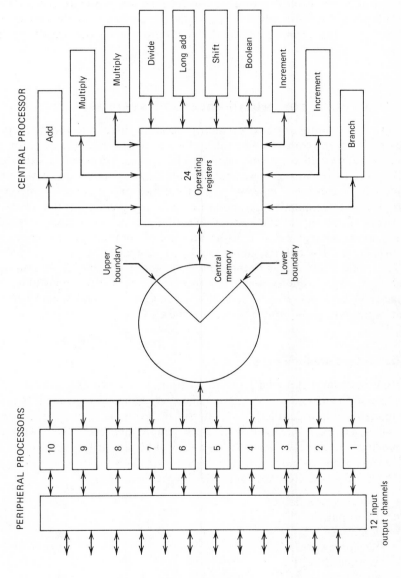

Figure 2-23 Block diagram of 6600 (illustrating the multiple arithmetic and logic units in the CPU).

57

pendent on the proper mix of instructions in a sequence and availability of the operands.

Obviously, the central processor control function is greatly complicated, since it must determine when the operands are available for use and are not subject to being changed by another operation being performed concurrently.

MAIN MEMORY FOR MULTIPROCESSOR SYSTEMS

In all of the configurations for multiprocessors discussed, the memory is shown as several separate modules. This is a standard practice for the central memory of uniprocessors also. The original purpose of establishing certain fixed-size modules was to standardize the production of the units while still permitting expansion of the total memory attached to any given system. Also economic considerations are involved with the trade-off between complexity of the address selection and read-out circuitry as opposed to the savings possible via greater use of common-use circuitry such as MARs, MORs, buffers, control and power supplies.

The availability of separate memory modules capable of autonomous and even asynchronous operation present yet another opportunity for concurrent or parallel operations. Consider first the breakdown of events that occur during one complete cycle of the CPU.

Overlapped Memory Access

During both the Fetch and Execute portion of the cycle (see Figure 2-24), two memory accesses are necessary. The first change in the timing that can be made to obtain parallel or overlapped operation is to overlap the I and E cycles as much as possible as shown in Figure 2-25. Even with this procedure, the overall system throughout will be primarily a function of the cycle time of the memory.

The normal cycle for core memories is (Figure 2–28*a*).

- Address selection.
- Read-pulses.
- Readout.
- Settling period.
- Write-pulses.
- Settling period.

If it is a WRITE operation, the results of the READ are discarded; if it is a READ, the results of the readout must be written back into the cores, since core readout is destructive.

Memory Access Conflicts

One factor that reduces the performance of a multiprocessor system is a memory access conflict. These are of two types—software and hardware. A software memory access conflict occurs when a processor attempts to use a table or data set that is currently in use by another processor which has activated the "lock" to preclude access by anyone else. Such locks are necessary for the proper execution and integrity of both control routines and applications programs. Software memory conflicts, better known as "memory lockout," are discussed in the section on software problems in Chapter 3. When a processor encounters a memory lockout, it may be able to switch to some other task which does not utilize that particular table or data set; however, most of the time it is forced to go into a WAIT loop checking the status of the lock which is often kept set for relatively long periods.

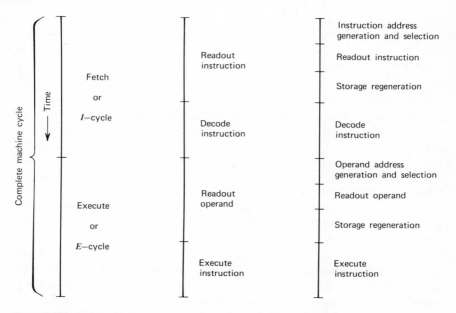

Figure 2-24   Memory access actions occurring in a complete machine cycle.

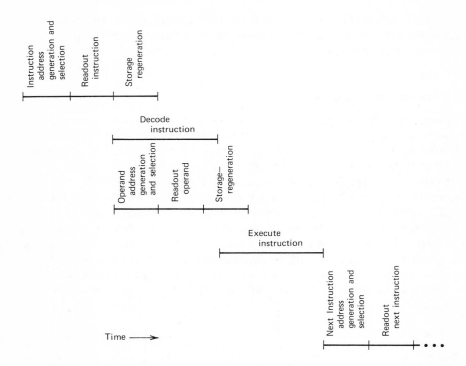

Figure 2-25   Overlapped fetch and execute cycles.

A hardware memory conflict occurs when two or more processors or an I/O unit and a processor attempt to access the same memory module simultaneously; "simultaneously" as used here means the conflicting requests are made during a single memory cycle. Since only one access can be made per memory cycle, the other request(s) must wait; however, in this case the wait will usually be only a cycle or two in each case. The problem occurs when the number of conflicts gets large. This form of degradation also known as "interprocessor interference" can become quite appreciable and present a real problem if the system (both hardware and software) is not specifically designed to cope with it.

There have been few actual measurements of this effect because of the difficulty in instrumenting the test as well as establishing the base for comparison. One estimate made for the two-processor S/360 Model 67 running under the University of Michigan UMMPS system was that it was "less than a few percent and probably less than one percent" [Alexander].

Some simulation studies were made of the quantitative effects of hardware conflicts on a crossbar system running real time tasks utilized a paging memory allocation procedure.

The number of memory modules was assumed to be equal to the number of processors. The memory conflict depends on the cycle time of the memory and the processor operating speed which determines the rate of memory accesses. Processor timing was assumed to be as in Figure 2-26.

The processors competed for each individual memory on a round-robin basis. A memory was attached to a particular processor for a memory cycle time (t_{mc}). If the required memory was unavailable, the processor cycle of Figure 2-26 would be lengthened accordingly. Values used in the simulation were:

$$t_{fO} = t_{fI} = t_{mc}/2$$
$$t_D = 1/\mu\text{sec}$$
$$t_E = 1 \ \mu\text{sec} \ (60\%), \ 9 \ \mu\text{sec} \ (40\%)$$

Both the instructions and data were considered to be randomly distributed in pages among the memory modules. [A somewhat unrealistic condition.] A total of 256 accesses was made from each page and then a new page was chosen at random. The resultant system through-put and percentage of a processor's time lost to a memory conflict appear in Figures 2-27a and b. For the processors assumed, the memory conflicts do not appear critical for 1 and 2 μsec memories. . . .

Since the scheduling algorithm . . . allows some measure of freedom in allocating the total system workload among the individual processors, one possible algorithm is to assign individual tasks to the processors so as to minimize potential memory conflicts. In this case, there would be a complex interaction between the task scheduling and memory allocation functions of the Executive. [Jordan]

The simulation indicates that the degradation effects that would occur with a memory operating with a cycle time the same as the average instruction execution time (4.2 μsec) are quite appreciable. This problem is definitely of major importance in any system design. The benefits of higher

Figure 2-26 Processor cycle times [Jordan]. t_{fI}-time to fetch an instruction from the memory; t_D-time to decode instruction address; t_{fO}-time to fetch an operand from memory; and t_E-time to execute an instruction.

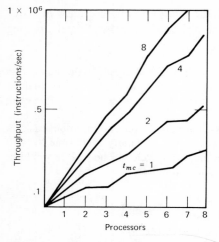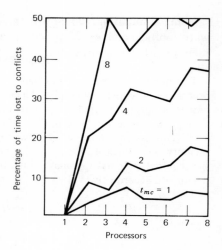

Figure 2-27 Effects of memory conflicts [Jordan].

speed memories are obvious. The effect of more, but perhaps smaller, memory modules is not.

One method that may be used to reduce performance degradation due to memory access conflicts as well as queueing delays when the same control or service program is being utilized by several different processors is the replication of the program code in different memory modules. This problem has been examined quantitatively by Covo, who determined that full replication is unnecessarily expensive. In fact, partial replication "may cause 30 to 40% reduction in the combined cost of CPUs and program memory, compared to full replication" [Covo].

A recent short note by Ravi examines the effective bandwidth of multiple memory modules with interleaved addresses using analythic methods and probability theory. His findings indicate that the number of words transferred per memory cycle will be higher than results obtained by the investigators [Ravi; Hellerman; and Burnett and Coffman]; however, his results are highly dependent on the probability distribution for the number of requests made during a single cycle. In any event, Ravi argues that if the average number of random requests exceeds the number of modules memory utilization is improved.

Physical and Logical Memory Address Assignments

Very early it was observed that the effective readout time could be greatly reduced if successive memory address were placed in different modules in an interleaved fashion. This is illustrated below:

	Memory Module No. 0	Memory Module No. 1
Address stored	0, 2, 4, 6, . . .	1, 3, 5, 7, . . .
Timing sequence:	Address selection	
	Read pulses	
	Read-out	
	Settling period	Address selection
	Write pulses	Read pulses
	Settling period	Read-out
	Address selection	Settling period
	Read pulses	Write pulses
	Read-out	Settling period
	Settling period	Address selection
	.	.
	.	.
	.	.

The use of two "interleaved" memories has effectively doubled the memory transfer rate with little increase in complexity other than the requirement that the interface for each module distinguishes between even and odd addresses (Figure 2-28 b and c). The basic timing relations for core memories actually permit effective pay-off from four-way interleaving; however, past that point, little advantage is gained.

This same technique can be utilized in multiprocessor systems also;* however, the results may well be counter-productive in these cases. The problems that may occur are the interference or conflicts between the accesses generated by the various processors, since they are all operating simultaneously and the interleaving technique requires that they use all or at least several of the memory modules. This problem is discussed below. The other drawback to the interleaving system of assigning addresses is a lowering of system availability. If a memory module goes down, then it is not possible to merely reallocate core assignments and continue, since a logical area of core is spread over several physical units. For this latter reason, as well as the interference factor, a multiprocessor system will often

---

* To be fully effective, the processor must have multiple memory paths or ports and normally have some mechanism for overlapped access between them.

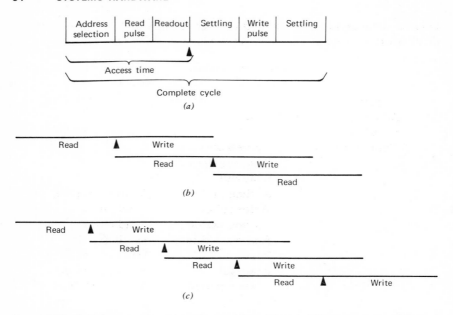

Figure 2-28 Full memory cycle and overlap conditions. (*a*) Basic full memory cycle. (*b*) Overlap with symmetric cycle. (*c*) Overlap exploiting shorter access time.

divide its addresses between the memory modules so that each module contains a series of consecutive addresses. This will slow down the effective transfer rate for each individual processor, but may well result in a higher overall system transfer rate and a greatly enhanced capability to reconfigure the system when one module fails.

Finally, a multiprocessing system with a large number of reasonably small memory modules may use a combination of both methods accepting the fact that when one module goes down, its companions (one to three) are also removed from service until all can be brought back up together.

An example of the various methods in which logical addresses can be assigned to the physical memory modules in the UNIVAC 1108 is shown in Figure 2-29*a, b*, and *c* for the 1108 multiprocessor. Address interleaving is quite common now and Table 2-1 lists several systems that have that capability. It should be noted that this capability is not always implemented for the reasons stated above, losing two to four times as much logical memory when one physical module fails.

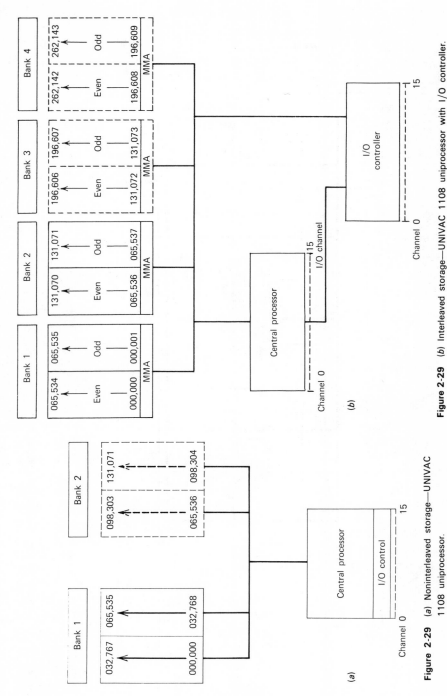

Figure 2-29 (*b*) Interleaved storage—UNIVAC 1108 uniprocessor with I/O controller.

Figure 2-29 (*a*) Noninterleaved storage—UNIVAC 1108 uniprocessor.

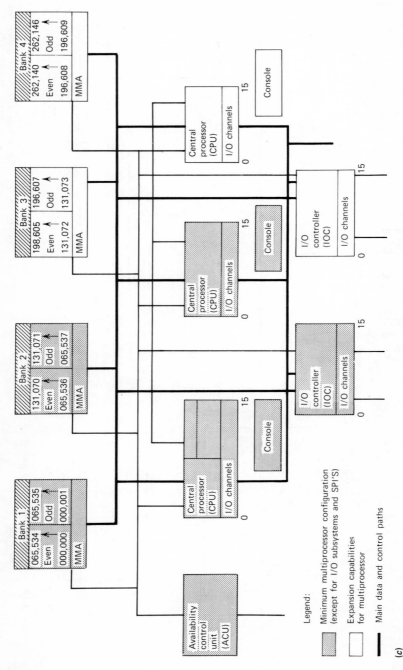

Figure 2-29 (c) Interleaved storage—Univac 1108 multiprocessor.

TABLE 2-1   EXAMPLES OF MAIN MEMORY BANK ADDRESS INTERLEAVING[a]

	Two-way	Four-way
Burroughs		
B6700	X	
B7700	X	X
Control Data		
Cyber 72/73/74	(max. of 10 concurrent accesses)	
STAR	(32-way)	
Digital Equipment		
System 10	X	X
Honeywell		
6050/60	X	
6070/80	X	X
IBM		
S/360–65/67	X	
75/85		X
195	(16-way)	
S/370–165		X
Texas Inst.		
ASC	(8-way)	
UNIVAC		
1108	X	
1110	X	
Xerox		
Sigma 6/7/8/9	X	X

[a] Possible—not always implemented.

INPUT/OUTPUT ORGANIZATION AND INTERFACES

Thus far, the discussions of various organizations have all emphasized the interconnection arrangements possible between processors, memories, and I/O channels or controllers. The interconnection with the individual I/O device control units and the devices themselves have been ignored except for the two examples shown in the section on the crossbar system (i.e., the use of a separate crossbar switch matrix between the channels and the devices on the standard Burroughs systems and the attachment of the devices directly to the basic switch matrix in the proposed Burroughs Multi-Interpreter System).

The ability to connect devices directly to a single time-shared bus, if that

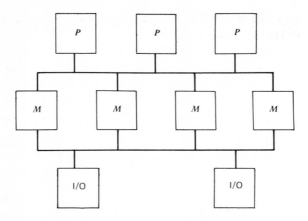

Figure 2-30   Dual time-shared bus system organization—separate processor and I/O buses.

is the basic organization of the system, has both advantages and disadvantages. The primary advantage is the flexibility and ease with which the I/O device complement can be changed. It can also be seen that any legitimate channel controller to device path can be established readily by using merely the proper addresses on the transfer bus. The major disadvantage of such an arrangement is the additional load placed on the single transfer bus by the I/O transfers. This can be overcome in part by a dual time-shared bus configuration (see Figure 2-30); however, the time-sharing of a single path is still a constraint.

Another more basic consideration often precludes the use of either the crossbar matrix or the common time-shared bus for I/O devices—most of the device control units and the devices themselves were designed for use in systems with a tree-like topology* and are not adaptable to anything else (Figure 2-31). It would be possible to configure a multiprocessor system with each processor having its own private set of channels, control units, and devices; however, this would be very inflexible, require detailed knowledge of the requirements of an unvarying workload, and negate many of the benefits of the multiprocessor organization. If there were private sets of I/O devices then there would be the additional, and unnecessary, expense of storing multiple copies of all of the system software at that level. A much better arrangement of the control units and devices is to make use of the dual connection capability that many of them already have or to use a special interface unit to permit sharing. The tree-like topology is still

---

* Physically or logically even though daisy-chained.

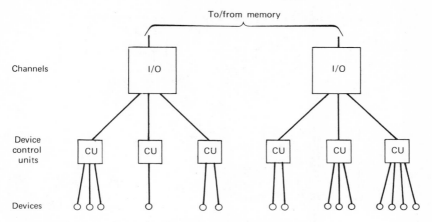

Figure 2-31   Connection of I/O devices by common tree-like topology.

retained. The dual connection can be made at either the control unit or the device level (Figure 2-32).

Multiple interconnection of control units is made possible in the UNIVAC 1108 system by the use of a Shared Peripheral Interface (SPI). The SPI can be used with single-channel peripheral units or with dual channel devices (Figure 2-33). Both types of connections are found in 1108 multiprocessor systems depending on the type of device being connected, its transfer rate, and other characteristics.

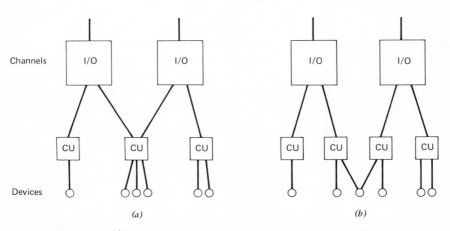

Figure 2-32   Sharing I/O devices by dual-connecting. (*a*) At control unit level. (*b*) At device level.

Each shared peripheral interface can be connected to up to four channels

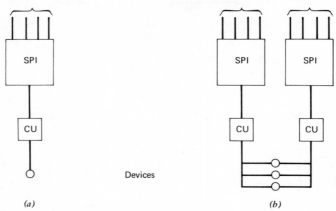

(a)   (b)

Figure 2-33 UNIVAC 1108 use of shared peripheral interface to permit sharing of I/O devices. (a) Single-channel system. (b) Dual-channel system.

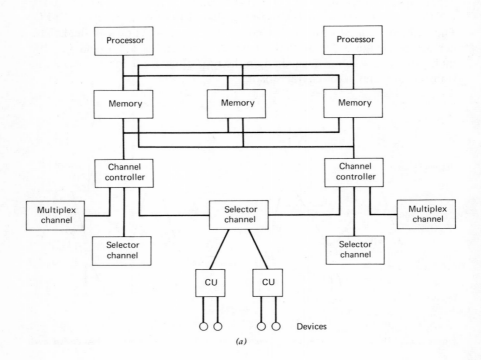

(a)

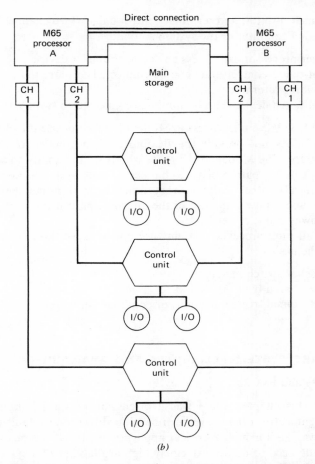

Figure 2-34 IBM multiprocessors and their I/O connections; (a) Model 67 multiprocessor for timesharing. (b) Model 65 multiprocessor [Witt].

IBM's 360/67 can be configured as a dual processor as well as a uni-processor. For the dual version each processor is connected through a crossbar to a special device called the channel controller (Figure 2-34a). The channel controller interfaces with one to six selector channels and one multiplexor channel. These channels operate in the normal manner. (Each selector channel has a high-speed path with up to eight control units on each and addressing capability for 256 devices. It is used for the high-speed devices while the multiplexor channels are used for slower units such as the reader, punch, printer, and terminal control units.) Two channel controllers then provide flexibility for the system so that:

- Either processor can access any control unit or device.
- Dual-tailed control units can be connected to more than one channel providing alternate paths.
- Dual-tailed devices can be similarly connected to two control units.

The IBM S/360 multiprocessor Model 65 does not use the channel controller and does not provide the flexibility of the model 67 I/O system (Figure 2-34b). The Model 65MP relies wholly on the ability to connect the control unit to a separate private channel on each system (known as dual-homing of a control unit). Direct communication between the two processors does allow some use of the alternate path if the channel busy is busy or down on one system.

Nearly all multiprocessor systems use one of these three basic interconnection schemes:

- Crossbar switch matrix.
- Time-shared bus.
- Dual-homed tree connections or combination thereof.

HARDWARE SYSTEM RELIABILITY AND AVAILABILITY

Fail-Safe and Fail-Soft

Earlier in this chapter, there was a discussion of special multiprocessor system organizations that have been developed to produce fault-tolerant or fail-safe systems for highly critical applications. Those designs were motivated by the need to obtain extremely high availability of a system capable of performing the total workload regardless of the cost, or at least not very strongly constrained by cost. [This high availability was attained through the use of duplicate or redundant functional units and interconnection schemes that could be switched as necessary to partition off a "complete" system.] This specific goal and the methods used to attain it are certainly at one extreme of the spectrum of reliability and availability; the other extreme is a straight-line system with only one unit of each type and no excess capacity.

Availability is certainly a function of the reliability of the system and its components; however, it is not always a simple relationship. In the straight-line collection of single units mentioned above, the relationship is quite clear with the overall system reliability being merely the product of the reliabilities of each unit in turn and the availability of the system being a simple function of its reliability, probability of failing, and mean time to repair (MTTR). When multiple identical units are available and a certain degree of flexibility of reconfiguration is possible as in most multiprocessors, the solution is not simple. One technique used to provide this capability is the use of a special control unit. This method is used in the UNIVAC 1108 which has an Availability Control Unit (ACU) and in the Bell Laboratories CLC system (safeguard computer). The UNIVAC 1108 ACU performs the following functions:

- Partitions the multiprocessor system hardware into independent systems.
- Takes units offline for maintenance without disrupting operation of the rest of the system.
- Protects main storage in event of a power failure in the CPU or I/O Controller.
- Automatically initiates a recovery sequence after a failure.

Multiple parallel units are definitely not new to the digital computer field, but their benefits have not always been exploited. Even the UNIVAC I contained two complete sets of duplicate arithmetic registers. (Remember, those were the days of unreliable vacuum-tube circuitry.) These were compared constantly, and the machine was stopped whenever a discrepancy was detected. However, the duplicate set of registers did not aid in restoring the machine to operation and, therefore, did not improve its availability, although there is no denying the value of knowing when incorrect results may be appearing. What was provided was an error- or failure-detection capability which is certainly the first step toward improved availability.

If there are multiple units in a system, then some operational capability may be retained if the failure of a unit can be detected *and if* the system can be reconfigured to operate without the downed unit. The capability of this new system will undoubtedly be less than the original unless there was redundancy or unused capacity in the original system, and it will then not be able to perform the entire workload. This leads to an extension of the "fail-safe" concept to one of "fail-soft" or graceful degradation. The various conditions that may occur and govern the success of the error-recovery procedure are discussed in Chapter 3. The subject of interest here is the hardware that provides the reconfiguration capability.

The UNIVAC ARTS III system found isolation to be impossible due to the nature of multiprocessor operation (e.g., can not tell which processor changed the table). It utilized another philosophy. When an error was detected, it found out who was still good and went with that set. The importance of this experience is quite significant.

Reconfiguration

Reconfiguration is a combination of several factors.

- Physical switches in the transfer or interconnection paths.
- Actions by the console operator using the system control language which occur automatically in a real-time system.
- Actions by the operating system.
- Control tables maintained by the operating system.

Any of the first three types of actions will probably require that changes be made in the tables which define the complete configuration of equipment available, processors, channels, control units, devices, and core, and the interconnection paths functioning. Some operating systems will sense automatically the operating environment by testing periodically a collection of "presence bits" that are set by each unit as it comes on-line. This procedure is employed in the Burrough Master Control Program (MCP). In this case, unit failures or operator changes to the system due to turning off a unit are detected quickly, and appropriate adjustments are made to the control tables which in turn drive the operating system in resource allocation and management.

In the IBM S/360, the operator has to tell the operating system that a unit is going off-line by the use of the VARY command from the console. Of course, unless it is absolutely necessary, he would not want to immediately suspend operation of a unit that has work in progress. The multiprocessor Model 65 has a control command to bring a processor to an "orderly halt," which means completing all I/O operations in progress that are under its control and completing other pending functions or transferring them to the remaining CPU.

A somewhat different approach is taken in the UNIVAC 1108 system which has a ACU to perform reconfiguration and partitioning as necessary. The ACU also allows units to be taken off-line for maintenance, protects main storage in case of power failures, and initiates automatically a recovery sequence after a failure. In fact, the ACU operates in a rather unusual mode with respect to this last function. It assumes continually that a malfunction has occurred and initiates automatically the error-correcting reinitialization of the entire system unless its internal timer is reset by the executive system within an interval that can be set from 1 to 15 sec. The ACU is an independently operating unit that can be interrogated by a processor to determine which units are on-line and available.

The IBM 9020 is a special multiprocessor developed for air traffic control. Since it is operating in an important and critical real-time environment, its reconfiguration actions must be executed automatically. The reconfiguration technique is based on a Configuration Control Register which is duplicated in the private memory (32 K bytes) of each I/O Control Element. The operation of this reconfiguration system is described by Lorin.

As anyone with digital hardware experience is well aware nearly every system is highly susceptible to "electrical noise" or extraneous impulses introduced into the system. For this reason there may be a unique distinction between logical and physical reconfiguration. Although a unit may be logically removed from the system while it is in an operational status by merely modifying the system tables, it is quite often necessary to require a pause in normal operation to guard against the effects of noise when a unit is physically disconnected. After the pause, jobs in progress could then be resumed without the necessity for a system restart.

Summary

Involved in the design of any high-availability system are four underlying concepts, which we present here in summary: (1) modularity—the definition of functonal elements that are assignable, connectable, and isolatable, (2) multiplicity—the replication of selected units to achieve fail-safe redundancy, (3) configurability—the ability quickly to reconnect modules in the face of detected error, (4) analysis and recoverability—the ability to detect errors and to minimize the impact of errors in the system. [Lorin]

All of these concepts are functions of the hardware, both the individual units, and the system organization. The last two also require a large amount of integration with the software.

MULTIPROCESSOR HARDWARE

Generalized guidelines to assist the designer of a multiprocessor have not yet been developed. There are no "cookbook rules"; however, the designs do not appear to be driven totally by *ad hoc* decisions (e.g., costs of different technologies). A number of trade-offs can be made. Perhaps the most significant of these is cost versus performance in a very general sense. Some of these factors are listed in Table 2-2.

There can be no better example of this than the interconnection or data transfer system. At one extreme, the highly sophisticated crossbar switch matrix provides almost complete hardware control over the transfer process but will contain as many components and active circuitry as two to three central processors. The other end of the spectrum is occupied by the totally passive time-shared, common-bus which is merely so many con-

TABLE 2-2   POINTS TO CONSIDER IN COMPARISON OF HARDWARE SYSTEM ORGANIZATIONS

Physical connection required.
- Number of wires connecting functional units (size of cables).

Complexity of control mechanism.
- Contention for a transfer path.
- Resolution of conflicts at data destination.
- Completion (connection) of transfer path.

Reliability.
- Not degraded by single unit failure of interconnection equipment.
- Ability to gracefully degrade.
- Ability to recover and complete task started by a failed processor.
- Ability to reconfigure.

Performance.
- Overall transfer rate possible.
- Overall effective utilization of equipment.

Hardware (functional unit) capabilities.
- Number of access ports available.
- Is system also to operate as a uniprocessor?
- Location of interconnection control: centralized switch; distributed in each unit.

Application/use to be made of the system.
- Software required: control system; application programs.

---

ductor paths. This is certainly a more reliable single-path transfer/interconnection system; however, its limitation in transfer rate have already been discussed, and some of the complexity has merely been moved to the interface required at each and every functional unit attached to the bus. Also, the fact that there is just a single path makes the total system subject to catastrophic failure based on one critical component or unit.

Comparing the three major organizations:
Time-shared/common-bus.

- Cheapest
- Least complex—bus may be totally passive although multiplexing on a single bus can add complexity.
- Easiest to physically modify system configuration by adding or removing functional units.
- System capacity limited by bus transfer rate.
- Failure of bus is catastrophic for the system.

- System expansion (addition of like units) may degrade overall system performance (throughput).
- System efficiency (simultaneous use of all available units) lowest.
- Usually confined to smaller systems.

Crossbar switch matrix.

- Most complex and most expensive interconnection system.
- Cheapest and simplest functional units since none of them require special switching circuitry.
- Configuration (and usually the modules used in it) suitable for multiprocessors only.
- Potential for highest total system transfer rate.
- System expansion usually improves overall system efficiency.
- Potential for expansion without reprogramming.
- Conceptually, expansion limited only by the size of the switch matrix which can usually be modularly expanded within engineering limits.
- Reliability of system dependent on operation of single functional unit, the switch; this weakness can be overcome to some degree by making the switch passive and/or subdividing it into autonomous blocks or by utilizing extensive redundancy in this key unit.

Multi-bus/multiport memory.

- Processor requires no special switching circuitry.
- Most expensive memory units.
- Allows low cost uniprocessor configuration of same functional units without redesign or wasted capabilities.
- Potential for high transfer rate.
- Limited in size and configuration options possible by the number and type of memory ports available.
- Large number of cables and connectors required.

A Functional View of Organization

Before concluding this discussion on system organizations, it should be pointed out that there is a totally different manner of approaching the subject. The basic theme in this chapter has been the topological arrangement of the functional units and their interconnection into a system. Another taxonomy is based on the number of instruction streams, the number of data streams, and their interaction. The basis of this classification scheme is attributable to some work several years ago by Michael Flynn. The more important members of this functional categorization of systems are:

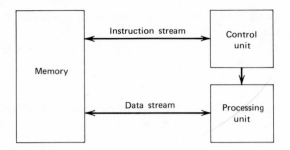

Figure 2-35 SIS-SDS Single-instruction-stream-single-data-stream system organization (examples: standard uniprocessors).

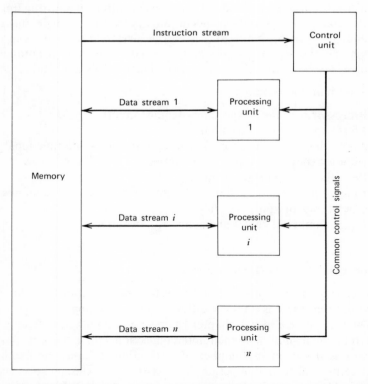

Figure 2-36 SIS-MDS Single-instruction-stream-multiple-data-stream system organization (examples: array and vector processors and other parallel systems).

SIS-SDS—SINGLE INSTRUCTION STREAM—SINGLE DATA STREAM

This is the basic uniprocessor (Figure 2-35).

SIS-MDS—SINGLE INSTRUCTION STREAM—MULTIPLE DATA STREAMS

These are the array, parallel, and associative processors (Figure 2-36). Prime examples of this class are ILLIAC IV, PEPE, and STARAN. The

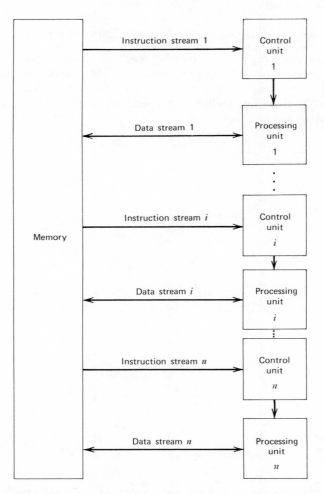

Figure 2-37 MIS-MDS Multiple-instruction-stream-multiple-data-stream system organization (examples: multiprocessors as defined in this book).

CDC 6600 and 7600 and the IBM S/360 Model 85 also fall into this class even though their execution units do not operate in lock step.

MIS-SDS—MULTIPLE INSTRUCTION STREAMS—SINGLE DATA STREAM

This is included more for completeness than any other reason. An example might be a multiprocessor system in which the memory was not segmented into parts. The peripheral processor units of the CDC 6000's and 7000's and the Texas Instruments ASC fall into this class.

MIS-MDS—MULTIPLE INSTRUCTION STREAMS—MULTIPLE DATA STREAMS

More than one program is executing each on its own data. There are multiple processors and multiple memories. Multiprogramming is also imployed. These are the classical multiprocessors as defined in this text (see Figure 2-37). However, multiple, independent uniprocessors could also be said to belong to this class.

CHAPTER 3

OPERATING SYSTEMS AND OTHER SYSTEM SOFTWARE FOR MULTIPROCESSORS

INTRODUCTION

The external differences in the basic characteristics and capabilities between an operating system for a multiprocessor and that for a third-generation uniprocessor are not readily apparent. Internally, there is a great amount of difference. In fact it has been operating system development that has often set the pace for the development and performance of the multiprocessor configuration. One aspect of the system software that sets multiprocessors apart from uniprocessors is the essential need for an extensive operating system to make effective use of the multiprocessor. It is possible for an experienced programmer to operate a uniprocessor without any system software, although the effective utilization of a third-generation machine operated in this manner will be quite low. Such is not the case with even the simplest multiprocessor system. An operating system is usually necessary to even start the system. In fact, it was the development of early multiprocessors such as the NBS PILOT, the Burroughs D 825 (AN/GYK-3), and the Ramo Wooldridge RW 400 (AN/FSQ-27) that first brought into focus many of the basic problems still encountered in operating system organization and operation even in uniprocessors. In fact AOSP, the "Automatic Operating and Scheduling Program" for the D 825, is considered a landmark in the development of operating systems in general. The reader should realize that multiprogramming (i.e., the concurrent execution on a single processor of several simultaneously resident programs) is an almost essential capability of a multiprocessor operating system, and, in fact, multiprogramming might be considered a subset of the total multiprocessor operating system.

The purpose of this chapter is not to cover in detail all the information one needs to have to fully understand even the basics of multiprocessor operating systems. Because of the great similarity to uniprocessor operating systems, the reader is referred to material already available on that subject [COMTRE]. The primary emphasis of this chapter is on those requirements, features, and operations peculiar to multiprocessors.

Although the hardware ensemble may be more complex, the reader should not assume that the system software will be. The availability of additional, redundant functional units often makes it possible to provide better solutions to some of the major problems faced in the uniprocessor, such as:

- Adaptability to changing demands both in quantity and in nature of job mix.
- Availability of at least a minimal operational system for the completion of critical functions.
- Expansion to a larger system with no effect on presently operational programs.
- Response time, etc.

On the other hand, the presence of those additional units complicates several other important functions:

- Utilization of all resources to the maximum extent possible.
- Error recovery to save work in progress.
- Synchronization.
- Structuring application programs to run efficiently.
- Reentrancy.

to list only a few.

ORGANIZATION OF MULTIPROCESSOR OPERATING SYSTEMS

Although many minor variations are possible, there are three basic organizations and modes of operation for the operating system executive of a multiprocessor:

- Master slave.
- Separate executive for each processor.
- Symmetric or anonymous treatment of all processors.

The primary characteristics of these organizations are summarized in Table 3-1 discussed in detail below.

TABLE 3-1 CHARACTERISTICS OF THREE ORGANIZATIONS OF MULTIPROCESSOR OPERATING SYSTEMS

Master Slave	Separate Executive for Each Processor	Symmetric or Anonymous Treatment of All Processors
• Executive always runs in one (the same) processor.	• Each processor services its own needs.	• Master floats from one processor to another.
• Executive routines do not need to be reentrant.	• Supervisory code must be reentrant or replicated.	• Better load balancing.
• No problem of table conflict or lockout for the Executive. (Applications programs will still conflict over table accesses.)	• Each processor has own set of of private tables.	• Conflicts in service requests resolved by priorities.
• Subject to catastrophic failure.	• Not subject to catastrophic failure from single failure; however, restart of a failed processor will probably be very difficult.	• Code must be reentrant since several processors can be executing same service routine.
• Comparatively inflexible.		• Since several processors can be in supervisory state simultaneously, access conflicts can occur.
• Idle time on slave can build up if master is not fast enough.	• In effect, each processor has own set of I/O equipment, files, etc.	• Advantages:
• Most effective for special applications and asymmetric systems.	• Reconfiguration of I/O usually requires manual switching.	Provides graceful degradation.
• Comparatively simpler software and hardware.		Better availability potential.
		Real redundancy.
		Most efficient use of resources.

Master Slave

The master-slave mode may be dictated by the different character of the processors in the system such as the NBS PILOT system which included one processor designed especially for supervisory control and dedicated to that function. The master-slave technique has also been used in other applications because of its simplicity and the fact that it usually allows maximum use of the software that may have already been developed for the processor units operating in a uniprocessor system. It was used in the early TRW 400 system and is currently used in systems such as the SEL 86 for its expediency although there are often plans for replacing it on systems currently being marketed as full-fledged multiprocessors. A current example of this type of operating system organization and operation is the RCA-215 which maintains a single executive in a reserved portion of memory unit 1 with the recovery nucleus in memory unit 2 basing its reliability on the unlikely probability of both failing at the same time.

The primary characteristics of the master-slave mode of operation are summarized below:

- The supervisor always runs in only one of the processors that is selected by the operator. This processor may be of special a design configured just to run the supervisor or it may be similar to all of the others in the system. A special design supervisor processor will probably be dedicated solely to performing that function; however, if the processor is of the general-purpose type it can also be used to run production programs when not involved in performing supervisory actions.
- It is not necessary that all of the supervisory routines be written in reentrant code, since only one processor will be executing them. Reentrant coding will still be necessary for some of the common routines that are used recursively or are subject to multiple activations.
- There will be no problem of conflict or lock-out of Executive tables, since only one processor will be accessing them.
- The system is subject to catastrophic failure if the master fails. If it is not of special design, it may be possible for the operator to restart the system using another processor as the new master.
- The system is inflexible consisting of a main processor with one or more dependent processors.
- The master must be able to execute its supervisory functions fast enough to stay ahead of the demand. Efficiency of system utilization can become quite low if this condition is not met. Even when the

master is a special supervisory computer design, overall system performance can be quite low if it is heavily occupied performing executive functions. A slave that becomes free while the master is busy must wait for a new task assignment. A large proportion of short tasks will create problems for this type of operation because of the large demand for executive functions that they create.

- The idle time that does accumulate in the slaves makes this mode of operation most appropriate for special-purpose applications. It is also applicable to asymmetrical systems which contain processors of greatly different power.
- Examples of master/slave operating systems are the IBM S/360 TSS for the Model 67, the Burroughs B5500 Master Control Program (MCP) and the Texas Instruments Advanced Scientific Computer (ASC). From the user's point of view, the CDC 6600 also falls into this category although it does not operate internally exactly in the master/slave mode.
- "As a rule master-slave can have simpler hardware and software structures, but at the cost of flexibility." [Cohen]

Separate Executive for Each Processor

Since memory is shared, there is no need for completely separate copies of the coding for the operating system for each processor. However, in this type of operating system organization that might as well be the situation for each processor operates autonomously and executes all of its own executive, supervisory, and support functions just as if it were a uniprocessor. Each task is assigned to a particular processor and runs to completion on that unit. The characteristic of this type of operating system organization and operation are summarized below:

- Supervisory functions are executed by each processor as required to service its *own* needs and those of the programs *assigned to it*.
- Since several processors are executing it, the code for the supervisor must be reentrant, or private copies will have to be loaded for each processor. A combination of these two procedures is sometimes used.
- There will be less conflict on system table lock-outs, since each processor will have its own private set. There will not be as many common executive tables.
- The total system is not subject to catastrophic failure due to the failure of any one processor; however, recovery and restart of the work in progress on the failed unit will usually be very difficult.

- All I/O operations for a given task are executed by the processor to which it is assigned.
- I/O interrupts are directed to the processor initiating the I/O operation.
- In effect, each processor has its own private set of I/O equipment, files, etc.
- Sharing of auxilliary storage is not possible without special coding.
- In this case, the efficiency can be low if one processor has several long jobs in progress while others sit idle.
- Reconfiguration of I/O may require manual switching.

Symmetric or Anonymous Processors

The most "pure" hardware configuration for a multiprocessor is an ensemble of identical processing units. Since this group of identical processors share common memory, I/O channels, and I/O devices, there is no reason that they cannot all be treated symmetrically. Every processor can be equally effective in executing the supervisor and, for efficiency, this is what is done. The executive "floats" from one processor to another. There are certain executive functions that are inextricably associated with a task and are best executed by the same processor that is executing the task; however, there are many others such as the handling of interrupts for asynchronous I/O operations that can be handled by any processor. The primary motivation for this mode of operation is the overall system efficiency achieved in spite of the difficulties discussed below. It is probably the most commonly written-about system.

The characteristics of symmetric operation are as follows:

Each processor executes those supervisory functions inextricably connected with the task that it is currently executing and those functions necessary to get a new task when the current one is interrupted or completed. However, any processor can perform all or most of the general-purpose functions.

Because of the anonymity of processors and the symmetry of their treatment, a task may be executed on various units during its progress through the system. On successive executions, a different set of processors can be utilized.

Overall system control floats between processors.

- The one in control of system tables and functions such as scheduling is called the executive processor.
- Only one at a time can be *the* executive to prevent conflicts.
- Each processor may be assigned a priority.

- • Main reason is to resolve conflicts.
- • Ranked executive control seems most effective in a system working on a very large number of short tasks. If the tasks were not ranked, a large amount of time would be taken up in resolving conflicts and breaking up deadlocks [Irwin and Blanco].

Better load balancing and system utilization is possible, since non-specific functions such as I/O interrupts can be directed to the units least busy at that specific time.

Although only one processor is the Executive in "overall control," several of them may be executing the same supervisory code simultaneously and the coding must be reentrant or provide for separate copies for each activation.

Since more than one processor can be in the supervisory state at the same time, there are very real problems of conflicts in the access of tables and data sets.

- • Excessive lock-outs on system control tables can greatly affect overall efficiency.
- • Lock-outs on each data set are essential, and the time delays have to be accepted, since one processor might try to access a record being modified by another.

Several important advantages are realized.

- • Can provide graceful degradation.
- • Better uptime potential than separate backup system, provided that system is designed properly.
- • Only way to get real redundancy.
- • Most efficient use of resources.

Although this organization is the most aesthetically satisfying concept, most systems have had to back down when they have become operational (e.g., IBM's 9020 system for the FAA). However, one project is primarily devoted to developing a very definitely hardware and software symmetric system, the Carnegie Multi-Mini-Processor (C.mmp) [Cohen].

BASIC FUNCTIONAL CAPABILITIES REQUIRED

Although both multiprogramming-uniprocessor and multiprocessor operating systems have very similar functional capabilities, there are several important differences. One of the most important of these is software reliability. Software crashes (failures that can not be recovered from automatically by the software recovery routines) on a uniprocessor usually do not leave the system down too long. However, in a multiprocessor, several of the central processing units may all be executing the same or different portions of the executive code and a software error, or transient hardware failure in a single CPU can quickly propogate throughout the entire system, creating immediately many conditions that are difficult, or at least time-consuming, to recover from.

The multiprocessor operating system has to do everything the uniprocessor OS does and also has the ability to perform several other important tasks that result from the nature of the hardware configuration. These functional tasks are discussed below.

Resource Allocation and Management

The major resource allocation and management tasks can be categorized in the same manner as those found in a uniprocessor:

- *Scheduling.*   The selection of jobs from the input queue(s) to form the active mix.
- *Memory management.*   Allocation, deallocation, and control of the main memory required for both application programs and systems software.
- *Dispatching.*   The assignment of a processor unit to the execution of a task. (Or you might consider dispatching in a multiprocessor system to be the assignment of a task to a processor; however, this point of view may create some confusion, for in most current systems a task may be executed on several processors before it is completed.)

The similarity to uniprocessor systems is very high especially when compared with some of the extremely comprehensive and sophisticated uniprocessor operating systems now being developed. The traditional problem is the conflict between several simultaneously executing processes for common resources including memory, processors themselves, data, procedures, tables, I/O, and so on. There are, however, a few special aspects to providing this functional capability for the multiprocessor.

MEMORY ALLOCATION AND CONTROL

For user or application programs the problems are almost identical to those of uniprocessor systems, and similar solutions have been employed, such as partitioning, segmenting, and paging.

System routines (e.g., the supervisory and support software) face the identical problem of providing both resident and transient areas. Also, depending on the type of executive control employed (see the preceeding section), each processor may need some private memory (i.e., a memory not physically accessible by the other processors). This private memory is particularly important for recovery routines, private tables, and so on.

Two of the major problems in performing memory allocation and control for multiprocessors are special aspects of both paging hardware and software that must be considered and the control of access to code or data that may be made available to more than one user. Perhaps the most ambitious, and most complete, approach to these problems in a multiprocessor system is the MULTICS system. For a thorough discussion of this rather complex paged memory allocation and access control system the reader is referred to Organick's text on MULTICS.

Since the efficient operation of any system utilizing a paged memory is highly dependent on the hardware available to perform "automatic" address translations, the ability to utilize paging is tied to the hardware system organization (i.e., multiport and single-bus) as well as the hardware capabilities of the functional units themselves.

In paging systems the key question with respect to address translation is whether memory mapping or processor mapping is employed. This characteristic, however, refers only to the logical operation; the physical location of the translation hardware is also important.

The three possible locations for the page tables, the hardware registers used to map logical address into physical ones, are in the memory units, in the processor units, or in a special mapping or address translation unit of very high speed logic, possibly utilizing associative memory tables.

If the registers are in the memory units, or at least logically associated with specific memory modules, this would imply only one set of registers and would necessitate a memory unit design with only a single port. This, in turn, would limit the system organization options to either the single-bus or the crossbar configurations. Of course, if the memory addresses are staggered between units so that interleaving may be employed; then it is not possible to have the mapping registers associated with a single unit, since they would have to be used with two or four different units, depending on the degree of interleaving implemented. (See the section on memory address assignment in Chapter 2.)

If the registers are in the processor units, then the maps of various programs must be properly meshed together. When executive or supervisory service calls or interrupts of any kind are handled, the processor responding to the call may need access to the map of the requesting program which is not necessarily in the servicing processor.

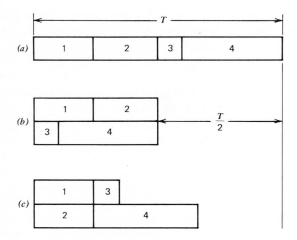

Figure 3-1 Multiprocessor dispatching anomaly [Jordan].

In any case, if the map can be changed dynamically; then errors can be generated through lack of synchronization.

When one considers the languages and compilers to be used with the multiprocessor system, the memory management system should also probably have the facility of handling common data pools (COMPOOLS).

SCHEDULING AND DISPATCHING

Even if the operating system is treating all processors symmetrically, it is still possible that the scheduling and dispatching algorithms will not exploit properly the fact that there are several processor units available. The most commonly encountered weakness in this area occurs when the scheduler assigns a given job or task to a particular processor and from that time on the dispatcher considers only that processor as being available for execution of the job/task. Obviously, under such circumstances there are periods during which a READY queue will develop on one processor while another is totally idle. This can be characterized as the "first-level" problem of multiprocessor scheduling and dispatching.

If the first-level problem is to be solved, the dispatcher as well as the scheduler must be much more sophisticated than those found in uni-processor systems. The scheduler must specify clearly the relationship between the various tasks that constitute a complete job, and the dispatcher must then handle the relatively simple operation of executing independent tasks as well as the much more complex function of coordinating the execution of tasks that are dependent on one another in some manner such as a sequence of operations on a single data set. The identification of those tasks as well as parts of tasks that can be executed in parallel is a major problem that must be solved if the full capabilities of the multiprocessor system are to be exploited. This "second-level" problem has been the subject of a large amount of study and research and is discussed in the section on special problems.

The "third-level" problem is centered on keeping all the processors busy over the same period of time. This problem which is often referred to as "dispatching anomalies" is well illustrated by an example from Jordan:

The literature . . . contains numerous examples where shortening the execution time of one or more tasks results in an increase in the overall execution time of a string of tasks. This counter-intuitive response can result when the shortened run time of a task alters the sequence in which subsequent tasks are executed, thus producing a complex re-ordering of the execution time history of the entire task string. . . . Decreasing the actual task run time, relaxing precedence relations between tasks and adding more processors can actually increase the overall time required to process a task string. . . . The problem is illustrated by Figure 3-1.

Figure 3.1a represents a multiprocessor with one processing unit. If a second processor were added to an "ideal" multiprocessor, the task list would be processed in half the time. However, for an actual multiprocessor, b and c clearly show that the time required is a function of the order in which the tasks are processed. What is required is to take the single task string of a of length T/N. In general, there is no procedure for doing this—optimal or otherwise. For some task strings it may not be possible; for example, if a consisted of one single task which could not be executed in parallel.

The solution of the third-level problem for indivisible tasks requires a sophisticated form of look-ahead to establish run-time estimates and other resources requirements.

Some examinations of the bounds or worst-case conditions that can occur in these situations have also been done by Graham. His conclusions are pessimistic in some respects; however, as always it is useful to examine the worst case to determine whether the area requires more detailed study. Some of the other empirical results that Graham cites are also interesting in assessing the probability of attaining "optimal" performance. One citation of particular interest was the simulation work of Manacher in 1967 in which he found that optimal scheduling lists fail to remain optimal 80% of the time if the execution times of each are slightly perturbed in a random manner as would normally be the situation.

Multiprocessors must be considered as multiserver queue systems as opposed to the simpler single-server queue models applicable to uniprocessors even when the uniprocessor is operating in the multiprogrammed mode.

Studies of the effect of queue disciplines on the utilization factor of the processors the mean response time for each task have been made by Regis. Although his results do give some insight into the problem, scheduling for multiprocessors still remains a "poorly optimized" procedure.

Processor Intercommunication

If two or more processors are to operate in collaboration in executing one or a series of jobs, they must have some means of intercommunication. Communication between the two may be planned, e.g. requesting another processor to execute an independent task of a larger job, or unplanned, reacting to a malfunction alert, or servicing an I/O interrupt.

This absolutely essential capability is usually provided by a combination of both hardware and software. It may be implemented by allowing one processor to interrupt another as in the IBM S/360 Model 65 MP. This method is known as the "shoulder tap." The actual message is then placed in a mailbox, a specific location in the memory allocated to the control system. The other method that is also often used is for each processor to poll its mailbox on a periodic basis, after being interrupted by a real-time clock set to a fairly low value such as 200 msec. In either case, the addressee modifies the contents of the mailbox to indicate that it has received the message and has already or will take the actions indicated. It is the responsibility of the originator of the message to check the mailbox for message acknowledgements and take appropriate action based on that test.

Abnormal Termination

Because of the nature of the system organization, if adequate processor intercommunication is not available, it is extremely difficult, if not impossible to terminate properly a multitask job if the tasks are being executed on separate processors. Again, rather than being a unique requirement of multiprocessor systems, it is more a matter of degree of complexity above the requirements of a uniprocessor.

Processor Load Balancing

This capability is highly dependent on the ability of the processors to intercommunicate and is the key factor in attaining increased performance from the multiprocessor configuration. Consider the following situation:

Job 1.
- High priority.
- Two tasks, A and B.

Job 2.
- Low priority.
- Task C.

Processor X executing task A.

Task B in a WAIT state due to I/O operation not yet completed.

Processor Y executing task C.

If processor X receives the interrupt indicating completion of the task B I/O operation, then X will be the only processor knowing that B, a high priority task, is ready for execution. This information must be given to processor Y so that it may temporarily suspend the execution of task C and switch to the higher priority work, task B.

Table and Data Set Protection

Although the protection of tables and data sets from illegal access is also required in a uniprocessor system, the presence of multiple processors, each of which may be executing the same or closely associated portions of the supervisor, complicates the procedures that must be employed to provide this capability. This is due to the fact that an illegal access to the table in a multiprocessor system may occur on the very next memory cycle following a legal one before a software routine can effectively lock the table. The multiprocessor system requires some hardware capabilities to support this functional capability.

Input/Output Load Balancing

This capability may be quite difficult to implement considering the configuration and I/O paths possible in the multiprocessor. If all I/O channels and equipment are in an anonymous pool, the procedure is to establish merely one priority driven queue for I/O requests with the detailed scheduling handled in the same manner as in a uniprocessor. The major difficulties arise when some of the I/O paths or equipment are assigned uniquely (and untransferably) to a single processor. This does occur in some multibus configurations, and the problem of I/O scheduling and control must then be handled through the interprocessor communications mechanism.

Reconfiguration

Although some uniprocessors do have limited capability to recognize changes in the equipment available for use, the ability to do this automatically and adjust all necessary control tables and routines is an absolutely essential requirement for a good multiprocessor operating system. Obviously, this capability is most important and most easily implemented in a system that is designed to operate in a truly symmetric mode.

System Deadlock*

System deadlock is also referred to as the "deadly embrace" problem. The problem occurs when two tasks, both in active execution, each need a resource currently assigned to the other, and neither can proceed further or relinquish the resource it holds that is in contention until it obtains the use of the requested one. Very often when the situation reaches this impasse the only way to restore any activity is to kill completely one of the jobs and release all of the resources assigned to it after first attempting to restore them to the state they were in before being utilized by the job being dropped. If the resource released is a data set in the process of being updated or modified by the dropped program, the problem of "restoration" may be a critical one and extremely difficult to accomplish without complete fallback. If both of the resources being contended for have been only "partially modified" by their first user, then probably both programs must be killed. In any event, a lot of completed work will be lost and a lot of additional work required to save what little can be saved. The high level of skill required by the console operator to know what to do and how to do it is obvious. What may not be so obvious is the fact that it usually takes a very alert and knowledgeable operator to even detect that deadlock has occurred.

All types of resources can be a party to a deadlock condition:

I/O devices.
- Specific units.
- Generic type (i.e., seven-track tape drive).

Data sets.

Nonreentrant programs.

Main Memory.

* Coffman, Elphick, and Soshani give a complete tutorial discussion of this subject.

Since there is really no cure for the situation created by deadlock, the important factor is to prevent it from occurring. Usually to do this, all "unique" resources such as specific data sets or special devices are assigned to a task before it is scheduled and initiated. For the remainder of the resources, however, it is impossible to know which ones may be potential deadlock items in order to avoid embrace.

A specific example of deadlock is given in another tutorial paper on the subject by Holt. Spooling systems, such as IBM's ASP or even OS/360 which utilize READER and WRITER programs, completely separate from the main programs for input and output, allocate only so much space on the disk for holding the input and output data sets. Since the READER is operating totally autonomously from the processing programs, it will continue to place new data sets on the disk as long as there is anything in the card reader or other input source. The problem occurs when the space is filled with input data sets for jobs that are yet to be executed, and output data sets for jobs only partially completed. Unfortunately, neither of the two operating systems mentioned above provide any procedures to recover spooling space from a partially completed job, and deadlock occurs. Then the system must be restarted, losing the work already completed but not yet outputted. Holt mentions:

a crude ad hoc solution to this problem . . . (manually) [prohibitting] the spooling of new jobs once the utilization of spooling space becomes too high, say above 80%.

In their general treatment of the subject, Coffman, Elphick, and Soshani identified the four general conditions that would permit deadlock to occur. These are all stated as necessary and essential conditions.

1. Tasks claim exclusive control of the resources they require ("mutual exclusion" condition).

2. Tasks hold resources already allocated to them while waiting for additional resources ("wait for" condition).

3. Resources cannot be forcibly removed from the tasks holding them until the resources are used to completion ("no preemption" condition).

4. A circular chain of tasks exists, such that each task holds one or more resources that are being requested by the next task in the chain ("circular wait" condition) [Coffman et al., p. 70].

Their paper also points out that it is impossible to prevent or avoid the first condition for all resources. The necessity for single access during the updating of a file or table is obvious. The other three conditions, however, can be avoided.

Havender suggests the following approaches which will, in effect, deny each of the three remaining conditions:

1. Each task must request all its required resources at once and cannot proceed until all have been granted ("wait-for" condition denied).

2. If a task holding certain resources is denied a further request, that task must release its original resources and, if necessary, request them again together with the additional resources ("no preemption" condition denied).

3. The imposition of a linear ordering of resource types on all tasks; i.e., if a task has been allocated resources of type r it may subsequently request only those resources of types following r in the ordering. In the case of only one resource of a type, the linear ordering is of resources. (It can be shown that under this condition the state graph cannot have circuits, and therefore circular wait conditions are prevented) [Coffman et al., p. 72].

It is important to point out that this is actually the "multiple active program" environment that creates the danger of deadlock, and both uniprocessors as well as multiprocessors are subject to it.

SPECIAL PROBLEMS FOR MULTIPROCESSOR SOFTWARE

Again, as has been mentioned earlier, the multiprocessor operating system faces almost the same problems as those encountered by a uniprocessor system. Even the same solutions are often applicable. The major difference is in degree or complexity of analyzing fully the problem in the multiprocessor and ensuring that the "solution" implemented does solve it.

The problems discussed below are those that have already or should receive special attention in multiprocessor systems. The list is by no means a complete one of all of the problems either common with uniprocessors or unique to multiprocessors—included are only a few of those primarily unique that have received the most attention in recent system development and research projects.

Memory Sharing and Accessing

Two access-sharing-conflict problems must be considered. The first of these is a characteristic of the hardware organization of the memory and the mechanism available to access each unit. The ability, or better stated, the limitation, of multiple processing units to concurrently share and access the same set of main memory units can greatly slow down the overall performance of the system due to memory access contention. "Delays caused by processor interference on memory reference have been estimated at as high as 20% in some studies [Lorin]." However, this has been a very difficult number to obtain or verify.

One approach to solving, or at least alleviating, this problem is the distribution of consecutive memory addresses between successive memory units. This technique at first appears to hold great promise; however, a large amount of conflict can still occur, although now it will be more random in nature and not come in extended bursts such as those that occur when two processors are both executing blocks of coding in the same unit. In symmetric operating systems it would not be at all unusual for two processors to execute the same block of supervisory code. This problem of access conflict also occurs in uniprocessors; however, there it is limited to conflicts between processor accesses and accesses requested by the I/O controllers. Of course, I/O access conflicts also occur in multiprocessors.

Another hardware solution requires much more circuitry than address distribution and interleaving; however, it does offer much higher pay-offs, since it permits true simultaneous access through two separate ports on the memory unit. This approach has been implemented on the System Engineering Laboratories SEL 85 to provide a direct and autonomous I/O channel; however, the two processor units still access through separate ports on a priority contention basis.

Another hardware organization technique that has been implemented on some uniprocessors is the local ("buffer" or "cache") storage associated with the processor unit (e.g., IBM S/360 models 85 and 195; S/370 Models 155, 158, 165, 168, and 195). This local store is private to the processor, and it usually is substantially faster than primary main memory. For example, the 370/165 CPU can obtain 8 bytes from its buffer in two cycles, or 160 nsec, and a request can be initiated every cycle. This compares with 1.44 μsec (or 18 cycles) required to obtain 8 bytes of data directly from processor storage.* The buffer is loaded in blocks on a look-ahead basis rather than by individual words so that if the code does not contain too many jumps, therefore, negating the value of the sequential locations loaded into the cache, the number of accesses to main memory can be greatly reduced. For the 360/85 with a 16,384 byte buffer, detailed analysis of 19 trace tapes (about 250,000 instructions each) gave an average probability of finding the data needed in the buffer of 0.968.† It should be noted that, if the addresses generated by a program were random, the probability would be much less than 0.01. Therefore, it can be said that what makes the buffer work is the fact that real programs are not random in their addressing patterns [Liptay, p. 19]. The total time spent in access

---

* "A guide to the IBM System/370 Model 165," IBM Form GC20–1730.
† "J. S. Liptay, "Structural Aspects of the System/360 Model 85, Part II—The Cache" *IBM Systems J.*, 7 (1), 15–21 (1968); IBM Form 321–0013.

will also be lowered, since the local store is loaded in a block transfer mode. The obvious major benefit of such an organization is if the local store is large enough to hold the code for an entire loop being executed several times in succession by the program. Performance studies of a 360/85 with a 16,384 byte buffer indicates that the system operates on representative work at a mean performance 81% of what would be achieved if the entire 1.04-μsec main storage operated at buffer speed. The 360/85 CPU has an 80-nsec cycle and can normally obtain 8 bytes from the buffer every cycle [Liptay, p. 17–19].

Software simulations of local store have also been attempted [Lorin, p. 267]. In this case the compiler must "unwind" the code and produce separate images to be loaded into a special memory bank if "useful" blocks of code can be recognized. The major drawback to the use of local or cache memory is the cost of the hardware required to make it fast enough and large enough to be useful. The rapidly dropping cost of fast monolithic storage has made it possible to include buffers ranging from 8 k to 32 kbytes in the IBM S/370 Models 155–195.

Table or Data Set Access and Protection

The second access conflict is strictly a software problem although some hardware has been used in its solution. The specific problem is the concurrent access to a table or dataset by two or more processors when there is the possibility that one of the processors may be changing the contents during its use of the material. These changes, not being synchronized with the logic of the use of the material being made by the other processors, create unrecoverable problems in the results or actions of the other processors. Since simultaneity of specific accesses is not what creates the problem—only access by one while another is still using the block of material—this exact same problem can and does occur in uniprocessors quite frequently, although it is separate processes or tasks running on the same machine that are involved there.

Since this was recognized some time ago in uniprocessor systems, it has been the subject of extensive study, the best known of which is the study of the use of "semaphores" by Dijkstra [1965]. Other work has been characterized by titles such as "synchronization," "table lock," or simply "lock." (Note that this problem is totally different from "system deadlock" discussed earlier, although deadlock may result from improper operations executed or the basis of bad data obtained when a partially modified control table is accessed.) In fact, it is the control tables, such as CPU and I/O dispatching queues and resource allocation tables, that are most important to protect from this problem, since they are so critical to the proper operation of the system and are accessed so frequently.

The solution is conceptually quite simple. Whenever a dataset is opened for a program that may make any modifications to it, a lock is set that must be checked by any other program before it can also OPEN that dataset. The new program cannot use the dataset in question until the lock is reset by the primary user as he CLOSES the dataset. A similar procedure is followed in accessing tables, although there is no OPEN procedure necessary before each is used. This explanation makes the problem sound deceptively simple as a little experience in trying to write the actual test and lock routines quickly reveals.

To assist in preparing efficient lock checking/setting routines, a basic instruction is now found in most processors, TEST and SET. This is a test of a control bit in memory assigned to a specific dataset or table. If that bit is OFF, it is turned ON, and the program is allowed to access the material in question. If it is already ON, it is not changed, and the program requesting access must transfer to some other routine or go into a WAIT state if nothing else productive can be accomplished at this time. The latter is usually the case, since the material being requested is often an essential control table used by the operating system. A large amount of WAIT time can be accumulated in this manner. This is particularly true if the processor is also locked out of the dispatcher.

There are some situations where a second user must be denied access to a table even if it is strictly a read request. A specific example of this is described below (based in part on Madnick).

Situation

- All jobs ready to be served are listed in the work queue.
- The next job to be served is selected in a round-robin or first-in-first-out fashion and is indicated by a pointer into the work queue.
- When a processor is free, it goes to the work queue to determine which job to start next.
- The SELECT ROUTINE selects the top entry in the work queue as the "next job to be served."
- The ADVANCE ROUTINE moves the pointer in the work queue down to the next job.
- The operating system is distributed between the various processors at least to the point that each selects its own "next job to be served."

Steps in creating the problem:

1. Almost simultaneously, both processors *A* and *B* become free.

2. Processor *A* SELECT ROUTINE notes "next job to be served" as job 12.

3. Processor *B* SELECT ROUTINE notes "next job to be served" as job 12.

4. Processor *A* ADVANCE ROUTINE advances "next job to be served" pointer to job 13.

5. Processor *B* ADVANCE ROUTINE advances "next job to be served" pointer to job 14.

6. Processor *A* starts execution of job 12.

7. Processor *B* starts execution of job 12.

Results:

> *Both* processors executing job 12.
> *Job 13 skipped.*

One method to avoid this occurring is to utilize interlocks on the dispatching tables or queues.*

Error Recovery

Since one of the main features of multiprocessor systems is the ability to sustain equipment failures in individual units and reconfigure so as to continue in operation, it may seem that error recovery is not a special "problem" of the multiprocessor operating system. In fact, nothing could be further from the truth. All of the potential capabilities of the system for reconfiguration, fail-soft degradation, and such,would be worthless without the software necessary to exploit them.

Some specific techniques or considerations for error recovery are as follows:

- All system and task control tables are maintained in duplicate in separate memory banks. (An example of a complete implementation of this is the Burroughs Multi-Interpreter System [Davis et al.].

- The operating system should be written to accommodate (control effectively) the maximum configuration as well as any usable subsets. The actual operating environment should be indicated automatically by the functional units utilizing some procedure such as setting an indicator bit in a main memory control word which is checked by the operating system so that the current environment is known. (An

---

* A further discussion of some other aspects of this "lock problem" are presented in Section 18.8 of *Parallelism in Hardware and Software: Real and Apparent Concurrency* [Lorin].

example of this is the Burroughs B 6500 as well as other Burroughs systems.)

- Hardware failure error detection and correction should be as extensive as possible. Checks should be made at all points that will not interfere with the efficient operation of the machine, for example, parity check on memory reads, parity check on all data transfers, self-checking hardware in arithmetic and logic unit, and I/O device checks such as read-after-write or punch.

- Extensive checkout routines should be available and run on idle processors to detect failures before they occur during an operational run.

- The processor should assume the task in progress on a malfunctioning unit to have access to all of the tables and control information in use by the failed machine. The successor should also have the ability to sense the complete "state" of the failed unit so that it knows where to pick up the execution.

Whenever an error or failure condition is detected, usually by the occurrence of an interrupt, the effects of the failure are most important for recovery purposes even though the determination of its cause is important for repair purposes. In this section the subject of interrupt is recovery so the comments will be confined to that area. When the failure, its effects, and the condition governing reconfiguration are analyzed, two questions must be answered leading to four recovery states [Dancy].

		Has the Data Base remained valid	
		Yes	No
Can the system be reconfigured so that it retains some	Yes	I	III
minimally acceptable processing capacity	No	II	IV

State I.   The system can be quickly reconfigured and control returned to the dispatcher to continue with the normal workload.

State II.   Even after reconfiguration it will be necessary to drop completely nonessential tasks and curtail or delay the execution of low-priority tasks.

State III.   After reconfiguration and the reattainment of full computing power, the system will have to be reloaded and restarted (hopefully at a checkpoint).

State IV.   After reconfiguring and reloading, the system output will still be below the normal levels.

Recognition and Exploitation of Parallelism

This topic is so important and so essential to the performance of complete multiprocessor systems that it could easily be the subject of a complete chapter or even a book itself; something along the lines of the latter has already been published [Lorin]. The problem can be factored into several parts for basic considerations, although there are obviously interactions between the various items and how they are accomplished.

Statements or other mechanisms are required in the programming language to identify tasks or subtasks that may be executed in parallel and provide the other information necessary for the operating system to control their execution.
- Specification of the starting and ending points of the portions that can be executed in parallel.
- Special conditions governing or restricting parallel execution if any exist.
- Conditions that must be met so that all results will by synchronized properly with one another and other parts of the program.

Capabilities within the supervisior to create, schedule, dispatch, and recombine "independent-parallel" tasks spawned by a single program.

Ability to recognize parallelism and its extent.
- By the programmer.
- By the language translator automatically.

There has been a large amount of research on the recognition aspect of the problem; however, complete solutions have not yet been found and the research continues [Ramamorthy and Gonzalez, Gonzalez and D. E. Wilson specifically for the PEPE system]. A very likely candidate for parallel execution is a loop, if each separate pass uses completely different data elements such as is usually the situation in vector and matrix operations or multiple inquiries to a data base. In fact, the FORTRAN DO loop statement is often a user expression of parallelism. However, there are many more instances where it is possible to exploit the ability to have several processors working on the same problem. It is not always possible to identify easily sections that can be executed independently even using the program flow charts. It requires a much more sophisticated use of graph theory to accomplish this, and much of the research has centered on that technique and its use. Even with the use of graphs, it is still very difficult for a programmer to detect parallelism because of the many combinations that have to be checked. It appears that it will eventually have to be an automated process.

Most multiprocessor systems can be utilized fairly efficiently even if there is no use made of the parallelism existing within each program. In this situation each processor is kept busy by having a large pool of programs, each being executed in a straight-line fashion, all available for dispatching on any unit. The pool has to contain enough programs in the active mix for the entire system so that there are always enough jobs in the READY state to have one available for each processor. Obviously, even a very large collection of I/O-bound jobs would probably be unsatisfactory because of the proportion in an I/O WAIT state at any given time.

In contrast to the fairly straightforward problem of loading a "standard" multiprocessor, the array, vector, and pipeline systems all present special problems. Basically, the program *must* contain inherent parallelism or these machines are almost valueless. There has been a significant amount of work done by the Department of Defense on identifying specific application areas where the ILLIAC IV and the CDC STAR systems provide the greatest pay-off. The obviously ideal situation for an array processor is a large quantity of matrix operations such as those found in nuclear energy calculations or large weather simulations based on observations taken over a grid of stations. What is not as obvious is the fact that even a payroll program contains a large amount of parallelism. The identical operations are executed for each employee with only the data elements such as hours worked and rate being different. Since each Processing Element of the ILLIAC IV has its own small private memory for current operands, the ILLIAC IV can easily handle a problem like payroll keeping all of the PEs busy, although the full capabilities of the system are probably not being utilized very well.

One example of language statements that can be used to request parallel processing is the FORK-JOIN pair of instructions in the Gamma-60. A FORK statement has the following form

$$L1 \quad \text{FORK} \quad L2, J, N$$

and states that there are N independent tasks available for parallel processing. The code for these tasks starts at location $L1 + 1$, $L2$, and so on. All of the tasks must rejoin at the statement labeled J, and the program must wait there until all N are complete. A JOIN statement can similarly be defined. Another example is a statement at the compiler level. In $PL/1$, if the TASK attribute is used in calling a procedure, a two-way fork is implied and the join is controlled by the WAIT statement. This statement is not very apropriate for multiprocessors, however, because of the limitations on multiple forks. It is really meant for use in a uniprocessor multiprogramming environment to exploit the overlap of I/O and CPU operations.

Even one of the earliest multiprocessors, the Burroughs D 825, included in its AOSP operating system the capability for the programmer to segment his program and identify those segments that could be processed in parallel [Anderson et al., 1962]. It was also the programmer's responsibility to specify the join points following the parallel processing.

The material in this paragraph can be summarized by observing that the existence of parallelism, hence the ability to exploit it, can be handled by one of three methods:

- Stated by the user.
- Found by analysis.
- A combination of these two methods.

Development and Test of System Software

System software is the control software required to provide the programmer as well as the machine operator the means to utilize and control the hardware system effectively. The major component of the systems software is the operating system. Certainly every comment made about the difficulty of actually preparing and debugging a uniprocessor operating system apply here; however, the problem is increased greatly. Not only is the logic and analysis more difficult, but also testing is more difficult, and complete checkout is almost impossible because of the difficulty of making certain specific series of events occur in precisely the desired order and at exactly the desired time. And, of course, the number of conditions or combinations of conditions that may occur in a multiprocessor is almost limitless so that the checkout is never complete.

The actual checking of the code is a formidable task, and the primary objective during the preparation of the code should be attention to detail and constant emphasis on accurracy. This approach can be highly successful as pointed out by Dijkstra in describing the development of the T.H.E. Operating System [Dijkstra, 1968].

To relieve or eliminate as many operating restrictions as possible, as much of the code as possible should be in the form of reentrant routines. This procedure will not only ease the checkout process but it will allow the maximum flexibility in the method of organizing and the mode of operation of the completed system.

Finally, since the system will undoubtedly be a team effort, it is extremely important that clearly defined functional modules be established as the basic building blocks for the software system. It is not enough to specify that "module five will handle scheduling." The specifications must be made quite detailed as to exactly what the module does and the totality of its interface with other modules. This latter point is worthy of a great deal of emphasis. Much programming is done in modules; however, the techniques of "modular programming" are not properly adherred to. Often a program failure is caused by something happening internally to a module as a result of a new version of some other module being added to the system. In "true modular programming" this is not likely to occur, since all modules communicate *only* through a *fully specified interface* and that *specification* is *common to all interfaces*. This means that one module will never reach down inside another to obtain a data element or change one. Any transfer must be done across the interface where it will be fully visible to any and all persons examining the flow of the program and data. The benefits of following these procedures are manyfold, both at program preparation and checkout as well as at a later point in time when the logic or coding of one of the modules must be changed or a new one added.

The discussion above has been centered on the preparation and checkout of the actual code. This is not meant to subordinate the problem of systems analysis and design. As pointed out in the first paragraph, it will probably be a relatively simple task to specify what the operating system should do, and it will not be too difficult to design the logic to accomplish these goals. The real problem is in verifying that the logic actually does conform to the desired results and that it performs its work in an efficient manner. Even after the routines are all coded and running, those questions will probably still not be answered. The only suitable approach known to this author is the use of simulation to conduct controlled experiments that can be repeated in the same exact form often enough to obtain statistical validity. For this purpose, an exact event and time driver simulation must be used. This can be prepared utilizing a general-purpose simulation language such as GPSS or any other event oriented system. However, several special-purpose simulation languages and systems have been focused entirely on this type of problem. Some examples of these are System and Software Simulator (S3), System Analysis Machine (SAM), and Operating System Language (OSL). A software and hardware systems simulation is very useful to checkout error recovery, reconfiguration control, interrupt handling, and other operating system functions that are highly time dependent or occur only under very special conditions, because the simulator allows complete control to any degree desired of both time factors and operating conditions.

A production cycle based roughly on the following outline will probably produce a good multiprocessor operating system in the minimum amount of time with minimum total effort.

1. Define hardware operating configuration(s).
2. Establish the overall operating and performance specifications.
3. Define the modules, their functions, specifications, and the standard interface.
4. Determine the detailed logic of each module.
5. Prepare the simulation models of the individual modules and the overall control logic.
6. Run extensive system operation and performance checkout tests utilizing the simulator, ensuring that all specifications are met.
7. Make the changes necessary in the functional description of each module and its logic as required.
8. Repeat steps 5 through 7 until all specifications are met.
9. Code the "debugged" logic of each module and checkout each module of code as much as possible for accuracy.
10. Assemble the complete system and run verification tests.

SUMMARY

In summarizing this extremely brief introduction and discussion of multiprocessor system software, there is a great temptation to close with an observation that has been made individually in almost every section of the chapter—the multiprocessor system software has the same general problems, objectives, and capabilities as a multiprogramming operating system for a uniprocessor; however, it is more complex. However, this statement is an oversimplification of the situation.

Certainly, stated in broad and very general terms, functions such as resource management and control in the two classes of systems bear strong resemblances. However, the differences are more than just subtle degrees of complexity, and it is most useful to focus on those differences.

The first and foremost of these distinctions is the difference between the *concurrent interleaved* execution of several programs on the multiprogrammed uniprocessor and the *simultaneous, parallel* execution of more than one program on the multiprocessor. One characteristic is obvious—a poorly performing scheduler or dispatcher will result in more idle resources on the multiprocessor.

The second, and perhaps only other truly significant, difference is in the interaction of the software with its hardware operating environment. The uniprocessor software system is usually designed for a specific complement of hardware units connected in a fixed configuration. This is certainly true of the system after it has been tailored or adapted to the specific installation and its requirements by the procedure of "system generation". *All* of the multiprocessor software, on the other hand, must be designed to operate in an extremely fluid environment, and not only must it be able to exist under those conditions, it must also be able to control the units on-line as well as all those which represent the configuration with maximum system expansion.

These two differences then give substance and meaning to the general observation—similar, but more complex.

CHAPTER 4
TODAY AND THE FUTURE

Several sets of comparison charts, each purporting to show the performance or cost-effectiveness advantages of one system organization over another, have been reviewed. Unfortunately each set was usually prepared by the proponent for a specific system, and it is an almost impossible task to evaluate comparatively all the conditions and assumptions used to make his system attain the highest rating. This is no reflection on the veracity of the information presented, only on its comprehensibility—particularly when nearly all results conflict. The answer is obvious. The performance of any system that has been developed explicitly to provide and exploit concurrent and parallel processing is almost totally dependent on subtle factors in the workload description. This may explain the relatively small number of multiprocessor systems operating in general-purpose environments, although certainly several are available for such applications.

Because of the complexities involved and the strong interactions with the specific characteristics of the workload, it would be impossible for this short introduction to provide specific guidelines as to the applications in which multiprocessors should be used and why. Unfortunately, the remarks have to be confined to generalization about their advantages, disadvantages, and other rather nonspecific matters.

COMPARATIVE CHARACERISTICS OF CURRENT
MULTIPROCESSOR AND PARALLEL PROCESSING SYSTEMS

Perhaps the best way to assess the value of a specific technique or technology in an area as dynamic as digital computers is by its popularity.

Despite many shortcomings and unsolved problems, the organization of functional units into multiprocessor systems has become an accepted technique. These systems are available in all sizes and can be obtained from every major mainframe manufacturer (Table E 4-1).

The Table 4-1 lists the hardware characteristics of over 50 multiprocessor and parallel processing systems. Some of the systems in the table are no longer in production, and others are still in development. All of them have been included to provide a better representation of the state-of-the-art. The type of system organization/interconnection scheme is indicated for both the memory to processor and memory to I/O paths. Also given are the *maximum* hardware capabilities of each system. It should be noted definitely that the hardware often has a greater expansion capability than that supported by the operating system available. Unfortunately, it has not been possible to develop similar entries for the capabilities of the system software for each system. If the operating system supports only a reduced configuration, a footnote is given.

ATTAINING MULTIPROCESSOR SYSTEM DESIGN OBJECTIVES

Objectives/Advantages

The three basic design objectives for multiprocessors compare almost exactly to the three "advantages" claimed for such systems:

- High availability/reliability.
- Flexibility in system operations.
- Improved performance (efficiency and increased throughput).

Availability

Based purely on the hardware and topology involved, there is little argument that multiprocessor system organization is the best means to obtain a high availability of a system capable of performing an essential workload. The only other approach is to completely duplicate the minimal system and utilize the extra equipment as a separate stand-alone system or perhaps as just a stand-by. What is the comparative efficiency of such an approach?

Consider an application that requires a minimum of one processor, six memory modules, and two I/O subsystems. Illustrative values for the

TABLE 4-1 CHARACTERISTICS OF MULTIPROCESSOR AND PARALLEL PROCESSING SYSTEMS

Name	System Organization[a]		Maximum Number of Functional Units		Memory[c]
	Proc	I/O	Proc	I/O[b]	
Minicomputers					
Microdata MICRO 1600D	TS	TS (separate)	2	One TS bus per CPU and one DMA per system / —	$\{16 \times 4K\} \times 8b$, $8 \times 8K$ (max 64K)
Small					
EMR 6155 (UNIVAC) Series-60)	TS[f]	TS[f] (common)	2	—/6 per CPU[f] / 63 per chnl	$6 \times 8K \times 16b$
Xerox SIGMA—5[g]	MP	MP	5[h]	5[h]/8 per IOP / 32 per chnl	$\{32 \times 4K\} \times 32b$, $16 \times 8K$ (max 131K)
Medium					
Digital equipment DECsystem-10/1055	TS	TS (multiple)	2	—/4[i]/126	$16 \times 16K \times 36b$
Honeywell HIS 2088	MP	MP	2	—/16[e]/96[e]	$4 \times 131K \times 8b$ (max 64K bytes)
Memorex MRX/40 & 50	TS	TS (common)	7[j]	7[j]/—/—	—
RCA model 215	CB	CB	4	4 / 1 mux or 2 selec. per IOC / —	$8 \times 32K \times 36b$
Systems Engineering Labs SEL 88	MP	MP	3[k]	3[k]/—/—	$16 \times 8K \times 32b$

System	Type		Number		Memory
Xerox SIGMA—6 and 7[v]	MP	MP	7^l	7^l |8 per IOP| / 32 per chnl	$8 \times 16K \times 32b$
Medium-to-large					
Burroughs B 5700 (B 5500)[m]	CB (common)	CB	2	4/4/—	$8 \times 4K \times 48b$
Digital Equipment DECsystem-10/1077 UNIVAC model 498	TS (multiple)	TS	2	—/4^i/126	$64 \times 64K \times 36b$
Xerox SIGMA—8[g]	MP	MP	11^n	11^n |8 per IOP| / 32 per chnl	$8 \times 16K \times 32b$
Xerox SIGMA—9[g]	MP	MP	11^n	11^n |8 per IOP| / 32 per chnl	$32 \times 16K \times 32b$
Large					
Burroughs B 6700 (B 6500)	CB (common)	CB	3	$3/36^o/256$	$\begin{Bmatrix}64 \times 16K\\ 16 \times 64K\end{Bmatrix} \times 48b$ (max 1048K)
Control Data CYBER 72 (equivalent to CDC 6200)	CB	TS	2	20/24/—	$32 \times 4K \times 60b$
Control Data CYBER 73 (equivalent to CDC 6400 & 6500)	CB	TS	2	20/24/—	$32 \times 4K \times 60b$
Honeywell HIS 6050/6060	MP	MP	4	4/96/—	$16 \times 32K \times 36b$
Honeywell HIS 6070/6080	MP	MP	4	4/96/—	$16 \times 64K \times 36b$
Honeywell HIS 6180	MP	MP	4	4/96/—	$32 \times 64K \times 36b$

TABLE 4-1 (*Continued*)

Name	System Organization[a]		Maximum Number of Functional Units		Memory[c]
	Proc	I/O	Proc	I/O[b]	
Honeywell HIS 635	MP	MP	4	4/64/—	8 × 32K × 36b
Honeywell HIS 645 (MULTICS)	MP	MP	4	4/64/—	8 × 32K × 36b
IBM S/360, Model 65 MP	MP	MP	2[p]	—/12 (selec)/— 2 (mux)/—	8 × 256K × 8b
IBM S/360, Model 67	MP	MP	2	2/12 (selec)/— 2 (mux)/—	8 × 256K × 8b
UNIVAC 1108	MP	MP	3	2/32/	4 × 65K × 36b
Large-to-extra large					
Burroughs B7700	CB	CB	7[j]	7[j]/224/255	{8 × 131K} × 48B {4 × 262K} (max 1048K)
Control data CDC 6500	CB	TS	2	20/24/—	32 × 4K × 60b
Control data CDC 6600	CB	TS	1	20/24/—	32 × 4K × 60b
Control data CDC 6700	CB	TS	2	20/24/—	32 × 4K × 60b
Control data CYBER—74 (equivalent to CDC 6600 and 6700)	CB	TS	2	20/24/—	32 × 4K × 60b

System					Memory
IBM S/370 model 158 MP	MP	MP	2	—/10 blk mux/— /4 mux	8 × 1024K × 8b
Extra large					
Control data CDC 7600	CB	TS	1	13/15/—	SCM^q 32 × 2K × 60b LCM 8 × 64K × 60b
Control data CYBER—76 (equivalent to CDC 7600)	CB	TS	1	13/15/—	SCM 32 × 2K × 60b LCM 8 × 64K × 60b
IBM S/370 model 168 MP	MP	MP	2	—/24 (max 22)/— /blk mux	16 × 1024K × 8b
UNIVAC 1110	MP	MP	6^r	4/96/—	8 × 32K × 36b^s
Giant and special systems					
U.S. Army Adv. Ballistic Missile Defense Agency PEPE]^t	AV	MP	288^u	3^v/—/—	Data memories: PE 1 × 1K × 32b, ACU 1 × 4K × 32b, CCU 1 × 2K × 32b, AOCU 1 × 2K × 32b Program memories: ACU 2 × 32K × 32b, CCU 1 × 2K × 32b, AOCU 1 × 2K × 32b
Bell Labs CLC (SAFEGUARD)	MP	MP	10	5/80/80	63 × 4K × 64b^w
Burroughs D 825	CB	CB	4	2/20/128	32 × 4K × 64b^x
Control data STAR-100	—	AV	—	—	16 × 4K × 48b
Goodyear Aerospace STARAN "S"	AV	AV	8192	—/2^y/—	1 × 32K × 32b^w
Burroughs ILLIAC IV	AV	TS	64^z	^{aa}	32 × 256K × 256b^x
Hughes H 4400	CB	CB	7^{bb}	7^{bb}/8 per IOP/—	1 × 2K × 64b (per processor) 16 × 16K × 32b
IBM 9020A (360/50) (special FAA system)	MP (common)	MP	4	3/—/—	24 × 32K × 32b

TABLE 4-1 *(Continued)*

Name	System Organization[a]		Maximum Number of Functional Units		
	Proc	I/O	Proc	I/O[b]	Memory[c]
IBM 9020D (360/65) (special FAA system)	MP	MP	4	3/—/—	40 × 32K × 32b
IBM 4-pi, EP/MP	MP	MP	3	2/(na)/(na)	8 × 16K × 32b
IBM 4-pi, CC-1 (AWACS)	MP	MP	2	2/2 per IOU^{cc}/(na)	11 × 16K × 32b
Texas Instruments ASC (Advanced Scientific Computer)	PL	TS	2^{dd}	8^{ee}/—^{ff}/—^{ff}	8 × 512K × 32b^{gg} 8 × 256K × 32b^{hh}
Ramo-Wooldridge RW-400	CB	CB	—	—	—
U.S. Navy AADC (Advanced Airborne Digital Computer)	^{aa}		^{aa}	^{aa}	^{aa}
UNIVAC ARTS III (Air Traffic Control)					
UNIVAC AN/UYK-7	MP	MP	3	2/ /	16 × 16K × 32b
UNIVAC Model 1832 (avionics computer)	MP	MP	2	2/18/—	3 × 32K × 32b

[a] Abbreviations used:
TS: time-shared/common-bus
CB: crossbar
MP: multiport

AV: array/vector
PL: pipeline

[b] Expressed as [[(I/O processors]]/[I/O channels)/(I/O devices) [(I/O controllers]] Dashes have two meanings:
In the IOP position: System does not utilize separately identifiable I/O Processors. The channels communicate directly with memory.

In the channel or
device position: The maximum number is not firmly established or limited by the basic system design.

[c] Expressed as: (number of modules) × (size of module) × (size of memory word).

[d] Multiprocessor communications adapter required for each processor system to interface it to a common system bus. All transfers on system bus have to be cooperative, that is, explicit program action at both transmitters and receivers.

[e] Per processor system.

[f] Separate bus per system. Allows private and shared core and shared disk with six private I/O multiplex channels. There is also low-speed I/O direct to processor by-passing bus.

[g] The SIGMA-5 and larger models are designed to permit the attachment of multiple CPU's and I/O processor up to the capacity of the memory ports available; however, the standard Xerox software supports only the uniprocessor configuration.

[h] Sum of number of CPUs and IOPs cannot exceed six due to memory port limitations.

[i] Plus a dedicated data communications channel and a low-speed channel connected directly to one of the processors.

[j] Total number of CPUs plus IOPs must not exceed eight.

[k] Any combination of CPUs and DMAs up to total of four.

[l] Sum of number of CPUs and IOPs cannot exceed eight due to memory port limitations.

[m] The B5700 is an upgrade of the B5500 with a shared disk available.

[n] Sum of number of CPUs and IOPs cannot exceed 12 due to memory port limitations.

[o] Floating data switching channels.

[p] "Because of the design of the 360 I/O control units, connection to more than two processors is not feasible. Also, because of the nature of the direct control feature for communications between processors, the system is limited to two processors. Thus the system is restricted by its hardware design from expansion beyond a two-CPU configuration, although the principles upon which the system is based are not as restricted." [Miller]

[q] Main memory is divided into two parts: small core memory (SCM), which is executable, and large core memory (LCM), which is used as bulk core storage for very high speed on-line operations such as swapping.

FOOTNOTES TO TABLE 4-1 (Continued)

[r] Only four being supported at this time.

[s] Can also have $16 \times 65K \times 36b$ of magnetic core high-speed Extended Storage.

[t] PEPE is an architecture to augment a host general purpose computer such as the CDC 7600.

[u] The MSI Model PEPE is designed for 288 Processing Elements. The architecture does not limit the number of processing elements.

[v] PEPE attaches to a host computer via three control units. No peripherals are directly attached to the PEPE computer system.

[w] Program store.

[x] Variable store.

[y] One 1-Gbit channel and one 1-Mbit channel.

[z] For present implementation of one quadrant.

[aa] Characteristics not established at this time.

[bb] Total number of CPUs plus IOPs must not exceed eight.

[cc] One high-speed channel and one low-speed channel.

[dd] Each central processor can have one, two, three, or four arithmetic units all controlled by a single instruction processing unit.

[ee] The peripheral processors are virtual processors. (The operating system executes entirely in a peripheral processor.)

[ff] Not set by system design but rather by memory port transfer capacities.

[gg] Central memory.

[hh] Central memory extension (directly executable).

system requirements and the availability of various configurations that will meet these requirements are given below.

	Single Unit Availability	Required for One System	Required for Two Separate or Duplexed Systems	Required for Multi-processor System	Required for Three Separate Systems
Processor	0.98	1	2	2	3
Memory	0.97	6	12	8	18
I/O	0.9	2	4	3	6
System availability (to perform basic workload,	0.66		0.88	0.951	0.95

Then the overall reliability of a single system would be 0.66. Having an identical system as a back-up spare would provide an improvement of the system availability to 0.88. The number applicable to the multiprocessor system shown would be 0.95. To attain this with more independent systems would require another complete back-up system. Two factors should be added to these comments focused primarily on hardware. The first is that there were no reductions made to the multiprocessor system figure to take into the account the reliability of the interconnection system used which will certainly be more complex and less reliable than that of a uni-processor. The other factor is the cost of an additional system as compared to the cost of the interconnection system, which, as has been pointed out, can be quite appreciable.

The system control software required to exploit this inherently higher hardware reliability is more complex, more costly, and less reliable when compared to the system software required by a uniprocessor. These systems are very difficult to integrate into one single evaluation; however, experience has shown the system software factors to be significant enough to negate the numerical improvement in reliability shown above.

It is probable that this latter factor coupled with the possibility of catastrophic failure of an integrated memory has lead some [Weitzman] to claim higher reliability for several interconnected uniprocessors with independent memories. This may be true in an examination of reliability alone; however, when other factors, such as all processors having access to all memory and to the programs and data stored there, and the ability to reconfigure quickly in a real-time situation, are considered, the evaluation of system availability to perform a minimal set of essential tasks still gives a slight cost-effective advantage to a suitable multiprocessor configuration.

Flexibility

What immediately comes to mind when flexibility is mentioned is the ability of the system to reconfigure itself, but this is really a functional capability that provides high availability and system reliability for the minimum system. With appropriate software, the basic flexibility of the system to perform actions, such as respond to unusually large machine requirements, is available at all times.

System operations are greatly improved by the flexibility available in the utilization of all system resources by every task. Of particular significance is the ability for several programs to have access to a large data base.

Performance

There is only one reason to utilize a multiprocessor for its performance or throughput characteristics; that reason is that no single processor is large enough to handle a single large task in the time available. All other strictly throughput requirements can be met with a combination of uniprocessors.

Much to the sorrow, and perhaps amazement, of developers of multiprocessors, the addition of extra processors along with appropriate increases in memory and I/O capabilities did not result in a linear increase in performance.* A commonly quoted figure for the second processor of a large system is 60 to 80% improvement.† For the third processor the appropriate increase is only 30 to 50%. One of the best performance increase figures the author has seen was 0.8 for the second system; however, when a third processor was added to this *same* system the total performance (throughput) was only 2.1 times that for a single processor configuration of the same equipment components.‡

Obviously this performance is the result of the system software, because the operating system did not utilize effectively the functional units available. There is little question that usually one and often two of the processors were sitting idly awaiting the assignment of a task to be performed.

It is interesting to note that in one simulation analysis of a multiprocessor for the Apollo project, the results indicated that performance was better with "many slow processors" as opposed to "a few fast processors" [Mallach]. Since a major-time-consuming function of the operating system that greatly affects processor utilization is scheduling and dispatching, this

---

* Note that these figures do not apply to array or vector systems.
† On one specific 10-hr special job stream benchmark run on the B6700, a factor of 90% improvement was observed.

result may merely be reflecting that that operation has to be executed less often. However, such a situation does present the additional requirement that long jobs must be broken down into short independent tasks, and that problem has certainly not been solved by any of the known software.

One specific area in which the performance benefits of multiprocessors can be utilized, even with the limitations discussed above, is in closing a gap in the cost performance curves of the various systems offered by a manufacturer. Consider the IBM S/370 line as an example. If the basic Model 155 is assigned a relative cost and a relative performance of unity, various configurations of the 155 will provide cost-performance factors generally following the solid line shown in Figure 4-1. The next step up, the Model 165, can be configured to provide the cost-performance factors shown by its curve. Note that the basic 155 cost and performance are still the basis for comparison. Assume that a multiprocessor could be assembled utilizing Model 155 components. It would cost more than a collection of separate 155's and not exhibit linear performance increases; however, the multiprocessor 155 system could still be used to fill the gap and provide a more cost-effective alternative than changing to the 165 until

---

† From Miller *et al.*

Univac has prepared a formula for use in evaluating the performance improvement realizable from addition of processors to a system, and supplied numbers for the 1108 system. The formula is

$$N = \frac{P \times 10^6}{C + Q + D + E}$$

where N is the instruction rate, P is the number of processors, C is the memory cycle time, Q is delay due to queues at memory units, D is the delay due to hardware (multiple module adapters, etc.), and E is the time added due to extended sequence instructions.

For one processor,

$$N = \frac{1 \times 10^6}{0.75} = 1.33 \times 10^6$$

With extended instructions,

$$N = \frac{1 \times 10^6}{0.75 + 0.30} = 0.95 \times 10^6$$

For two processors,

$$N = \frac{2 \times 10^6}{0.75 + 0.05 + 0.125 + 0.30} = 1.63 \times 10^6$$

Thus the gain for the second processor is

$$\frac{1.63 - 0.95}{0.95} = 0.71.$$

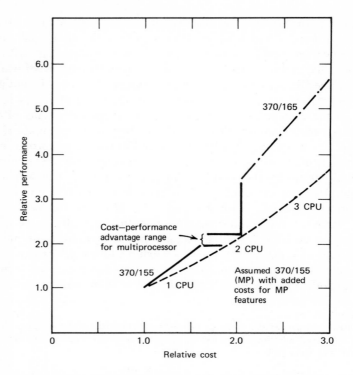

Figure 4-1   Cost-performance comparison. (Based on data from Quantum Science Corp.)

the workload exceeds 2.2. This is a very hypothetical example, but it does illustrate the point that there is often a range in which the multiprocessor is the most cost-effective option. Of course, the seemingly small range for multiprocessor advantage must also be balanced with the other benefits that the multiprocessor configuration offers.

Witt's Comparative Evaluation

In his paper discussing the IBM S/360 Model 65 multiprocessor and multiprocessors in general, B. Witt, one of its developers, presented an evaluation or comparison of the ability of several system organizations to meet a given set of design objectives. He compared five configurations:

- $p + s$

$$\boxed{\begin{array}{c} \boxed{s} \\ | \\ \boxed{p} \end{array}}$$

A standard processor with standard memory.

- $p + S$

A standard processor with double the standard memory.

- $P + S$

A "double power" processor with double the standard memory.

- $2(p + s)$

Two stand-alone configurations each with a standard processor with the standard memory.

- $2p + S$

The multiprocessor consisting of two standard processors sharing a double size memory, where p and P represent two different types of processors, the first with the capabilities of the standard machine, the second a theoretical processor exactly twice as fast as the standard; and s and S represent the storage and channel capacities, the first half the size of the second.

The results of Witt's comparative evaluation were presented in the matrix shown below:

Table entries have the following meaning:
    0: a standard, against which the other configurations may be judged.
    1: better
    2: best

If two systems have the same number, they are judged equally effective.

	$2p + S$	$p + S$	$2(p + s)$	$P + S$
Protection of critical data (safe from loss)	0	0	2 (if systems are duplexed)	0
Frequency of system/job restarts	0	2	1	Unknown
Critical system availability	2	0	1	0
Exceptional jobs/peak loads	2	1	0	2
System operations	2	2	0	2
Performance	1[a]	0[a]	1[a]	2

[a] Measured; all other comparisons were estimated.

All of the criteria are almost self-explanatory except "systems operations." The difference in ratings here is attributed to the problem of not having a single data base. (Note that for configuration 2 $(p + s)$, memories are totally disjoint.)

The reader is cautioned against assigning absolute values to the numbers used in the table. Although the multiprocessor configuration does exhibit some advantages over the others in certain areas, its peak load capacity is definitely not twice that of a single unit. More realistic estimates of this exact factor are given elsewhere in this text. What is pointed out is that the multiprocessor is at least as good if not better in all categories except restart. This latter weakness of the multiprocessor configuration can be attributed to the increased complexity of the operating system and other control mechanisms.

The various methods and techniques that can be utilized to improve the performance of a multiprocessor system are almost the same as those that are found in uniprocessors.

- Separate sets of control and operating registers can be used to facilitate the switching from one program to another as each individual processor operates in a multiprogrammed mode.
- Memory banking for overlapped access as described in detail earlier.
- The use of microprogramming (and a read-only-memory) tailoring the instruction set to the specific application area.
- Special instructions included for repetitive operations such as looping.
- The use of a hierarchy of memory down to the use of a high-speed solid-state cache memory acting as an anticipatory high-speed block buffer. (The use of a cache can introduce additional complications and problems in maintaining the integrity of the contents of the cache if the block of data it contains are used by more then one processor.)

Disadvantages of Multiprocessors

Several of the disadvantages have already been mentioned above, but the list below is complete in itself.

- System software is quite complex, difficult to design, expensive to produce, and difficult to check-out.
- By the very nature of the software and hardware systems and their numerous interactions, the checkout of the system software is very difficult and time consuming.
- The performance increases attained as additional components or functional units are added is nonlinear with respect to the added cost. For some workloads of numerous small tasks, a greater increase in performance for the same cost may be attained with uniprocessors. (A theoretical analysis of the situation supports this conclusion.)
- The configurations possible are severely limited by the hardware capabilities of the functional units.

    Ability to time-share a common bus.

    Number of access ports available.

    Electrical interface requirements.

    Limitations on cable lengths between units because of transfer delays added.

    Availability of suitable interconnection/switch mechanism.
- The potential advantages of the hardware and the systems organization may not be attained because of limitations of the system software.

SOME OTHER THOUGHTS ON CONCURRENCY AND PARALLEL PROCESSING

Other Taxonomies

A very basic taxonomy to describe the organization and mode of operation of systems containing multiple functional units was presented by Crenshaw in a NATO conference paper. Although his paper discussed primarily space and aircraft on-board systems, the terminology appears equally appropriate to systems in general. The two classes he defined were "federated" and "integrated" systems.

FEDERATED COMPUTER SYSTEM

A federated system consists of several computers, each dedicated to a particular task. The computers communicate through their I/O channels for normal functions. Redundancy may be provided, as in the case of the dual federated system, where each computer can perform backup functions in addition to its normal functions in the event of malfunction of the other computer. Individual elements of a federated system may have all the characteristics of an integrated system. Federated computers can be standardized in which all of the processors are identical, or they may be customized in which each processor is designed for the specific task. The second approach gives greater computational efficiency, but the first approach provides advantages in training, test equipment, maintenance and logistics.

INTEGRATED COMPUTER SYSTEM

An integrated system is defined as one which performs unrelated tasks in a multi-programmed mode of operation. The system may contain one central processor unit (CPU), the simplex system, or two CPU's sharing common main storage operating in a multiprocessing mode. The number of job queues distinguishes a federated system from an integrated system. A federated system requires a job queue and executive program in each computer, while an integrated system has only one job queue and executive program residing in the common storage. [Crenshaw]

Crenshaw also presented his estimates of the relative advantages of the two classes of systems. Except for the comment on battle damage, these comments are also applicable to systems in general.

FEDERATED SYSTEM ADVANTAGES

Less complex software including the operational program and the executive program
Simple reconfiguration
Lower vulnerability to battle damage
No storage interference
Higher reliability for critical functions

INTEGRATED SYSTEM ADVANTAGES

More efficient load sharing
Greater flexibility
More efficient communication
Less redundancy of storage
Greater total computational capacity
Higher total system reliability [Crenshaw]

Obviously, the multiprocessor and parallel processing systems as defined in this monograph are integrated computer systems, while all of the other multicomputer system configurations fall into the classification of federated systems. The naming of each class of system does reinforce the comments made here on the hardware and software characteristics that distinguish them.

John Shore has given up attempting to clarify terms such as parallel, orthogonal, associative, array, vector, and such. He attempted to clarify his own thoughts on the subject by establishing six types of machines.

Machine I. Conventional sequential processor (word serial, bit parallel operation).

Machine II. A parallel processor that operates on the same bit in all data words at the same time; example is Goodyear STARAN (word parallel, bit serial operation).

Machine III. Capabilities of I or II at will.

Machine IV. Multiple data memories, multiple processors, one control unit; example unit; example PEPE.

Machine V. Machine IV with linear array connnections of the processors and data memories; example ILLIAC IV.

Machine VI. Associative memories and processors utilizing logic-in-memory-arrays (LIMA).

Shore then closed his short paper on parallel processing with the following observations.

1. Most of the advanced, high-throughput computer organizations being proposed and built today are usefully viewed as alternate ways of increasing the amount of processing hardware relative to the amount of memory hardware, i.e., increasing the processing ratio.

2. In comparing alternate ways of increasing the processing ratio; a useful criterion is the duty cycle of the processing hardware; i.e., the proportion of the total rate of arithmetic and logical activity that is meaningful.

3. The higher the processing ratio, the fewer and more special purpose are the applications capable of using this ratio with a high duty cycle.

4. An important consideration in the choice between hardware or software implementions of parallel instruction sequences is the amount of meaningful arithmetic and logical activity resulting from these sequences.

5. An inability to find other than low duty cycle hardware implementations of "parallel" processes probably indicates a poor choice of algorithms and the possibility of attaining the same speed with less hardware in a Machine I design using appropriate software. [Shore]

It is difficult to see where the rather conventional multiprocessors that have been discussed fit into Shore's categorization, although his observations on the effects of various organizations on the "processing ratio" are of interest.

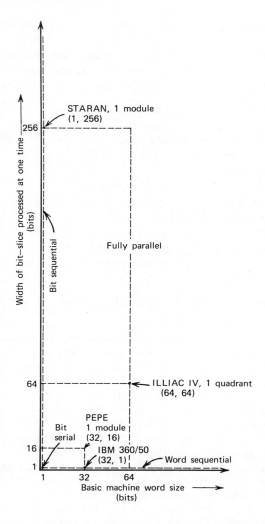

Figure 4-2   Maximum parallelism possible with various processing systems [Feng].

Degree of Parallel Operation

Professor Tse-yun Feng in introducing a special conference session on parallel processing systems presented an overview of the major parallel systems, emphasizing their degree of parallelism but not necessarily their overall throughput capabilities (which of course depend on clock rates also)

[Feng]. Each processing element may execute serial arithmetic-logic operations (i.e., a one-bit slice of each word being processed is handled) or it may execute fully parallel arithmetic-logic operations. The former case requires only a single storage register (either a word or a bit-slice of several words), while the latter system, the fully parallel processor, requires a number of registers. It is then possible to plot the maximum parallelism on a chart, comparing the machine's basic word size to the size of the bit-slice processed at one time (Figure 4-2).

THE FUTURE OF MULTIPROCESSORS

There is no question that we will continue to see multiprocessors utilized in applications where high availability and high reliability are of paramount importance. The development of smaller and lighter weight units has now made it possible to plan on their use as the standard airborne avionics computer for combat aircraft where only a few years ago the technology had just reached the point where even a uniprocessor avionics computer was possible.

One might expect that the driving function for multiprocessors would be applications such as process control where availability and reliability are principle requirements; however, the limited market for special systems of that type would not be enough incentive to develope a standard product specifically for those applications. The commercial motivations are always cost and performance in every applications sector, and the multiprocessor has a lot to offer. The primary characeristic of multiprocessors that contributes to this goal is the modularity of the system, providing the capability to better match the resources to the job.

- There can be a better utilization of the resources that the customer buys, since the system can literally be tailored to his specific needs.
- The incremental modularity of all of the major functions (processing, memory, and I/O) will provide the customer with a smoother price/performance curve to select his system.
- Development, engineering, production, and maintenance costs can all be reduced, since a few of the models of each functional unit will provide a broad range of performance capabilities.
- For special extra-large jobs, the multiprocessor system organization may be the only way to assemble sufficient power in any one system at a given point in time.

As the prices for hardware decrease and the cost of producing software increases, one of the few promising approaches is greater standardization of both across very wide ranges of both applications and system capacities. Multiprocessing and parallel systems hold that promise. They are applicable to single systems physically concentrated at one point as well as to cooperative networks of functional units interconnected by communication lines. The manufacturers of these systems must find more cost-effective solutions to the problem of system development.

Although there are certainly some cost advantages for multiprocessors in meeting certain classes of operational requirements, it is most probable that issues other than cost will be emphasized in the future. The multiprocessor will surely captalize on reliability and flexibility as well as the growth capabilities provided by its system organization.

REFERENCES

Alexander, Michael T., "Time Sharing Supervisor Programs," Class Notes, Computing Center, University of Michigan, Ann Arbor, Mich., May 1969, revised May 1970, 62 pp.

Anderson, J. P., S. A. Hoffman, J. Shifman, and R. J. Williams, "D825-A Multiple Computer System for Command and Control," *Proc. FJCC* **22,** 86–96 (1962).

Aschenbrenner, R. A., M. J. Flynn, and G. A. Robinson, "Intrinsic Multi-Processing," *Proc. SJCC,* **30,** 81–86 (1967).

Avizienis, Aigirdas, "Design of Fault-Tolerant Computers," *Proc. FJCC (1967),*

———, F. P. Mathur, and D. A. Rennels, "Automatic Maintenance of Aerospace Computers and Spacecraft Information and Control Systems," AIAA Paper 69–966, AIAA Aerospace Computer Systems Conference, Los Angeles, Calif., September 1969.

Baer, Jean-Loup, "Large Scale Systems," Chapter 5 in A. F. Cardenor, L. Presser, and M. A., Marin, eds., *Computer Science*, Wiley-Interscience, New York, 1972.

———, and D. P. Bovet, "Compilation of Arithmetic Expressions for Parallel Computations," *Proc. IFIP Congress*, Booklet B, 4–10 (1968).

Barnes, G., R. Brown, M. Kato, D. Kuck, D. Slotnick, and R. Stokes, "The Illiac IV Computer," *IEEE Trans.*, C–17, 746–757 (August 1968).

Baskin, H. B., B. R. Borgenon, R. Roberts, "PRIME—A Modular Architecture for Terminal-Oriented System," *Proc. SJCC*, 431–437 (1972).

Bell, C. Gordon, and Allen Newell, *Computer Structures: Readings and Examples*, McGraw-Hill, New York, 1971.

Burnett, G. J., and E. G. Coffman, Jr., "A Study of Interleaved Memory Systems," *Proc. SJCC,* **36,** 367–374 (1970).

Coffman, E. G., Jr., M. J. Elphick, and A. Soshani, "System Deadlocks," *ACM Comput. Surv.*, 3 (2), 67–78 (June 1971).

Cohen, Ellis, "Symmetric Multi-Mini-Processors: A Better Way to Go?," *Comput. Decis.*, 16–20 (January 1973).

COMTRE Corp, Sayers, Anthony P., ed., *Operating Systems Survey,* Princeton, Auerbach, 1971.

Covo, A. A., "Analysis of Multiprocessor Control Organizations with Partial Program Memory Replication," to be published (short version published in *Proc. IEEE COMPCON 1972*).

Crenshaw, James H., "Federated vs Integrated Computer Systems," in C. T. Leondes, ed., *Computers in the Guidance and Control of Aerospace Vehicles*, NATO, AGARDograph 158, February 1972, pp. 9–22.

Dancy, Charles, A., III, "System Reliability and Recovery," Department of Transportation Systems Center, Cambridge, Mass. 02142, Report DOT-TSC-FAA-71-16, June 15, 1971, AD 733760.

Davis, R. L., S. Tucker, and C. M. Campbell, "A Building Block Approach to Multi-processing," *Proc. SJCC*, 685–703 (1972).

Dijkstra, E. W., "Solution of a Problem in Concurrent Programming," *Commun. ACM* (September 1965).

Feng, Tse-yun, "An Overview of Parallel Processing Systems," *1972 WESCON Tech. Papers*, Session 1—"Parallel Processing Systems," (September 19–22, 1972).

Filene, Robert J., and William Weinstien, "The Regional Computer," Section 2.2, in *STS Data Management System Design (Task 2)*, Charles Stark Draper Laboratory, Massachusetts Institute of Technology, Cambridge, Mass., E-2529, June 1970.

Flynn, Michael J., "Some Computer Organizations and Their Effectiveness," *IEEE Trans. Comput.*, C-21 (9) 948–960 (September 1972).

Flores, Ivan, *Computer Organization*, Prentice-Hall, Englewood Cliffs, N. J., 1969.

Gonzalez, Jr., Mario, J., and C. V. Ramamoorthy, "Program Suitability for Parallel Processing," *IEEE Trans. Comput.*, C-20 (6) 647–654 (June 1971); AD 730 210.

Hellerman, H., *Digital Computer System Principles*, McGraw-Hill, New York, 1967, pp. 228–229.

Holt, Richard C., "Comments on Prevention of System Deadlocks," *Commun. ACM*. 14 (1), 36–38 (January, 1971).

Hopkins, A. L., Jr., "A Fault-Tolerant Information Processing Concept for Space Vehicles," Charles Stark Draper Laboratory, Massachusetts Institute of Technology, Cambridge, Mass., R-682, December 1970.

Irwin, J. D., J. M. Thorington, Jr., and V. S. Blanco, "Multiprocessing Computer Systems," Project Themis, Digital Systems Laboratory, Auburn University, Auburn, Ala., Technical Report AU-T-12, July 1970, 97 pp.

Jordan, John W., "Task Scheduling For a Real Time Multiprocessor," Electronics Research Center, Cambridge, Mass., NASA TN-D-5786.

Mallach, Efrem G., "Analysis of a Multiprocessor Guidance Computer," Instrumentation Laboratories, MIT, T-515, June 1969, 113 pp. (Ph.D. dissertation).

Miller, James S., Daniel J. Lickly, Alex L. Kosmala, and Joseph A. Saponaro, "Multi-processor Computer System Study—Final Report," Intermetrics, Inc., Cambridge, Mass., March 1970, 161 pp.

Murtha, J. C., "Highly Parallel Information Processing Systems," *Adv. Comput.*, 7, 2–116 (1966).

Quatse, Jesse T., P. Gaulene, and D. Dodge, "The External Access Network of a Modular Computer System," *Proc. SJCC*, 783–790 (1972).

Ramamoorthy, C. V., and M. J. Gonzalez, "A Survey of Techniques for Recognizing Parallel Processable Streams in Computer Programs," *FJCC Proc.*, 35 (1969).

Ravi, C. V., "On the Bandwidth and Interference in Interleaved Memory Systems," IEE *Trans. Comput.*, 899–901 (August 1972).

Seligman, L., "LSI and Minicomputer System Architecture," *Proc. SJCC*, 767–773 (1972).

Shore, John E., "Second Thoughts on Parallel Processing," *Proc. 1972 IEEE INTERCON*, pp. 358–359.

Slotnick, D. L., W. C. Borck, and R. C. McReynolds, "The SOLOMON Computer," *Proc. FJCC (1962)*.

Witt, B. I., "M65: An Experiment in OS/360 Multiprocessing "presented at Information Systems Symposium, September 4–6, 1968, Washington, D.C., also presented at 1968 ACM Conference.

Wang, Gary Y., "An In-House Experimental Air Space Multiprocessor—EXAM," ERC Memo KC-T-031, September 20, 1967.

Weitzman, Cay, "Aerospace Computer Technology Catches Up With Ground Gear," *Electronics* 112–119 (September 11, 1972).

Wilson, D. E., "The PEPE Support Software System," *COMPCON '72 IEEE Comput. Soc. Int. Conf.*, pp. 61–64.

Wood, Paul E., Jr., "Interconnection of Processors and Memory in the Multiprocessor System," ERC Memo KC-T-041, February 5, 1968.

———, "Input/Output System for An Aerospace Multiprocessor," ERC Memo RC-T-062, May 19, 1969.

GLOSSARY

This glossary is included for *one purpose only*—to assist the reader in understanding the material presented in the text. This caveat is necessary, since many of the terms defined below have additional meanings that are not appropriate here, and no attempt has been made to make the glossary general-purpose in nature.

algorithm   A prescribed set of well-defined rules or processes for the solution of a problem in a finite number of steps, for example, a full statement of an arithmetic procedure for evaluating sin x to a stated precision or the complete definition of the hardware operation involved in executing a basic arithmetic or logic operation.

arithmetic and logic unit   The *functional unit* of a computing system that contains the circuits that perform arithmetic and logical operations.

array processor   A computer system with multiple *arithmetic and logic units* (or portions thereof) sometimes referred to as *processing elements* organized so that operations may be executed *simultaneously* on an array of data elements.

associative   Normally used to refer to memory that is accessed by the value of its contents rather than its location designation. Locations are therefore identified by their contents, not by names or physical positions. Synonymous with content addressed memory (CAM) or storage. Associative is also used to refer to a mode of operation of a computer in which logical decisions are made based on the contents of a group of memory cells.

ASP   See *attached support processor*.

asymmetrical systems   A multicomputer system in which there is a significant variation between the capabilities of the various *processor units* compromising the total system.

ATC The Air Traffic Control System installed and operated by the Federal Aviation Authority (FAA).

attached support processor A *multicomputer system* organization in which one computer functions primarily as the I/O processor for the other computer which does the computations. (Term primarily used by IBM.)

availability A measure of the capability of a system to be used for performing its intended function as a result of the system being in an operational state.

bi-directonal bus A *bus* that permits the transfer of data signals in either direction.

blocking Collecting together and recording several logical records as one physical record or block on tape, disk, or drum to better utilize storage space and increase effective rate of I/O transfer.

BMEWS The U.S. Air Force Ballistic Missile Early Warning System.

bus One or more conductors used for transmitting data signals or power. Often acts as a common connection among a number of locations.

central memory The *functional unit* containing the storage cells directly accessible by the *arithmetic and logic unit* and the *control unit*.

central processor unit A term commonly used to refer to the assemblage of the *arithmetic and logic unit*, the *control unit*, and the *central memory*.

channel A system component that performs the functions of an independent computer in controlling all I/O components (card, tape, disk, anddrum) under the control of channel commands. A channel permits simultaneous operation of I/O components and the main computer.

character-oriented machine A computer in which the normal size of the unit of the data element accessed in memory and processed in the *arithmetic and logic unit* is one character. Synonomous with byte-oriented machine.

common-bus system A system organization in which all *functional units* are connected to a single common interconnection *bus*. It refers to any organization, even those having multiple buses, if there are not sufficient paths available to permit all *functional units* to be active at the same time.

concurrency Pertaining to the occurrence of two or more events or activities within the same specified interval of time. Contrast with consecutive, sequential, *simultaneous*.

control unit That portion of the hardware of an automatic digital computer that directs the sequence of operations, interprets the coded instructions, and initiates the proper commands to the computer circuits to execute the instructions.

crossbar switch system   A *multiprocessor system* in which the interconnection system is an orthogonal system of transfer *busses* that can be connected at any "crosspoint." The interconnection system is "nonblocking" in that transfers will never be inhibited due to the lack of a transfer path (although it may be blocked if one of the units is already busy).

data-interlock   The protection of a *data set* by inhibiting access to it by all processes except the single current user.

data set   A major unit of data storage and retrieval in the operating system, consisting of a collection of data in one of several prescribed arrangements and described by control information that is accessible by the system. (An IBM term primarily. Others often refer to this simply as a file.)

deblocking   The separation of a combined physical record into its constituent logical records. See *blocking*.

direct memory access   The ability of the system to transfer data directly from an I/O device to the *central memory* without using the *arithmetic/logic unit*. It may involve a complete *channel* or only an interface of more limited capability.

directly coupled systems   A coupled system in which the common storage media used for data transfer is high-speed *central memory*.

duplexed systems   A system with two distinct and separate sets of facilities, each of which is capable of assuming the system function while the other assumes a standby status. Usually, both sets are identical in nature.

fault-tolerant systems   Any system organization in which the motivation for the use of redundant *functional units* and the design of the interconnection system is to allow the system to overcome the effects of failures in either the units or the interconnect system. It often meets all of the criteria for being a multiprocessor; however, the motivations are not primarily those applicable to other *multiprocessor systems*.

functional units   The major operational units of a digital computer; for example, *central memory, arithmetic and logic, control, input/output controller or processor*.

indirectly coupled system   A coupled system in which the common storage media utilized for data transfer is an on-line device such as a tape, drum, or disk.

input/output channel A device which allows independent communication between the *central memory* and the I/O equipment. It controls any *peripheral* device and performs all validity checking on information transfers.

input/output controller Performs the same function as an *input/output channel*; however, it may have more logic capability to facilitate its operation in a multiprocessor system.

input/output processor Synonomous with *input/output controller*.

"interleaved" memories (1) To arrange parts of the sequence of memory addresses so that they alternate with parts of one or more other sequences of addresses and so that each sequence retains its identity. (2) To organize storage into banks with independent *busses* so that sequential data references may be overlapped in a given period of time.

interprocessor interference A reduction in the effective speed of a *processor* due to delays in accesses to *central memory* caused by the memory being in use by other *processors* or the I/O.

interrupts A break in the normal flow of a system or program occurring in such a way that the flow can be resumed from that point at a later time. Interrupts are initiated by signals of two types. (1) Signals originating within the computer system to synchronize the operation of various components. (2) Signals originating exterior to the computer system to synchronize the operation of the computer system with the outside world (e.g., an operator or a physical process).

memory access conflicts Degradation in the performance of the overall system caused by two or more *processors* trying to access the same *memory module* during the same memory cycle. When this does occur, it is necessary that one *processor* "idle" until the next cycle. Synonomous with *interprocessor interference*.

memory lockout Synonomous with *data interlock*.

memory module The physical block or assembly of *central memory*. The typical memory module is capable of executing only one access operation (READ or WRITE) at a time.

multicomputer system A system having more than one *processor* but not meeting all of the criteria of a *multiprocessor*.

multiple-bus/multiport systems A *multiprocessor system* in which interconnection is implemented by individual *busses* connecting each *processor* and *input/output controller* to a separate *port* on the *central memory*.

multiprocessor (The definition given in this text is quite explicit) A multiprocessor computer is a system—containing two or more *processor units* of approximately comparable capabilities:

- All having access to shared common *central memory*.
- All having common access to at least a portion of the I/O devices.
- All being controlled by one operating system that provides interaction as required between the processors and the programs they are executing at the job, task, step, *data set*, data element, and hardware (*interrupt*) levels.

multiprogramming pertaining to the *concurrent* execution of two or more programs on a single *processor*. The separate programs must be *simultaneously* resident in *central memory* (at least a portion of each program), and the control of the *processor* must oscillate between the various programs in the active mix.

nonhomogeneous systems A *multicomputer* or *multiprocessor system* composed of nonidentical *processors*.

normalization To adjust the exponent and fraction of the floating point representation of the value of a number so that the fraction lies within the prescribed normal standard range. This usually involves shifting the fraction to the left to remove all leading zeros and appropriately adjusting the exponent.

overlapped input/output capabilities A data channel that allows asynchronous operation of its I/O devices and program processing by the central processing unit.

parallel executive of tasks Processing more than one program at a time on a parallel basis, where more than one *processor* is active at one time.

peripheral systems A generic term referring to devices that are not a part of the computer main frame (e.g., card readers, printers, and tape units).

pipelining The fragmentation of an arithmetic or logic operation into distinct steps executed by separate hardware modules within the *processor*.

pipeline systems Systems designed to exploit the parallelism possible by utilizing a *pipeline* to execute the same operation on a series of data elements.

Polymorphic System An early U.S. Air Force system designed by Ramo-Wooldridge that exhibited many of the characteristics of present *crossbar multiprocessor systems*.

port An interconnection point or interface to a *functional unit*.

PP   Peripheral processors. Found in the CDC 6000 and 7000 systems.

PPU   Synonomous with *PP*.

private memory   The interconnection system is designed so that a portion of the *central memory* is accessible to only a single *processor*.

processing element   Used to refer to the limited capability *arithmetic and logic units* sometimes utilized in *array* and *vector processors*.

processor   Synonomous with *processor unit*.

processor unit   The *functional unit* of the computer that performs the programmed operations. It consists of the *arithmetic and logic unit* and *control unit*.

Project MAC   A remote-terminal computing system developed at the Massachusetts Institute of Technology. (Actually, MAC refers to the parent project "Machine Aided Cognition.")

reconfigure   Changes in the *system organization* that may be achieved by either manual or automatic means.

reliability   A measure of the ability to function without failure.

SAGE   The Semi-Automatic Ground Environment. The first U.S. Air Force major air defense system making extensive use of digital computers.

satellite computers   A *multicomputer system* in which the satellites act as "slaves" to the main *processor*.

simultaneity   The ability of a computer to allow I/O operations on its *peripherals* to continue in parallel with operations in the *central processor*.

simultaneous   Pertaining to the occurrence of two or more events existing or occurring at the same instant of time. (contrast with concurrent.)

simultaneous input/output capabilities   See *overlapped input/output capabilities*.

switch matrix   The assemblage of gates and other logic circuitry that allows the interconnection of *functional* and other operational units.

systems architecture   That portion of computer system design that pertains to the implementation of the operational *algorithms* in the hardware within each *functional unit*.

systems organization   That portion of computer system design that pertains to the selection of the number and type of *functional units* and how they will be interconnected.

system software   The software that is prepared for the primary purpose of controlling the hardware and providing the man-machine interface.

time-shared-bus system   A multiprocessor system in which the interconnecting *buses* are shared on a time-division basis.

unidirectonal bus   An interconnecting *bus* on which the control circuitry and amplifiers, if any, will support transmission of signals in only one direction. Reversible flow is not possible even on a time-shared basis.

uniprocessor system   A digital computer system having only one *central processor*.

unit-record I/O   Input/output devices such as the card reader, card punch, and printer.

vector processor   A computer system with multiple *arithmetic and logic units* (or portions thereof) organized so that operations may be executed *simultaneously* on a single dimension vector of data elements. Contrast to *array processor*.

von Neumann machine   As specifically used in this text, it refers to the system organization consisting of five distinct and identifiable *functional units: central memory, control, arithmetic and logic, input*, and *output*.

word-oriented machine   A computer in which the normal size of the unit of data accessed in memory and processed in the arithmetic and logic unit is a complete data word.

APPENDIX A

U.S. ARMY ADVANCED BALLISTIC MISSILE DEFENSE AGENCY

PARALLEL ELEMENT PROCESSING ENSEMBLE (PEPE)*

SYSTEM ORGANIZATION

The Parallel Element Processing Ensemble (PEPE) is a high-speed computing machine employing unconventional architectural concepts designed specifically to augment sequential general purpose computers in ballistic missile defense (BMD) radar data processing applications. PEPE is programmable using procedural languages and is operated under the control of the general purpose or host computer. PEPE's effectiveness as an augmentation comes from using highly parallel and associative processing techniques realized through an unstructured ensemble consisting of an indefinite number of Processing Elements governed by common global control units.

The PEPE organization and BMD system interconnection for radar data processing is shown in Figure A-1. PEPE is composed of the following functional subsystems:

1. Arithmetic control unit (ACU), one per system.

* U.S. Army Advanced Ballistic Missile Defense Agency. Organizations that have been associated with the PEPE Program are the following. Bell Telephone Laboratories developed the basic concepts and the design of the feasibility model. System Development Corporation was the prime contractor for the software and system design during the design and implementation phases. Honeywell was the hardware subcontractor for the design phase. Burroughs was the hardware subcontractor for the implementation phase.

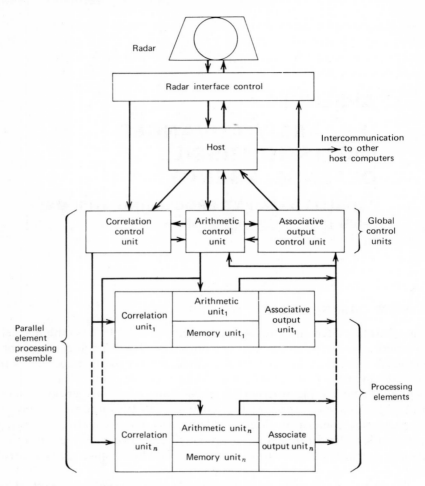

Figure A-1   PEPE organization and BMD system interconnections.

2. Correlation control unit (CCU), one per system.
3. Associative output control unit (AOCU), one per system.
4. Processing elements, an indefinite number each consisting of:
    1. Arithmetic unit (AU).
    2. Correlation unit (CU).
    3. Associative output unit (AOU).
    4. Memory unit (MU).

In addition, there are primary power and signal/power distribution subsystems to convert and route power and control and data signals between the various functional subsystems.

The Processing Elements (PEs) are the main computational component of PEPE. Selected portions of the BMD data processing load are offloaded from the general-purpose host computer to the PEs. The offloading selection process is determined by the inherent parallelism of the task and the ability of PEPE's unique architecture to manipulate the task more efficiently than the host. Specifically each PE is delegated the responsibility of an object under observation by the radar system. Each PE maintains a data file for specific objects within its memory and uses its arithmetic capability to continually update its respective file.

The number of PEs used in the PEPE is variable and may be expanded or contracted to meet the requirements of the application. This variability has no impact on the PEPE system performance except that enough PEs must be available to meet the computational load. PE operation and control is directed by the three global control units: ACU, AOCU, and CCU.

The operational portions of the PE are controlled by the respective global control units; the CU is controlled by the CCU, and AU is controlled by the ACU, and the AOU is controlled by the AOCU.

Arithmetic processes such as track updating, track prediction, discrimination, and interceptor guidance are performed in parallel by the AUs. All, or any selected subset, of the AUs execute simultaneously instruction signals issued by the ACU, depending on the elements' activity flip-flop condition.

Input of new information to the PEs is handled by the CU under control of the CCU. The CU correlation processes consist of comparing newly received object position information (as derived from radar returns) with predicted object position information generated by the processing element AUs and transferred to the respective CUs. Information on one object at a time is broadcast by the CCU to all CUs simultaneously, and all or a selected subset of CUs compare their stored data with the broadcast data. The object information is input to the CU (or CUs) where correlation occurs or into the first empty PE memory in those cases where no correlation occurs.

Output information sent to the radar is handled by the AOU under the control of the AOCU. Allocation of pulses for the radar consists of ordering pulse requests generated by the PEs as the result of object file updates calculated by the AUs and stored in the respective MUs for access by the APUs. The ordered retrieval of the pulse requests from the APUs on one object at a time are handled by the AOCU using a maximum-minimum search for associatively addressing data.

The AU, AOU, and CU and their respective control units are designed to allow independent and concurrent operation. Program memories in each of the control units permit the entire PEPE ensemble to operate concurrently with the host and require only minimal supervision by the host for scheduling tasks.

PEPE programs are loaded from the host into the ACU and then from the ACU to the program or data memory of each control unit. PEPE programs and most parameters are loaded at initialization time; thereafter, only occasional changes in parameters are sent from the host to PEPE.

Radar data sent to/from PEPE is handled by two PEPE connections. The CCU and AOCU transfer data from/to the host or the RIC, the Radar Interfare Control. The initial PEPE implementation will have the CCU and AOCU connected to a CDC 7600 host which will simulate the RIC functions. In a deployed configuration, the AOCU and CCU will have connections to both the host and the RIC. Radar data and orders will be transferred across the PEPE-RIC interface while netting and other communications and status information will utilize the HOST-PEPE interface.

The functions of the ACU, AOCU, CCU, AU, AOU, CU, and MU are described in detail in the following paragraphs.

FUNCTIONAL UNITS

Arithmetic Control Unit (ACU)

The functions of the ACU are:

1. Provide storage for the programs, global data base, and data required for operations of the ACU and AUs.

2. Decode AU parallel program instructions received from program memory and send the resulting microprogram sequence control signals to the AUs.

3. Provide PEPE with an I/O access to the host for sending summary PEPE status back to the host so that the host may properly schedule future tasks both within the host and PEPE under host control.

4. Provide the necessary arithmetic and logical operations for efficient control of parallel program instruction execution within the AUs.

5. Provide a route from the host to the CCU, ACU, and AOCU program and data memories so that they may be loaded and initialized.

6. Supervisor of interrupts from the host, CCU, AOCU, interval timers (clocks), and certain error conditions within the ensemble.

The ACU contains a 32K word (32-bit) program memory and a 2K word (32-bit) data memory loaded from the host at initialization. The sequential control logic (SCL) portion of the ACU retrieves instructions from the program memory and either executes them in the SCL for program control or sends them to the PICU, where they are converted to microprogram sequences and sent to the AUs for parallel execution. This allows computations to proceed within the element AUs with minimal intervention or control from the host. When the CCU or AOCU needs to perform operations requiring AU computations, they interrupt the normal ACU operation, initiate execution of AU programs stored in the ACU, and when the AU program is finished, return control to the normal ACU program.

The ACU is the global control unit for the AUs. All three of the global control units are similar in architecture and function. The control unit details are discussed in this paragraph and sections common to other control units reference this section. (A functional block diagram of the ACU is shown in Figure A-2.) The relationship of all three global control units is shown in Figure A-3. The other blocks are discussed below.

INPUT/OUTPUT UNIT (IOU)

The IOU provides the interface between the ACU and the host computer I/O multiplexer channel (MUX). The IOU is a 12-bit full duplex channel using a communication scheme compatible with the CDC 7600 host. The IOU performs all of the necessary operations to ensure that word format differences between the host and PEPE are resolved. The conversions performed on all data transfers are such that only the conversions to be performed need be specified by the programmer and the conversions themselves are performed by hardware. The IOU is divided into two subsections; a read interface unit (RDIU) and a write interface unit (WRIU). Both units are controlled by a common set of controls from the sequential control logic (SCL). These controls specify conversion and transmission start functions as derived from I/O instructions executed in the SCL.

SEQUENTIAL CONTROL LOGIC (SCL)

The SCL controls all of the ACU and AU operations. The SCL obtains parallel instructions from the Program Memory and sends them to the PICU which generates the appropriate microsequence signals for the element AUs. Additionally, the SCL obtains sequential instructions from program memory for internal execution.

PARALLEL INSTRUCTION CONTROL UNIT (PICU)

The PICU receives instructions from the SCL that are to be executed in the AUs. the PICU generates the necessary control microstep sequences required for the parallel instruction execution.

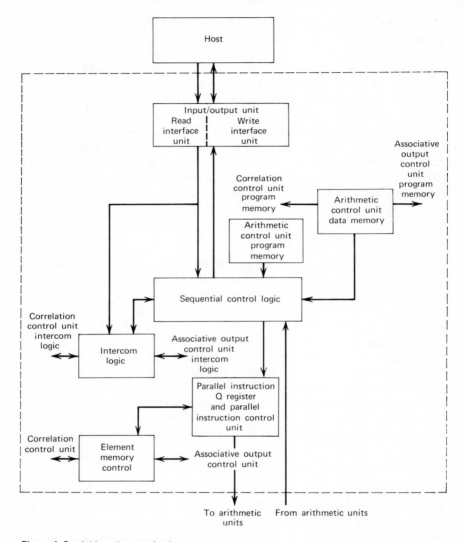

Figure A-2   Arithmetic control unit.

ACU PROGRAM MEMORY (PM)

The ACU PM is a 32K word by 32-bit, location addressed memory with a read/write cycle time of less than 600 nsec. The ACU is designed such that a 32K word increment of identical type memory may be added at a later date with no modification of existing hardware. The ACU PM is accessible by the ACU SCL only. The function of the PM is to store all programs required by the AUs under ACU control to execute necessary BMD algorithms allocated to the AU.

ACU DATA MEMORY (DM)

The ACU DM is a 2048 word by 32-bit, location addressed memory with an access time of less than 100 nsec. The ACU DM is accessible from the AOCU AND CCU by using an extended addressing format. The control unit memory interconnections are shown in Figure A-4. The function of the ACU DM is to store global variables and parameters required during the execution of programs stored in the ACU PM.

INTERCOM LOGIC (ICL)

The ICL maintains control over the nonnormal processing problems that are encountered within the ACU. These problems include loading of programs and initiation for normal execution, control unit intercommunications for interrupts, host interrupts, and timing and statistical data collection. Since the ACU is the supervisor control unit, it handles all of

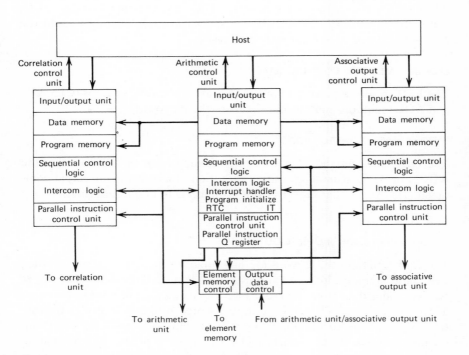

Figure A-3 Global control unit interconnections.

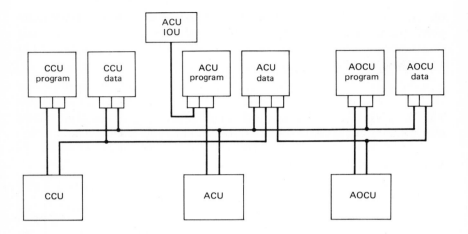

Figure A-4   Control unit memory bussing.

the interrupts. Note that under normal operation the CCU and AOCU can interrupt the ACU, but not vice-versa. The only interrupt that the ACU can affect in the CCU or AOCU is a special override operation, used for hardware debugging and software diagnostics.

ELEMENT MEMORY CONTROL (EMC)

The EMC resolved priority conflicts that arise when PE sections (CU, AU, and AOU) require simultaneous access to the PE MU.

OUTPUT DATA CONTROL (ODC)

The ODC switches the 32 output lines coming from the PE to either the AOCU or ACU accumulator upon execution of a control unit output command. The AOCU has higher priority for access to output information.

Correlation Control Unit (CCU)

The CCU contains a 2K word (32-bit) program memory and an identical size data memory loaded from the ACU at initialization. The CCU receives radar data from the radar interface containing new information on a particular object. The CCU, using its stored program, executes instructions in the CUs to correlate this information with predicted object information stored in the element CUs. The updated prediction information is obtained by interrupting the ACU. The ACU executes an AU program out of ACU program memory for this purpose. The CCU also inputs radar object track information from the RIC, or from the host when netted radar data is being used, and executes associative match instructions in the CU to store rapidly the data.

INPUT/OUTPUT UNIT (IOU)

The CCU IOU is identical to the ACU IOU in design and function except that it interfaces the CCU to the host Computer (see p. 143).

SEQUENTIAL CONTROL LOGIC (SCL)

The SCL is the portion of the CCU that controls all of the CCU and CU operations. See p. 143 for general description.

PARALLEL INSTRUCTION CONTROL UNIT (PICU)

The CCU-PICU function is functionally identical to the ACU-PICU except that the CCU-PICU has no PIQ.

CCU PROGRAM MEMORY (PM)

The CCU PM is a 2048 word (32-bit) location addressed memory with an access time of less than 100 nsec. Also the CCU design provides addressing and related control capability such that a 2048 word increment of identical memory may be added with no modifications to existing hardware. The CCU PM is accessible by the CCU or the ACU. The system functions are identical to the ACU-PM.

CCU DATA MEMORY (DM)

The CCU DM is a 2048 word (32-bit) location addressed memory identical in design and function to the ACU DM (see p. 145). The CCU DM is accessible by the CCU and the ACU.

INTERCOM LOGIC (ICL)

The functions of the ICL are to:

- Control the initiation of program executions within the CCU upon command from the host.
- Control the initiation of program executions within the CCU upon command from the ACU for diagnostic testing purposes.
- Send a request interrupt or trigger interrupt command to the ACU to initiate ACU programs.

Associative Output Control Unit (AOCU)

The AOCU contains a 2K word (32-bit) program memory and an identical size data memory loaded from the ACU at initialization. The primary purpose of the AOCU is to control all or a selected subset of the AOUs during execution of programs stored in the AOCU program memory. A maximum-minimum search algorithm is used in the AOCU to associatively retrieve and output data from the AOUs in an ordered manner. Once obtained from the AOUs, the AOCU sends the data to the RIC. The AOCU also controls the retrieval of object information from the PEs and transmission of the data to the host.

INPUT/OUTPUT UNIT (IOU)

The AOCU IOU is identical to the ACU IOU in design and function except that it interfaces the AOCU to the host computer.

SEQUENTIAL CONTROL LOGIC (SCL)

The Instruction Buffer, Index Adder, A, B, and Q Registers and the Adder are identical to the ACU SCL. The Index Registers (XR) and the Program Counter (PCTR) are identical to those in the CCU.

PARALLEL INSTRUCTION CONTROL UNIT (PICU)

The AOCU-PICU is identical to the CCU-PICU.

AOCU PROGRAM MEMORY (PM)

The AOCU-PICU is identical to the CCU PM except that it is accessible by the AOCU or ACU.

AOCU DATA MEMORY (DM)

The AOCU-DM is identical to the CCU-DM except that it is accessible by the AOCU and ACU.

INTERCOM LOGIC (ICL)

The AOCU-ICL is identical in function to the CCU-ICL except that it controls AOCU operation.

Arithmetic Unit (AU)

The functions of the AU are to:

- Execute integer and floating-point arithmetic and logical instructions on object data files stored in the element MU or on operands obtained from ACU data memory.
- Execute activity and select instructions.

The AU is a 32-bit, 2's complement, fractional binary arithmetic, and logical computation unit capable of executing single-address instructions issued by the ACU. The purpose of the AU computations is to update the object file information stored in the MU. Arithmetic computations are performed on floating point data so that logical decisions regarding future element computations can be made. Once AU computations are completed, results are stored in the MU.

Correlation Unit (CU)

The CU is the input portion of the element. The CU architecture and instruction set are designed specifically to enhance the input process. The CU is designed such that CU instructions shall be executed at the highest possible speed commensurate with existing technologies.

Associative Output Unit (AOU)

The functions of the AOU are to:

- Execute integer add, subtract, and logical operations on object data files stored in the element MU or on operands obtained from the AOCU data memory.
- Execute activity and select instruction.

The AOU is similar to the AU in that identical word size and formats are used in an identical arithmetic and logic unit with the exception that only integer arithmetic is used. The purpose of the AOU is to perform computations required for outputting data from the element.

Memory Unit (MU)

The functions of the MU are to:

- Store all object data files required by the AU, CU and AOU for element computations offloaded to the PEPE machine.
- Provide a local data base for the AU, CU and AOU such that references to other portions of the PEPE machine (global control units, the host or RIC) for element computations is minimized.

The MU is a 1024 (32-bit) location addressed memory with an access time of less than 75 nsec. The MU is shared on a cycle-stealing basis by the AU, CU, and AOU. The priority for access is determined by the PE Memory Control in the Global Control Units (see p. 146). All MU locations are accessible by the AU, CU, or AOU.

APPENDIX B
BURROUGHS CORPORATION*
D825 MULTIPROCESSOR SYSTEM

The D825 Modular Data Processing System is the result of a Burroughs study, initiated several years ago, of the data processing requirements for command and control systems. The D825 has been developed for operation in the military environment. The initial system, constructed for the Naval Research Laboratory with the designation AN/GYK–3(V), has been completed and tested. This paper reviews the design criteria analysis and design rationale that led to the system structure of the D825. The implementation and operation of the system are also described. Of particular interest is the role that developed for an operating system program in coordinating the system components.

FUNCTIONAL REQUIREMENTS OF COMMAND AND CONTROL DATA PROCESSING

By "command and control system" is meant a system having the capacity to monitor and direct all aspects of the operation of a large man and machine complex. Until now, the term has been applied exclusively to certain military complexes, but could as well be applied to a fully integrated air traffic control system or even to the operation of a large industrial complex. Operation of command and control systems in characterized by an enormous quantity of diverse but interrelated tasks—generally arising in real time—which are best performed by automatic dataprocessing equipment,

* This paper reprinted with permission of the Burroughs Corporation. It also appeared in the *1962 FJCC Procs*.

Appendix B   D 825 computer, memory, and I/O control modules, the status display console, and supervisory printer.

and are most effectively controlled in a fully integrated central data processing facility. The data processing functions alluded to are those typical of data processing, plus special functions associated with servicing displays, responding to manual insertion (through consoles) of data, and dealing with communications facilities. The design implications of these functions will be considered here.

Availability Criteria

The primary requirement of the data-processing facility is availability. This requirement, essentially a function of hardware reliability and maintainability, is simply the percentage of available, on-line, operation time during a given period. Every system designer must trade off the costs of designing for reliability against those incurred by unavailability, but in no other application are the costs of unavailability so high as those presented in command and control. Not only is the requirement for hardware reliability greater than that of commercial systems, but downtime for the complete system for preventive maintenance cannot be permitted. Depending upon the application, some greater or lesser portion of the complete system must *always* be available for primary system functions, and *all* of the system must be available *most* of the time.

The data processing facility may also be called upon to take part in exercising and evaluating the operation of some parts of the system or in actual simulation of system functions. During such exercises and simulations the system must maintain some (although perhaps partially and temporarily degraded) real-life capability, and must be able to return quickly to full operation. An implication here, of profound significance in system design, is, again, the requirement that *most* of the system be *always* available; there must be no system elements (unsupported by alternates) performing functions so critical that failure at these points could compromise the primary system functions.

Adaptability Criteria

Another requirement, equally difficult to achieve, is that the computer system must be able to analyze the demands being made upon it, and determine from this analysis the attention and emphasis that should be given to the individual tasks of the problem mix presented. The working configuration of the system must be completely adaptable so as to accomodate the diverse problem mixes, and, moreover, must respond quickly to important changes, such as might be indicated by external alarms or the results of internal computations (exceeding of certain thresholds, for example), or to changes in the hardware configuration resulting from the failure of a system component or from its intentional removal from the system. The system must have the ability to be dynamically and automatically restructured to a working configuration that is responsive to the problem-mix environment.

Expansibility Criteria

The requirement of expansibility is not unique to command and control, but is a desirable feature in any application of data processing equipment. However, the need for expansibility is more acute in command and control because of the dependence of much of the efficacy of the system upon an ability to meet the changing requirements brought on by the very rapidly changing technology of warfare. Further, it must be possible to incorporate new functions in such a way that little or no transitional downtime results in any hardware area.

Expansion should be possible without incurring the costs of providing more capability than is needed at the time. This ability of the system to grow to meet demands should apply not only to the conventionally expansible areas of memory and I/O but to computational devices as well.

Programming Criteria

Expansion of the data-processing facility should require no reprogramming of old functions, and programs for new functions should be easily incorporated into the overall system. To achieve this capability, programs must be written in a manner which is independent of system configuration or problem mix, and should even be interchangeable between different geographic sites performing like tasks. Finally, because of the large volume of routines that must be written for a command and control system it should be possible for many different people, in different locations and of different areas of responsibility, to write portions of programs, and for the programs to be subsequently linked together by a suitable operating system.

Concomitant with the latter requirement and with that of configuration-independent programs is the desirability of orienting system design and operation toward the use of a high-level, procedure-oriented language. The language should have the features of the usual algorithmic languages for scientific computations, but should also include provisions for maintaining large files of data sets which may, in fact, be ill-structured. It is also desirable that the language reflect the special nature of the application; this is especially true when the language is used to direct the storage and retrieval of data.

DESIGN RATIONALE FOR THE DATA-PROCESSING FACILITY

The three requirements of availability, adaptability, and expansibility were the motivating considerations in developing the D825 design. In arriving at the final systems design, several existing and proposed schemes for the organization of data processing systems were evaluated in light of the requirements listed above. Many of the same conclusions regarding these and other schemes in the use of computers in command and control were reached independently in a more recent study conducted for the Department of Defense by the Institute for Defense Analysis [Kroger *et al.*].

The Single-Computer System

The most obvious system scheme, and the least acceptable for command and control, is the single-computer system. This scheme fails to meet the availability requirement simply because the failure of any part, computer, memory, or I/O control disables the entire system. Such a system was not given serious consideration.

Replicated Single-Computer Systems

A system organization that had been well known at the time these considerations were active involves the duplication (or triplication, etc.) of single-computer systems to obtain availability and greater processing rates. This approach appears initially attractive, inasmuch as programs for the application may be split among two or more independent single-computer systems, using as many such systems as needed to perform all of the required computation. Even the availability requirement seems satisfied, since a redundant system may be kept in idle reserve as backup for the main function.

On closer examination, however, it was perceived that such a system had many disadvantages for command and control applications. Besides requiring considerable human effort to coordinate the operation of the systems, and considerable waste of available machine time, the replicated single computers were found to be ineffective because of the highly interrelated way in which data and programs are frequently used in command and control applications. Further, the steps necessary to have the redundant or backup system take over the main function, should the need arise, would prove too cumbersome, particularly in a time-critical application where constant monitoring of events is required.

Partially Shared Memory Schemes

It was seen that if the replicated computer scheme were to be modified by the use of partially shared memory, some important new capabilities would arise. A partially shared memory can take several forms, but provides principally for some shared storage and some storage privately allotted to individual computers. The shared storage may be of any kind—tapes, discs, or core—but most frequently is core. Such a system, by providing a direct path of communication between computers, goes a long way toward satisfying the requirements listed above.

The one advantage to be found in having some memory private to each computer is that of data protection. This advantage vanishes when it is necessary to exchange data between computers, for if a computer failure were to occur, the contents of the private memory of that computer would be lost to the system. Furthermore, many tasks in the command and control application require access to the same data. If, for example, it would be desirable to permit some privately stored data to be made available to the fully shared memory or to some other private memory, considerable time would be lost in transferring the data. It is also clear that a certain amount of utilization efficiency is lost, since some private memory may be unused, while another computer may require more memory than is directly available, and may be forced to transfer other blocks of data back to bulk storage to make way for the necessary storage. It might be added in passing that if private I/O complements are considered, the same questions of decreased overall availability and decreased efficiency arise.

Master/Slave Schemes

Another aspect of the partially shared memory system is that of control. A number of such systems employ a *master-slave* scheme to achieve control, a technique wherein one computer, designated the master computer, coordinates the work done by the others. The master computer might be of a different character than the others, as in the PILOT system, developed by the National Bureau of Standards [Leiner *et al.*], or it may be of the same basic design, differing only in its prescribed role, as in the Thompson Ramo Woolridge TRW400 (AN/FSQ-27) [Porter]. Such a scheme does recognize the importance, for multicomputer systems, of the problem of coordinating the processing effort; the master computer is an effective means of accomplishing the coordination. However, there are several difficulties in such a design. The loss of the master computer would down the whole system, and the command and control availability requirement could not, consequently, be met. If this weakness is countered by providing the ability for the master control function to be automatically switched to another processor, there still remains an inherent inefficiency. If, for example, the workload of the master computer becomes very large, the master becomes a system bottleneck resulting in inefficient use of all other system elements; and, on the other hand, if the workload fails to keep the master busy, a waste of computing power results. The conclusion is then reached that a master should be established only when needed; this is what has been done in the design of the D825.

The Totally Modular Scheme

As a result of these analyses, certain implications became clear. The availability requirement dictated a decentralization of the computing function—that is, a multiplicity of computing units. However, the nature of the problem required that data be freely communicable among these several computers. It was decided, therefore, that the memory system would be completely shared by all computers. And, from the point of view of availability and efficiency, it was also seen to be undesirable to associate I/O with a particular computer; the I/O control was, therefore, also decoupled from the computers.

Furthermore, a system with several computers, totally shared memory, and decoupled I/O seemed a perfect structure for satisfying the adaptability requirements of command and control. Such a structure resulted in a flexibility of control which was a fine match for the dynamic, highly variable, processing requirements to be encountered.

The major problem remaining to realize the computational potential represented by such a system was, of course, that of coordinating the many system elements to behave, at any given time, as a system specifically designed to handle the set of tasks with which it was faced at that time. Because of the limitations of previously available equipment, an operating system program had always been identified with the equipment running the program. However, in the proposed design, the entire memory was to be directly accessible to all computer modules, and the operating system could, therefore, be decoupled from any specific computer. The operation of the system could be coordinated by having any processor in the complement run the operating system only as the need arose. It became clear that the master computer had actually become a program stored in totally shared memory, a transformation which was also seen to offer enhanced programming flexibility.

Up to this point, the need for identical computer modules had not been established. The equality of responsibility among computing units, which allowed each computer to perform as the master when running the operating system, led finally to the design specification of identical computer modules. These were freely interconnected to a set of identical memory modules and a set of identical I/O control modules, the latter, in turn, freely interconnected to a highly variable and diverse I/O device complement. It was clear that the complete modularity of system elements was an effective solution to the problem of expansibility, inasmuch as expansion could be accomplished simply by adding modules identical to those in the existing complement. It was also clear that important advantages and economies resulting from the manufacture, maintenance, and spare parts provisioning for identical modules also accrue to such a system. Perhaps the most important result of a totally modular organization is that redundancy of the required complement of any module type, for greater reliability, is easily achieved by incorporating as little as one additional module of that type in the system. Furthermore, the additional module of each type need not be idle; the system may be looked upon as operating with active spares.

Thus, a design structure based upon complete modularity was set. Two items remained to weld the various functional modules into a coordinated system—a device to electronically interconnect the modules, and an operating system program with the effect of a master computer, to coordinate the activities of the modules into fully integrated system operation.

In the D825, these two tasks are carried out by the *switching interlock* and the *Automatic Operating and Scheduling Program* (AOSP), respectively.

SYSTEM IMPLEMENTATION

Most important in the design implementation of the D825 were studies toward practical realization of the switching interlock and the AOSP. The computer, memory, and I/O control modules permitted more conventional solutions, but were each to incorporate some unusual features, while many of the I/O devices were selected from existing equipment. With the exception of the latter, all of these elements are discussed here briefly. (A summary of D825 characteristics and specifications is included in Table B-1.)

Switching Interlock

Having determined that only a completely shared memory system would be adequate, it was necessary to find some way to permit access to any memory by any processor and, in fact, to permit sharing of a memory module by two or more processors or I/O control modules.

A function distributed physically through all of the modules of a D825 system, but which has been designated in aggregate, "the switching interlock," effects electronically each of the many brief interconnections by which all information is transferred among computer, memory, and I/O control modules. In addition to the electronic switching function, the switching interlock has the ability to detect and resolve conflicts such as occur when two or more computer modules attempt access to the same memory module.

TABLE B-1 SPECIFICATIONS, D825 MODULAR DATA PROCESSING SYSTEM

Computer module	Four maximum complement
Computer module, type	Digital, binary, parallel, solid-state
Word length	48 bits including sign, (8 characters, 6 bits each) plus parity
Index registers (in each computer module	15
Magnetic thin-film registers (in each computer module)	128 words, 16 bits per word, 0.33-μsec read/write cycle time
Real-time clock (in each computer module)	10-msec resolution
Binary add	1.67 μsec (average)
Binary multiply	36.0 μsec (average)
Floating-point add	7.0 μsec (average)
Floating-point multiply	34.0 μsec (average)
Logical AND	0.33 μsec
Memory type	Homogeneous, modular, random-access, linear-select, ferrite-core
Memory capacity	65,536 words (16 modules maximum, 4096 words each)
I/O exchanges per system	1 or 2
I/O control modules	10 per exchange, maximum
I/O devices	64 per exchange, maximum
Access to I/O devices	All I/O devices available to every I/O control module in exchange
Transfer rate per I/O exchange	2,000,000 characters/sec
I/O device complement	All standard I/O types, including 67 kc magnetic tapes, magnetic drums and discs, card and paper tape punches and readers, character and line printers, communications and display equipment

The switching interlock consists functionally of a crosspoint switch matrix which effects the actual switching of bus interconnections, and a bus allocator which resolves all time conflicts resulting from simultaneous requests for access to the same bus or system module. Conflicting requests are queued up according to the priority assigned to the requestors. Priorities are pre-emptive in that the appearance of a higher priority request will cause service of that request before service of a lower priority request already in the queue. Analyses of queueing probabilities have shown that queues longer than one are extremely unlikely.

The priority scheduling function is performed by the bus allocator, essentially a set of logical matrices. The conflict matrix detects the presence of conflicts in requests for interconnection. The priority matrix resolves the priority of each request. The logical product of the states of the conflict and priority matrices determines the state of the queue matrix, which in turn governs the setting of the crosspoint switch, unless the requested module is busy.

The AOSP

The AOSP is an operating system program stored in totally shared memory and therefore available to any computer. The program is run only as needed to exert control over the system. The AOSP includes its own executive routine, an operating system for an operating system, calling out additional routines as required. The configuration of the AOSP thus permits variation from application to application, both in sequence and quantity of available routines and in disposition of AOSP storage.

The AOSP operates effectively on two levels, one for system control, the other for task processing.

The system control function embodies all that is necessary to call system programs and associated data from some location in the I/O complement, and to ready the programs for execution by finding and allocating space in memory, and initiating the processing. Most of the system control function (as well as the task processing function) consists of elaborate bookkeeping for: programs being run; programs that are active (that is, occupy memory space); I/O commands being executed; other I/O commands waiting; external data blocks to be received and decoded; and activation of the appropriate programs to handle such external data. It would be inappropriate here to discuss the myriad details of the AOSP; some idea of its scope, however, can be obtained from the following list of its major functions:

1. Configuration determination.

2. Memory allocation.
3. Scheduling.
4. Program readying and end-of-job cleanup.
5. Reporting and logging.
6. Diagnostics and confidence checking.
7. External interrupt processing.

The task processing function of the AOSP is to execute all program I/O requests in order to centralize scheduling problems and to protect the system from the possibility of data destruction by ill-structured or conflicting programs.

AOSP Response to Interrupts

The AOSP function depends heavily upon the comprehensive set of interrupts incorporated in the D825. All interrupt conditions are transmitted to all computer modules in the system, and each computer module can respond to all interrupt conditions. However, to make it possible to distribute the responsibility for various interrupt conditions, both system and local, each computer module has an interrupt mask register that controls the setting of individual bits of the interrupt register. The occurrence of any interrupt causes one of the system computer modules to leave the program it has been running and branch to the suitable AOSP entry, entering a *control mode* as it branches. The control mode differs from the normal mode of operation in that it locks out the response to some low-priority interrupts (although recording them) and enables the execution of some additional instructions reserved for AOSP use (such as setting an interrupt mask register or memory protection registers, or transmiting an I/O instruction to an I/O control module).

In responding to an interrupt, the AOSP transfers control to the appropriate routine handling the condition designated by the interrupt. When the interrupt condition has been satisfied, control is returned to the original object program. Interrupts caused by normal operating conditions include:

1. Sixteen different types of external requests.
2. Completion of an I/O operation.
3. Real-time clock overflow.
4. Array data absent.
5. Computer-to-computer interrupts.
6. Control mode entry (normal mode halt).

Interrupts related to abnormalties of either program or equipment include:

1. Attempt by program to write out of bounds.

2. Arithmetic overflow.

3. Illegal instruction.

4. Inability to access memory, or an internal parity error; parity error on an I/O operation causes termination of that operation with suitable indication to the AOSP.

5. Primary power failure.

6. Automatic restart after primary power failure.

7. I/O termination other than normal completion.

While the reasons for including most of the interrupts listed above are evident, a word of comment on some of them is in order.

The array-data-absent interrupt is initiated when a reference is made to data that is not present in the memory. Since all array references such as A [k] are made relative to the base (location of the first element) of the array, it is necessary to obtain this address and to index it by the value k. When the base of array A is fetched, hardware sensing of a presence bit either allows the operation to continue, or initiates the array data absent interrupt. In this way, keeping track of data in use by interacting programs can be simplified, as may the storage allocation problem.

The primary power failure interrupt is highest priority, and *always* preemptive. This interrupt causes all computer and I/O control modules to terminate operations, and to store all volatile information either in memory modules or in magnetic thin-film registers. (The latter are integral elements of computer modules.) This interrupt protects the system from transient power failure, and is initiated when the primary power source voltage drops below a predetermined limit.

The automatic restart after primary power failure interrupt is provided so that the previous state of the system can be reconstructed.

A description of how an external interrupt is handled might clarify the general interrupt procedure. Upon the presence of an external interrupt, the computer which has been assigned responsibility to handle such interrupts automatically stores the contents of those registers (such as the program counter) necessary to subsequently reconstitute its state, enters the control mode, and goes to a standard (hardware-determined) location where a branch to the external request routine is located. This routine has the responsibility of determining which external request line requires servicing, and, after consulting a table of external devices (teletype buffers, console keyboards, displays, etc.) associated with the interrupt lines, the computer constructs and transmits an input instruction to the requesting device for an initial message. The computer then makes an entry in the table of the I/O complete program (the program that handles I/O complete interrupts) to activate the appropriate responding routine when the message is read in. A check is then made for the occurrence of additional external requests. Finally, the computer restores the saved register contents and returns in normal mode to the interrupted program.

AOSP Control of I/O Activity

As mentioned above, control of all I/O activity is also within the province of the AOSP. Records are kept on the condition and availability of each I/O device. The locations of all files within the computer system, whether on magnetic tape, drum, disc file, card, or represented as external inputs, are also recorded. A request for input by file name is evaluated, and, if the device associated with this name is readily available, the action is initiated. If for any reason the request must be deferred, it is placed in a program queue to await conditions which permit its initiation. Typical conditions which would cause deferral of an I/O operation include:

1. No available I/O control module or channel.
2. The device in which the file is located is presently in use.
3. The file does not exist in the system.

In the later case, typically, a message would be typed out on the supervisory printer, asking for the missing file.

The I/O complete interrupt signals the completion of each I/O operation. Along with this interrupt, an I/O result descriptor is deposited in an AOSP table. The status relayed in this descriptor indicates whether or not the operation was successful. If not successful, what went wrong (such as a parity error, or tape break, card jams, etc.) is indicated so that the AOSP may initiate the appropriate action. If the operation was successful, any waiting I/O operations which can now proceed are initiated.

AOSP Control of Program Scheduling

Scheduling in the D825 relies upon a job table maintained by the AOSP. Each entry is identified with a name, priority, precedence requirements, and equipment requirements. Priority may be dynamic, depending upon time, external requests, other programs, or a function of many variable conditions. Each time the AOSP is called upon to select a program to be run, whether as a result of the completion of a program or of some other interrupt condition, the job table is evaluated. In a real-time system, situations occur wherein there is no system program to be run, and machine time is available for other uses. This time could be used for auxiliary functions, such as confidence routines.

The AOSP provides the capability for program segmentation at the discretion of the programmer. Control macros embedded in the program code inform the AOSP that parallel processing with two or more computers is possible at a given point. In addition, the programmer must specify where the branches indicated in this manner will join following the parallel processing.

Computer Module

The computer modules of the D825 system are identical, general-purpose, arithmetic and control units. In determining the internal structure of the computer modules, two considerations were uppermost. First, all programs and data had to be arbitrarily relocatable to simplify the storage allocation function of the AOSP; secondly, programs would not be modified during execution. The latter consideration was necessary to minimize the amount of work required to pre-empt a program, since all that would have to be saved to reinstate the interrupted program at a later time would be the data for that program and the register contents of the computer module running the program at the time it was dumped.

The D825 computer modules employ a variable-length instruction format made up of quarter-word syllables. Zero-, one-, two-, or three-address syllables, as required, can be associated with each basis command syllable. An implicitly addressed accumulator stack is used in conjunction with the arithmetic unit. Indexing of all addresses in a command is provided, as well as arbitrarily deep indirect addressing for data.

Each computer module includes a 128-position, thin-film memory used for the stack, and also for many of the registers of the machine, such as the program base register, data base register, the index registers, and limit registers.

The instruction complement of the D825 includes the usual fixed-point, floating-point, logical, and partialfield commands found in any reasonably large scientific data processor.

Memory Module

The memory modules consist of independent units storing 4096 words, each of 48 bits. Each unit has an individual power supply and all of the necessary electronics to control the reading, writing, and transmission of data. The size of the memory modules was established as a compromise between a module size small enough to minimize conflicts wherein two or more computer or I/O modules attempt access to the same memory module, and size large enough to keep the cost of duplicated power supplies and addressing logic within bounds.

It might be noted that for a larger modular processor system, these trade-offs might indicate that memory modules of 8192 words would be more suitable. Modules larger than this—of 16,384 or 32,768 words, for example—would make construction of relatively small equipment complements meeting the requirements set forth above quite difficult. The cost of smaller units of memory is offset by the lessening of catastrophe in the event of failure of a module.

I/O Control Module

The I/O control module executes I/O operations defined and initiated by computer module action. In keeping with the system objectives, I/O control modules are not assigned to any particular computer module, but rather are treated in much the same way as memory modules, with automatic resolution of conflicting attempted accesses via the switching interlock function. Once an I/O operation is initiated, it proceeds independently until completion.

I/O action is initiated by the execution of a transmit I/O instruction in one of the computer modules, which delivers an I/O descriptor word from the addressed memory location to an inactive I/O control module. The I/O descriptor is an instruction to the I/O control module that selects the device, determines the direction of data flow, the address of the first word, and the number of words to be transferred.

Interposed between the I/O control modules and the physical external devices is another crossbar switch designated the I/O exchange. This automatic exchange, similar in function to the switching interlock, permits two-way data flow between any I/O control module and any I/O device in the system. It further enhances the flexibility of the system by providing as many possible external data transfer paths as there are I/O control modules.

Equipment Complements

A D825 system can be assembled (or expanded) by selection of appropriate modules in any combination of: one to four computer modules, one to 16 memory modules, one to ten I/O control modules, one or two I/O exchanges, and one to 64 I/O devices per I/O exchange in any combination selected from: operating (or system status) consoles, magnetic tape transports, magnetic drums, magnetic disc files, card punches and readers, paper tape perforators and readers, supervisory printers, highspeed line printers, selected data converters, special real-time clocks, and intersystem data links. (See Figure B-1.)

SUMMARY AND CONCLUSION

It is the belief of the authors that modular systems (in the sense discussed above) are a natural solution to the problem of obtaining greater computational capacity—more natural than simply to build larger and faster machines. More specifically, the organizational structure of the D825 has been shown to be a suitable basis for the data processing facility for command and control. Although the investigation leading toward this structure proceeded as an attack upon a number of diverse problems, it has become evident that the requirements peculiar to this area of application are, in effect, aspects of a single characteristic, which might be called *structural freedom*. Furthermore, it is now clear that the most unique characteristic of the structure realized—intergrated operation of freely intercommunicating, totally modular elements—provides the means for achieving structural freedom.

For example, one requirement is that some specified minimum of data processing capability be always available, or that, under any conditions of system degradation due to failure or maintenance, the equipment remaining on line be sufficient to perform primary system functions. In the D825, module failure results in a reduction of the on-line equipment configuration but permits normal operation to continue, perhaps at a reduced rate. The individual modules are designed to be highly reliable and maintainable, but system availability is not derived solely from this source, as is necessarily the case with more conventional systems. The modular configuration permits operation, in effect, with active spares, eliminating the need for total redundancy.

A second requirement is that the working configuration of the system at a given moment be instantly reconstructable to new forms more suited to a dynamically and unpredictably changing work load. In the D825, all communication routes are public, all modules are functionally decoupled, all assignments are scheduled dynamically, and assignment patterns are totally fluid. The system of interrupts and priorities controlled by the AOSP and the switching interlock permits instant adaptation to any work load, without destruction of interrupted programs.

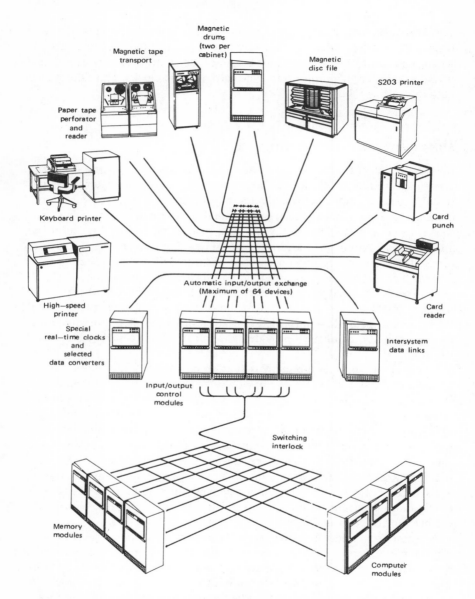

Figure B-1   System organization Burroughs D 825 modular data processing system.

The requirement for expansibility calls simply for adaptation on a greater time scale. Since all D825 modules are functionally decoupled, modules of any types may be added to the system simply by plugging into the switching interlock or the I/O exchange. Expansion in all functional areas may be pursued far beyond that possible with conventional systems.

It is clear, however, that the D825 system would have fallen far short of the goals set for it if only the hardware had been considered. The AOSP is as much a part of the D825 system structure as is the actual hardware. The concept of a "floating" AOSP as the force the molds the constituent modules of an equipment complement into a system is an important notion having an effect beyond the implementation of the D825. One interesting by-product of the design effort for the D825 has, in fact, been a change of perspective; it has become abundantly clear that computers do not run programs, but that programs control computers.

REFERENCES

Kroger, Marlin G., et al., "Computers in Command and Control," ITR61-12, prepared for DOD:ARPA by Digital Computer Application Study, Institute for Defense Analyses, Research and Engineering Support Division, November 1961.

Leiner, A. L., W. A. Notz, J. L. Smith, and A. Weinerger, "Organizing a Network of Computers to Meet Deadlines," *Proc. EJCC*, December 1957.

Porter, R. E. "The RW-400—A New Polymorphic Data System," *Datamation,* **6** No (1) 8-14, (January/February, 1960).

APPENDIX C

BURROUGHS CORPORATION
B6700 INFORMATION PROCESSING SYSTEMS

INTRODUCTION TO SYSTEM ORGANIZATION

The B6700 is described by Burroughs as a large scale processing system with these general features:

- Monolithic circuitry.
- Memory expandable to 1,048,576 words (6 EBCDIC characters per word).
- Memory cycle times of 1.5 μsec 1.2 μsec, or 500 nsec.
- Peripheral configuration expandable to 256 units.
- Triple I/O processor system permitting up to 36 simultaneous I/O operations.
- Data communication software for remote computing and file manipulation.
- Disk file storage or over 72 billion bytes (8-bit characters).

The configurations are organized in a central system exchange or crossbar architecture so that an array of memory modules, processing units, and I/O processors are connected in matrix fashion, as shown on the left side of the B6700 Schematic Diagram in Figure C-1. This diagram indicates the degree of modularity possible.

- One, two, or three central processors.
- Any combination of 16K or 64K word modules up to the maximum of 1,048,576 words.
- One, two, or three I/O processors.

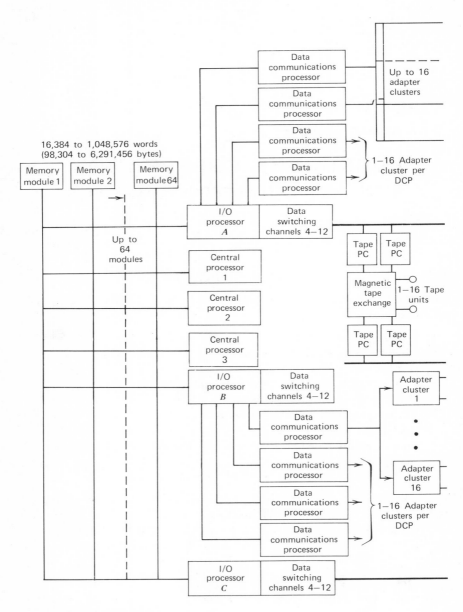

Figure C-1   B6500 block diagram.

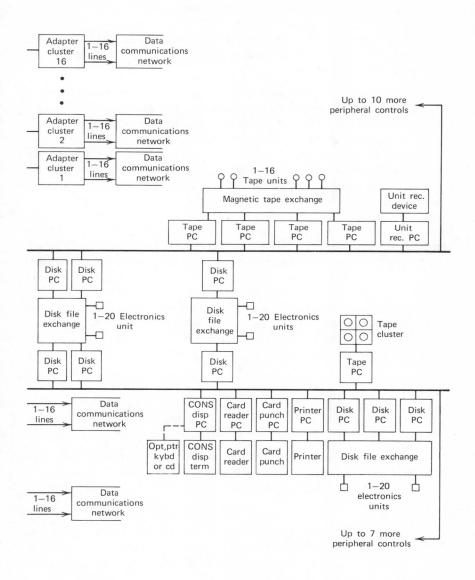

Adapter cluster 16 — 1–16 lines → Data communications network

Adapter cluster 2 — 1–16 lines → Data communications network

Adapter cluster 1 — 1–16 lines → Data communications network

1–16 Tape units

Magnetic tape exchange

Up to 10 more peripheral controls

Unit rec. device

Tape PC · Tape PC · Tape PC · Tape PC · Unit rec. PC

Disk PC · Disk PC

Disk file exchange — 1–20 Electronics unit

Disk PC

Disk file exchange — 1–20 Electronics units

Tape cluster

Disk PC · Disk PC

Disk PC

Tape PC

1–16 lines → Data communications network

CONS disp PC · Card reader PC · Card punch PC · Printer PC · Disk PC · Disk PC · Disk PC

Opt,ptr kybd or cd · CONS disp term · Card reader · Card punch · Printer · Disk file exchange

1–20 electronics units

1–16 lines → Data communications network

Up to 7 more peripheral controls

Up to 20 peripheral controls

171

- I/O channels, peripheral controls, peripheral devices and communication lines, connected according to the rules given in the discussion of the I/O processor.

Further reference to Figure C-1 indicates that independent access to main memory for each peripheral unit is provided, not under centralized I/O control using an I/O controller or data channel processor, but under distributed control by providing each peripheral unit with an associated control. Note that the maximum configuration with three I/O processor can be expanded further through the use of disk file and magnetic tape exchanges. These controls and exchanges are described further below under I/O processor.

Central processors are logically identical in a multiprocessor configuration; this way the three processors can service interrupt conditions and perform the executive services available in the Master Control Program required by multiple jobs in execution, without regard for the operational state of any other processor. Processors communicate with the I/O processor by use of the Scan Buss, which is a communications link consisting of 20 address lines, 48 data information lines, 1 parity line, and 11 control lines. Using this approach, the processors can issue I/O commands independent of the actual peripheral device configuration, as discussed below under I/O processor.

FUNCTIONAL UNITS

Central Processor

Each central processor is organized into two major divisions, called Functional Resources and Operator Algorithms. This organization leads to several system concepts, which appear to make the B6700 unique among other multiprocessors:

1. A processor command structure based on Polish string, operations which result in processor execution of successive instruction triplets, consisting of a string of 8-bit operator "syllables" which manipulate the contents of a hardware-implemented stock.
2. All programs, both user code and executive control code, are written in high-level procedure-oriented languages, and all compilations result in reentrant object code concurrently executable by multiple jobs, called "processes."

3. Unrestricted, and primarily automatic, recursive use of subroutines by multiple processes.

4. All data arrays, program segments, and character strings are initially addressed via descriptor words, which provides a hardware mechanism for program segmentation and for execution of programs whose instructions are not contiguous in main memory.

The stack operates as a last-in, first-out storage area, assigned to each process, for program variables and data references associated with the process. In addition, it provides a facility for the temporary storage of data and process history, such as declared/current process priority, authority, dynamic core estimate, process procedural depth, and time spent waiting for activation. A more detailed discussion of the stack mechanism is given later, after some of the hardware registers providing stack control are identified.

The processor data word is 51 bits long. The first 3 bits of the word are used as tag bits which identify the various word types as illustrated in Figure C-2. The remaining 48 bits are data or control information. These tag bits allow data to be addressed as an operand, with the processor determining whether the operand consists of one or two words; it also provides memory protection to the level of the basic machine data word, rather than using base registers or protection keys for protecting keys for protecting segments of memory of fixed minimal size. The 20-bit address field shown in the descriptor words provides for direct addressing of 1,048,576 words.

The processor contains a memory controller, unlike some multiprocessors where memory access priority is controlled by a separate module, such as the RCA 215 Signal Distribution or the Hughes 4400 Memory/Processor Switch. This does not mean that I/O channel data transfer into a memory module is dependent on central processor attention; however, it does mean that an I/O processor interface must be provided in each processor's memory controller, which contains the Scan Buss for asynchronous communication between processors and multiplexors. All this seems to indicate a duplication of control hardware, rather than a lack of modularity, when compared to the other systems. In addition to the I/O multiplexor interface, the Memory Controller contains the Address Processor Unit which consists of 32 object program address registers (D registers) and 16 base and index registers used by the Family Operator logic and Program Sequence Controller. Included in these 20-bit registers are five registers used by the Stack Controller for automatic stack adjustment, as required by the Operator Families and the other functional controllers. These

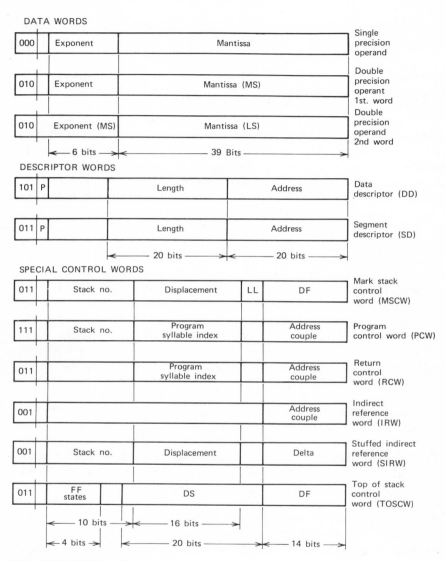

Figure C-2 B6500 word formats.

registers indicate to some extent the hardware control of the stack mechanism and are as follows:

Register	Function
S	Stack pointer register, giving top of stack address.
SNR	Stack number register, used to locate the data descriptor for the current active stack.
LOSR	Limit of stack register, one of the stack memory protection registers defining the upper address of the current active stack.
BOSR	Base of stack register, one of the stack memory protection registers defining the base address of the current active stack.
F	Pointer to top MSCW in the current active stack, indicating which procedure of the process is in execution.

The A, B, X, and Y data registers are referred to as top-of-stack registers and are the data path through which operands flow into the stack or out of the stack into the other data registers, as required by the current operator. This mechanism is shown in Figure C-3, where the MSCW word is the last Mark Stack Control Word entered in the stack, defining the current procedure in execution.

The relative addressing procedure used in the B6700 stack is an adoptation of the addressing environment of an ALGOL procedure, established when the program is structured by the programmer, and is referred to as the lexicographical ordering of the procedural blocks (see Figure C-4).

The address couple fields in the processor control words in Figure C-2 contain two items: the lexicographical level (LL) of the variable and an index value (1) used to locate the specific variable within a given lexicographical level. Since the ordering of the procedural blocks remains static as the program is executed, the variable can always be referenced via address couples. Note that the MSCW stack entry contains an LL field which denotes the lexicographical level of the procedure being entered. Given an ALGOL program structure as shown in Figure C-4, the current addressing environment for the process is depicted in Figure C-5, assuming that Procedure B is in execution. The D registers address the base of each addressing-level segment, so that the local variables of all procedures are addressed relative to the D registers.

The Stuffed Indirect Reference Word (SIRW of Figure C-2) is used to address beyond the immediate environment of the current procedures, and allows reference to variables in other stacks. Since all stacks for processes

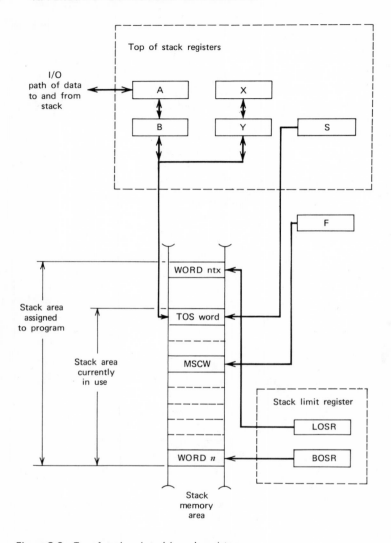

Figure C-3   Top of stack and stack bounds registers.

known to the system are organized in a tree structure, with the trunk of the tree a stack containing certain operating system global variables and segment descriptors describing the various procedures within the operating system, the reentrant program code produced by the compilers can be shared by multiple jobs executing the same program. This stack tree structure is depicted in Figure C-6 where a Stack Vector of data descriptors locates the stack branches of the tree. The display registers D0 and D1, representing lexicographical levels 0 and 1, point to Mark Stack Control Words in the operating system stack and in the stack of segment descriptors defining the location and size of all program code to be executed. It is the separation of the unmodifiable program code from the variables associated with a process, through a hardware-implemented stack mechanism, that

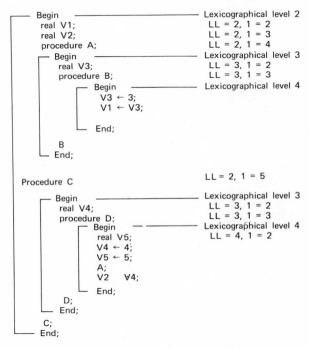

```
─  Begin  ──────────────────────  Lexicographical level 2
     real V1;                      LL = 2, 1 = 2
     real V2;                      LL = 2, 1 = 3
     procedure A;                  LL = 2, 1 = 4
   ─  Begin  ────────────────────  Lexicographical level 3
        real V3;                   LL = 3, 1 = 2
        procedure B;               LL = 3, 1 = 3
      ─  Begin  ──────────────────  Lexicographical level 4
           V3 ← 3;
           V1 ← V3;

      ─  End;

     B
   ─ End;

   Procedure C                     LL = 2, 1 = 5

   ─  Begin  ────────────────────  Lexicographical level 3
        real V4;                   LL = 3, 1 = 2
        procedure D;               LL = 3, 1 = 3
      ─  Begin  ── ───────────────  Lexicographical level 4
           real V5;                LL = 4, 1 = 2
           V4 ← 4;
           V5 ← 5;
           A;
           V2    ∀4;
      ─  End;

        D;
   ─ End;

     C;
─  End;
```

ALGOL Program with Lexicographical structure indicated

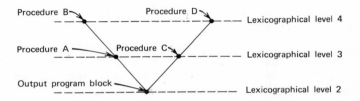

Procedure B — Procedure D — Lexicographical level 4

Procedure A — Procedure C — Lexicographical level 3

Output program block — Lexicographical level 2

Figure C-4   Addressing environment tree of ALGOL program.

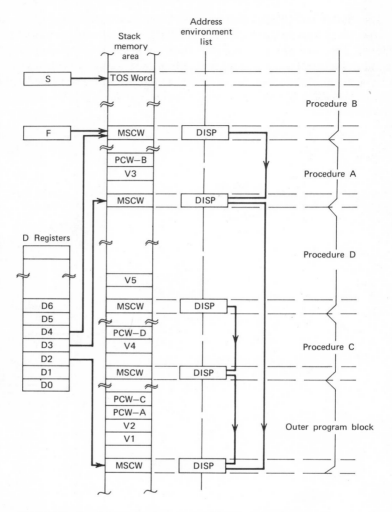

Figure C-5 *D* registers indicating current addressing environment.

provides a suitable processing environment for procedure-oriented language execution.

Three classes of interrupts are provided, allowing 25 different interrupts to be recognized by the processor, which includes four interrupt types for I/O processor operation. The classes of interrupts are syllable (instruction) dependent, alarm and external interrupts. The syllable dependent interrupts

(12 are recognized) are similar to other computer systems' program interrupts, such as exponent overflow, memory protection violation, and invalid operand, but they also provide two interrupt types for a mode of variable paging and segmentation mechanism, allowing program or data segments to be placed in main memory from secondary storage when they are referenced during process execution but are not present in memory. These interrupts are as follows.

- *Presence bit*, which occurs when the processor accesses a data or descriptor or segment descriptor with the "presence-bit" off, indi-

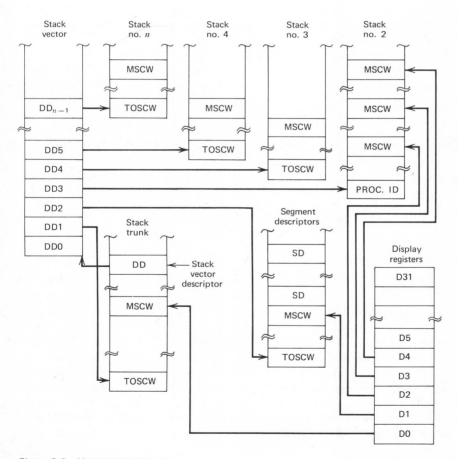

Figure C-6   Multiple linked stacks.

cating that whatever the descriptor references is not present in memory. This P-bit is shown in the descriptor words in Figure C-2.

⚬ *Segmented array*, indicating that the operating system has segmented an array row when storing it and has just attempted to index beyond the end of the current segment. The interrupt procedure must now replace the current segment by the proper segment, if one exists, and continue executing the process.

There are six alarm interrupts which are about the same as other system's processor fault interrupts, such as instruction not complete, memory parity, or invalid operator/operand. In addition, since the processor contains the Memory Controller (see Figure C-1), there is an I/O processor parity interrupt, an internal processor interrupt indicating faulty reception of data from an I/O processor.

There are seven external interrupt groups, for timer runout, process stack overflow, interprocessor communication, and I/O processor operation. The process stack overflow interrupt allows for the possibility of a process so complex that dynamic stack size growth is required to keep the process running.

Figure C-7 depicts a block diagram of the B6700 processor which summarizes pictorially the processor configuration presented. It indicates the relationship between the Functional Resources and Operator Algorithms comprising the processor and the flow of program syllables and data within the processor.

Primary Storage

Main memory in the B6700 is organized so that any memory module can send information to, or receive information from all processors over any one of six information busses (see Figure C-8). The modules examine each word that is placed on the buss to determine which particular module is being addressed. If a module is being addressed, it establishes the linkage to receive the word. This eliminates the need for a central control to establish a linkage directing the word to the proper module. Two hundred nanoseconds after the memory cycle is initiated, the module grants access. In another 200 nsec, the word is available to the buss, and 200 nsec later the word is in the central processor or I/O processor register. Operation of each memory module is independent of the operation of any other memory module.

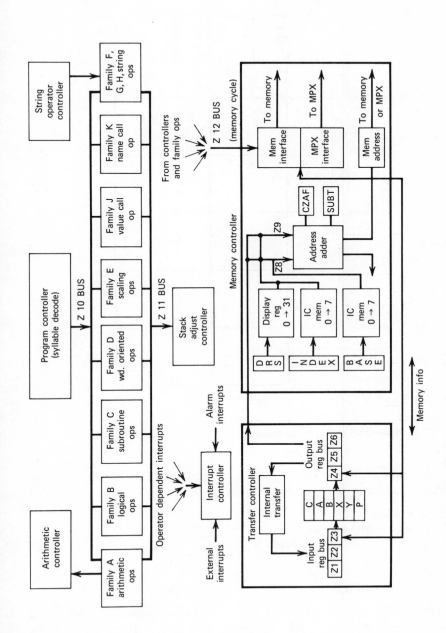

Figure C-7 B6700 processor block diagram.

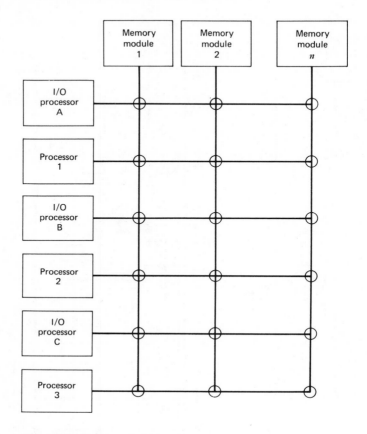

Figure C-8 Memory organization.

Information and control signals are transmitted along the 80-line bi-directional buss in parallel as illustrated below.

20 Bit Address
   6 bits for 0-63 modules.
   14 bits for memory addresses 0-16,383.
6 Control Bits
   (Read, write, busy, and such),
52 Information Bits

The B6700 Main Memory may consist of 1 to 64 memory modules each containing 16,384 words each. Although the diagrams depict the interconnection matrix as being external to both processors and memory, it is physically located within the memory cabinets and referred to as the Memory Controller.

Up to three modules and a Memory Controller can be housed in one Memory Cabinet (49, 152 words). The Memory Controller is able to respond to any of six requestors for memory access. The requestors are as follows:

1. Central processors 1, 2, and 3.
2. I/O processors A, B, and C.
3. Memory tester (connected through an I/O processor)
4. Maintenance diagnostic logic (MDL) processor A or B (connected through an I/O processor).

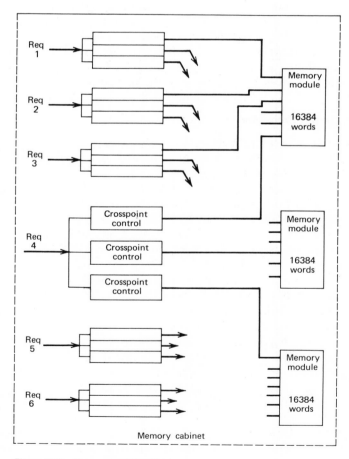

Figure C-9   Memory module selection.

Consider the example of a processor requesting access to memory module zero in cabinet zero. The processor places the address and information on the busses. It is seen by all of the memory controls, but only accepted by module zero because of the address decoding in memory cabinet zero. This means that each memory control must have the ability to accept addresses from six different requestors and connect them to one of three memory modules. This is accomplished by a crosspoint control located within the memory control (Figure C-9). There are three sets of crosspoint controls for each of the six possible requestors within each memory control. Three requestors may gain simultaneous access to the same memory cabinet if they are addressing separate memory modules.

A priority system, which is activated prior to the crosspoint controls, prevents conflicts when more than one requestor is addressing the same memory module. Memory modules are addressed by 2-bits, as indicated by the descriptor words in Figure C-2. Bits 0-13 are used for word selection and bits 14-19 are used for module selection. Each memory module has the ability to interleave every other word to the next consecutive module.

Input/Output Processor

The B6700 uses I/O processors and associated peripheral controls for transferring data between memory modules and peripherals, as indicated in the configuration schematic in Figure C-1.

Once an I/O processor receives an I/O command (from a processor), the transfer of data takes place independent of the central processors. One, two, or three I/O processors may be attached to a system. Any one of the central processors can initiate an I/O operation on any I/O processor.

Up to 20 peripheral controls can be connected to each I/O processor. Up to 256 peripheral units (numbered from 0 to 255) can be designated. The I/O processor also includes a time-of-day clock and character translators.

The IOP uses data switching channels for data transfer, a word buffer for each control which is transferring data. Each IOP can contain from 4 to 12 channels. These data-switching channels are "floating" so that any available channel may be used for any of the devices connected to the IOP. Thus a single IOP can handle up to 12 data operations simultaneously. The assignment of the data switching channels is performed by the IOP; upon initiation of an operation, the hardware assigns an available channel to the operation. An IOP service cycle (time 1.2 μsec) is required each time a peripheral control requires attention. During each service cycle 16 bits (2 bytes) are transferred between the IOP and high-speed device peripheral controls, for example, a disk or tape control. All other controls transfer 8 bits/cycle. I/O word formats are provided with an option of having all active IOPs or a particular IOP respond to the processor. Typical I/O functions are interrogate peripheral status, report a data path to a unit, initiate an I/O operation, and report the status of a completed operation. The interrogate I/O path function is of special interest, since it promotes modularity and reconfiguration possibilities. Issuance of this function determines if there is a path (an available control and a channel) through which an I/O operation can be initiated on the unit specified. The path can be checked for all IOPs, for a unit which is common to all IOPs, or for a particular IOP. The returned value indicates which IOP(s) contain such a path. The device configuration can be varied for each IOP without affecting the executive software when the peripheral changes are made.

Secondary Storage

Mass storage is accomodated by head-per-track disk files with average access times ranging from 20 to 40 msec and modular storage capacities ranging from 10 million to 72 billion eight-bit bytes and by disk-pack memory systems with average access times of 30 msec and modular storage capacities from 121 million to 1.6 billion bytes.

HEAD-PER-TRACK DISK FILE MEMORY SYSTEMS

Configuration rules for the B6700 disk files can be summarized as follows:

- A maximum of five disk file storage modules can be connected to a disk file electronic unit, providing up to 100 million bytes of storage per electronic unit.
- All disk modules connected to an electronic unit must be of the same type.
- One electronic unit can be connected directly to a disk file control.
- Alternatively, from 1 to 20 electronic units can be connected to a disk file control through the use of a disk file exchange.
- A disk file exchange permits a bank of up to 20 disk files to be serviced by one to four disk file controls.

A disk file optimizer which provides average access times of 2 to 6 msec on fixed-head-per-track disks by maintaining awareness of disk position relative to the heads is also available. The disk file optimizer queues disk file access requests according to their position on disk in relationship to the read/write heads. When a data path is opened, the requested record nearest the read head is accessed first; as the disk rotates, other records are accessed in their most efficient sequence. When the system is required to make many disk file accesses per second, this technique reduces latency and replaces the conventional software first-in-first-out queue.

DISK-PACK MEMORY SYSTEMS

Disk pack drives similar in design to the IBM 3300 disk are offered with 121 or 242 million bytes of storage per disk pack drive.

The disk-pack drive controller with single access capabilities may be used with eight disk-pack spindles (four dual drives) in a one-by-eight configuration, or two groups of eight disk-pack spindles (eight dual drives) in a one-by-16 configuration. Selection of each group is determined by a variant in the I/O descriptor. The disk-pack drive controller with dual access capability may be used in a two-by-eight configuration in which the disk-pack drive controller contains two internal control units. This allows the I/O processor to execute two simultaneous operations (two reads, two writes, or a read and a write). This configuration can be expanded to a two-by-16 configuration.

SYSTEM SOFTWARE

Job Control

Assuming sufficient core storage, up to 1,024 jobs or "processes" can be controlled in a multiprogramming fashion by the B6700 Master Control Program (MCP). The MCP is implemented entirely in a high-level language, ESPOL, with emphasis on dynamic memory allocation, reentrant object code, and parallel execution of independent object program sections. In conjunction with the hardware stack mechanism described earlier, the MCP is able to treat all processes, including its own resident executive, as if they were one large ALGOL program containing local and global variables, blocks and procedures in a unified software structure.

DISPATCHING CONTROL AND RESOURCE ALLOCATION

Resource allocation required for efficient scheduling deals with object code "segments" produced by all compilers running under MCP. The length of a program segment is variable depending on the program logic and language used. ALGOL program segmentation is based on the block structure of the source program, where each block is compiled into a code segment. COBOL programs are segmented by section level, unless specified otherwise by the programmer. FORTRAN program segmentation is by program unit (subroutine or main program) level and, if necessary, these units are further segmented to optimum segment size. In addition, the programmer has the option to segment his object code further, on the assumption that least used portions of his code can be run as transient segments.

The MCP schedules processes for execution according to a dynamic scheduling algorithm, consisting of priority equations used to order processes in an active queue, if all system resources required by the process are available, or a passive queue if sufficient resources are not currently free. As resources such as core storage and peripherals become available, a process is moved from the passive to the active queue and is selected for execution when its priority is highest according to an algorithm which takes into account these factors:

1. User declared priority.
2. Time spent in active queue.
3. Elapsed time spent in passive and active queues.
4. Total wait time in all system queues.
5. CPU time required for the process.
6. Core storage currently in use.
7. Difference between projected process start time and the current time.

Each of these factors has a coefficient applied to it which may be modified by the user to suit his own requirements. For instance, if the user wants to ensure that a processor-bound job does not take too large a portion of available processor time, he can supply an appropriate coefficient for factor 5 which he can later change through a console message to the MCP, if his estimate was off. The user may also supply a completely different scheduling algorithm, replacing the priority equations in the MCP, which are isolated in the code for ease of modification.

When a process is finally selected for execution, only the first segment of the process is in core. Each running process is controlled with a process stack, explained in detail above, which allows presence bit interrupts to be serviced whenever absent code segments or data array rows are referenced by the current segment. This approach provides a type of variable paging mechanism, allocating core storage dynamically for code segments and data arrays of variable size as they are referenced during execution. Since multiple code segments in memory need not be contiguous for a given process, memory compaction is held to a minimum.

Processes can also be scheduled for execution by another process spawning a job, through the issuance of a ZIP construct to the MCP, indicating the location of the control cards defining the job. An EXECUTE construct also exists, which may be issued by a process to cause an object code file to be loaded and placed into execution. These constructs are essentially high-level macro calls embedded in user source programs with appropriate arguments defining the job to be spawned.

SYSTEM COMMUNICATION

Operator communication with the MCP is through a modified BIDS display terminal, of which up to seven consoles may be configured, and through an on-line card reader using system control cards.

Normally, a mix table is displayed continuously, indicating the status of each job known to the MCP. If the job is active, the mix index (job number), job name, priority, compiler code, core used, processor time used, and status (beginning of job, running, end of job, discontinued) for the job is displayed in abbreviated form for each active job. In place of the mix table, various other tables can be displayed upon operator request, such as:

- Schedule table, indicating the status of each job waiting for execution.
- Peripheral unit table, indicating the status and mode of each configured peripheral.
- Label table, describing the files in use on a specified peripheral and which jobs are currently using the device.
- Disk directory table, which displays all file labels in the disk directory which are contained in the set specified by the input message.
- Job table, containing detailed information about each active job, such as the control cards associated with the job and a correlation of physical device units with file names used by the job.

In addition to these tables, a set of operator messages are defined, allowing the operator to delete selected jobs, raise or lower job priority, suspend jobs from execution, and so on.

I/O Control

I/O SCHEDULING AND DATA TRANSFER

All I/O operations are performed by the MCPs system of I/O routines, which are either file-oriented or peripheral oriented, depending on the logical level at which the user desires to access peripherals. Sets of MCP intrinsics, or common procedures accessible to all active processes on a reentrant basis, are referenced by the compilers generating object code, to produce I/O operations scheduled by a central MCP I/O procedure.

This procedure, called IOREQUEST, accepts all requests for I/O operations and schedules them according to these general considerations:

1. Each I/O must be associated with a particular buffer area of a particular program, since IOREQUEST schedules I/O operations on all programs.

2. Emphasis is on constructing an I/O operation sequence and returning control to the calling program as quickly as possible, even if the I/O request is on a device that cannot be initiated.

3. The scheduling procedure must include the ability to interlock the I/O buffer and later, when the I/O operation is complete, unlock the buffer.

This interlocking must be transparent to the programmer, and allow the program to run and be stopped only when the program attempts to process data in a buffer for which anI/O request has been made, but is not yet completed.

Two types of queues are associated with I/O scheduling, the unit queue, one for each peripheral unit, and the wait channel queue, one for each I/O channel. These queues are maintained as first-in first-out lists, with the unit queue emptying as the path to the device (any channel) becomes available. As mentioned earlier in the discussion of the I/O module, the channels are connected to the I/O processor in a floating fashion, so that any available channel may be used for data transfer on any of the devices connected to the IOP. The I/O scheduling and data transfer strategy incorporated into the MCP is designed to maximize the usefulness of this feature.

After IOREQUEST is initiated by another MCP procedure (INITIATEIO), the channel handles the I/O, as described above, and generates a result descripter as the operation is executed. An interrupt occurs upon completion of the operation, which activates an MCP procedure to check for I/O errors. If no errors occurred, and additional I/O requests are pending, new I/O operations are initiated on the last channel used, first taking requests from the wait channel queue, and then emptying entries from the unit queue into the wait channel queue, to optimize channel activity over device activity.

FILE HANDLING

All B6500 compilers allow the use of "symbolic files" or logical data sets referred to by a logical file name of up to 17 characters. "Label equation" control statements are available to relate the symbolic file name to the actual file name in the file header. The following file management capabilities are implemented:

1. A permanent file system, managed by a tree structured disk directory containing symbolic file names related to user file directories and three classes of security governing access to files at either file-open time or when accessing particular records.

2. A "volume" concept, allowing multiple files to reside on a single physical media, such as tape or disk pack.

3. Generations of files, allowing a "geneology" of files to be referenced through the same symbolic name qualified by generation numbers.

4. Files may be labeled according to a recommended ANSI standard or to a specified system standard, such that all labeled files are automatically assigned to object programs requesting symbolic files.

5. File records may be of five types—single precision, double precision, packed-decimal, BCL, EBCDIC, or ASCII.

6. File formats may be of eight types, such as fixed length, variable length binary or decimal, undefined format, variable length whose length is defined in the record, FORTRAN records, and so on.

7. File attributes are merged at execution time from Label Equation control statements, the Disk Directory and MCP operator messages into a File Information Block of variable length of up to 39 words.

An example of a symbolic file name is D/E/F, where D is the file directory identifier, E the volume identifier, and F is the file identifier. Item 4 should be expanded upon by noting that the MCP recognizes up to twelve different label types, including B5700 labels and B3700 ANSI labels.

APPENDIX D
CONTROL DATA CORPORATION
CDC 6500, CYBER-70/MODELS 72-2X, 73-2X, AND 74-2X

INTRODUCTION TO SYSTEM ORGANIZATION

Control Data has four systems that fall within the definition for a multi-processor as presented in this text. The CDC–6500 was introduced in 1966 followed by the CYBER–70 series in 1972. There are seven basic models in the CYBER–70 series but only three of these have dual central processors, the models 72, 73 (which is almost identical to the 6500), and 74 (which is essentially a dual processor CDC 6600). All four models are source code compatible at the assembly language level and, with the exception of certain efficiency features, are similarly compatible at the compiler source code level.

One interconnection path available in the CYBER–70 series, the distributive data path, is not found in the CDC 6500. Figure D-1 is the system organization applicable to all four systems. The systems differ only in certain features of the central processing unit (CPU). The rate at which instructions may be issued by the CPU differs for each of the three models. Also, the manner in which the CPU is organized, and therfore functions, is different in the Model 74 from that of the CPU organization of the Model 72 and the 6500.

Each of the systems have two large central processing units. These are accessible through a fast central memory and a group of 10, 14, 17, or 20 peripheral processors. Each of these peripheral processors has a separate memory and can execute programs independently of each other or of the central processors. Through the exchange jump feature and central memory

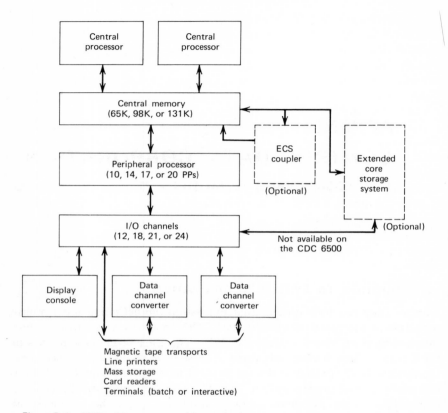

Figure D-1   CDC multiprocessor system organization.

communication, these peripheral processors control the central processors. They communicate with themselves through central memory, I/O channels, and the interlock register (not available on the 6500).

The basic functions of the CPs within the computer system are to perform arithmetic and logical problems, and, since there are two CPs, it is possible to support the simultaneous operations of two programs in the central memory. Under the SCOPE operating system, it is possible to have up to 15 jobs operating within central memory concurrently in a multiprogramming manner.

The functions of the peripheral and control processors within the computer system are to perform I/O operations for running central processor programs and to organize problem data (operands, addresses, constants, length of program, relative starting address, exit mode) and store it in central memory. Under the SCOPE operating system, two of the PPUs are used for operating system functions (PPU–0 is used as a computer system monitor and control processor and PPU–1 is used as the operator display console communication processor), while the other peripheral processors can be used for functions such as servicing standard peripherals (magnetic tapes, card punches/readers, line printers, disk files, etc.), communications systems, display systems, and graphic systems.

All PPUs communicate with external equipment on 12 independent bi-directional channels. These channels are 12 bits (plus control) and each may be connected to one or more external devices; however, only one equipment can communicate on any one channel at a particular time, but all 12 channels can be communicating with a different device at one time.

A real-time clock reading is available on a channel which is separate from the I/O channels. The clock starts with power on and runs continuously and cannot be preset or altered. This clock may be used to determine program running time or other functions, such as time-of-day, as required.

Central memory (CM) is accessed by all processors within the computer system and can consist of either 65K, 98K, or 131K words (60-bit) in 16, 24, or 32 banks of 4096 words each. The banks are logically independent and consecutive addresses go to different banks which decreases the probability of processor conflicts for memory and also allows each memory bank to be phased into operation every 100 nsec, resulting in very high CM operating speed. This allows a word (60–bits) to move to or from CM every 100 nsec.

Data flow control is exercised by the peripheral processor (PPU–0) which contains the system monitor (MTR). This PPU communicates with resident programs in the other PPUs and with active programs in the central processors through central memory communication locations, or, in the CYBER–70 models, through the interlock registers. The hardware functions that occur during the computer system operation can best be described by referencing Figure D-2.

References to central memory from all areas of the system (CPs and PPUs) go to a common address clearing house called a stunt box (lines B and C, Figure D-2), and are sent from there to all banks in central memory (line E, Figure D-2). As this address is being sent, if it is the address in which a data word is to be located, the data word is sent to the central data distributor via a 24–bit, bi-direction line (line A, Figure D-2), 12 parallel lines for write and 12 parallel lines for read. The stunt box accepts addresses from the various sources under a priority system and at a maximum rate of one address every 100 nsec. An address is sent to all banks, and the

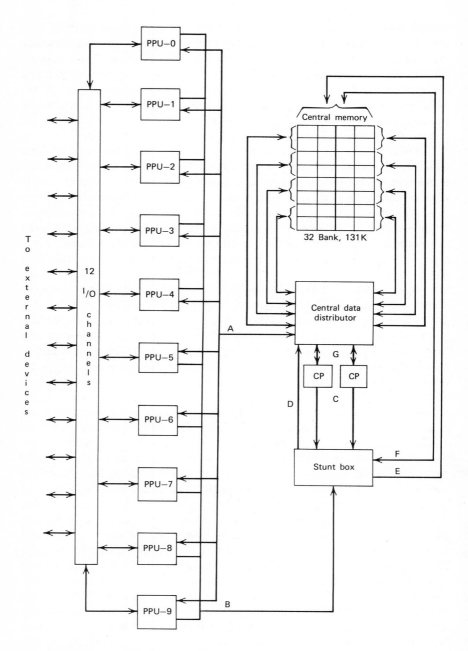

Figure D-2 Multiprocessor data flow diagram.

194

correct bank, if free, accepts the address and indicates to the central data distributor that the correct bank is free and the associated data word is then sent to or stored from the central data distributor via one of eight 60–bit lines one of each servicing a four-bank segment of memory. Central memory access by the central processors is performed in the same manner as PPU access in that the address is sent to the stunt box (line C, Figure D-2), and data words then pass through the central data distributor to and from the CPs (line G, Figure D-2).

The stunt box saves, in a hopper mechanism, each address that it sends to CM and then reissues it (and again saves it) under priority control in the event that it is not accepted because of bank conflict. This address issue-save process repeats until the address is accepted, at which time the address is dropped from the hopper and the read or store data word is distributed. The hopper (i.e., a previously unaccepted address) has the highest priority in issuing addresses to CM. The CPs and PPUs follow in that order.

The data distributor which is common to all processors handles all data words to and from CM. A series of buffer registers in the distributor provides temporary storage for words to be written into storage when the addresses are not immediately accepted due to bank conflict. As was stated previously, each group of four banks of CM communicates with the distributor on separate 60–bit read and write paths, but only one word moves on the data paths at one time. However, words can move at 100-nsec intervals between the distributor and CM or distributor and address-sender.

FUNCTIONAL UNITS

Central Processor

The central processor is a high-speed arithmetic unit which communicates only with central memory. It is isolated from the peripheral processors and is free to carry on computation unencumbered by I/O requirements.

Each processor consists (functionally) of an arithmetic and control unit. The arithmetic unit contains all logic necessary to execute the arithmetic, manipulation, and logical operations. The control unit directs the arithmetic operations and provides the interface between the arithmetic unit and central memory. It also performs instruction retrieving, address preparation, memory protection, and data retrieving and storing.

The CYBER model 74 central processor is organized differently from the CPs in the other systems. It is basically the CP of the CDC 6600. It is composed of 10 separate functional processors which operate in parallel. The 10 arithmetic and logical units (add, long add, increment-2, shift, multiply-2, divide, boolean, and branch) execute the arithmetic, manipulative, and logical operations. The control unit directs the arithmetic operations and provides the interface between the functional units and central memory.

The arithmetic section of the 6500, model 72, and model 73 executes instructions serially with little concurrency. Execution time for instructions is decreased by using an overlap feature in which the next instruction to be executed is being read during the previous instructions execution.

The instruction repertoire of the CP includes arithmetic, logical, indexing, and branch instructions as well as single and double precision floating-point arithmetic with optional rounding and normalizing; formats supporting integer coefficients of 48 bits, biased exponent of 11 bits (2^{10}), and the sign of the coefficient is 1 bit; fixed-point arithmetic allowing full 60-bit add/subtract.

Detecting and handling interrupt conditions involves both hardware and software. An Exchange Jump instruction issued by a PPU initiates hardware action in the CP to interrupt the current CP program and substitute a program, the parameters of which are defined within the exchange jump package. Also, the exchange jump instruction is used to start the CPs from a stop condition. CP hardware provides for three types of error halt conditions:

- Address out of range
- Operand out of range
- Indefinite result

Halting on any of these conditions is selectable. When an exchange jump interrupts the CP, several steps occur to leave the interrupted program in a usable state for re-entry:

1. Issue of instructions halts after issuing all instructions from the current instruction word in the instruction stack.

2. The program address register is set to the address of the next instruction word to be executed.

3. The issued instructions are executed.

4. The parameters for the two programs are exchanged.

A subsequent exchange jump can then re-enter the interrupted program at the point it was interrupted.

SUMMARY OF CENTRAL PROCESSOR CHARACTERISTICS:

24 operating registers per central processor to lower memory reference requirements

- 8 operand (60-bit).

- 8 address (18-bit).
- 8 increment (18-bit).

Instruction Issue Rate (million instructions/sec)	Model 72	Model 73	Model 74	Model 6500
One processor	0.9	1.2	3.0	—
Two processors	1.5	2.0	3.7	2.0

- Integer multiply (except 6500).
- Central exchange jump.
- Move and compare instructions (except 6500 and model 74).

Peripheral Processors

The peripheral processors are identical and operate independently and simultaneously as stored-program computers. Many programs may be running at one time or a combination of processors can be involved in one problem which may require a variety of I/O tasks as well as use of the central memory and the central processor(s).

The peripheral processors act as system control computers and I/O processors. This permits the central processor to continue computation while the peripheral processors do the slower I/O and supervisory operations.

Each processor has a 12-bit, 4096 word random-access memory (independent of central memory) with a cycle time of 1000 nsec. Execution time of processor instructions is dependent on memory cycle time.

Each PPU can execute approximately 500,000 instructions/sec. All PPUs share a common facility for add/subtract, I/O, data transfer to/from CM, and other necessary instruciton control facilities. This means that the programs within the PPUs are executed in a multiplexing arrangement which uses the principle of time-sharing. The multiplex consists of a 10-position barrel, which stores information about the instruction in each of 10 programs, and a common instruction control device. The 10 program steps move around the barrel in series and each step is presented to the control device. Thus up to 10 programs are in operation at one time, and each program is acted upon every microsecond. Instructions in the barrel are interpreted at critical time intervals so that information is available in the control device at the time the instruction is to enter the control device. Hence, a reference to memory for data is determined ahead of time and the data word is available when the instruction arrives. Similarly, instructions are interpreted before they arrive at the control device so that control paths are established when the instruction arrives.

For I/O instructions or communications with CM, one pass through the control device transfers one 12-bit word to or from a peripheral memory. Thus block transfer of data requires a number of trips around the barrel.

Each PPU exchanges data with CM in blocks of N words. Five successive 12-bit PPU words are assembled into one 60-bit CM word and conversely a 60-bit CM word is disassembled into five 12-bit words and sent to successive locations in PPU memory. Separate assembly (write) and disassembly (read) paths to CM are shared by all PPUs. Up to four PPUs may be writing in CM while another four are simultaneously reading from CM.

Within the PPUs, hardware flages indicate the state of various conditions within data channels, for example, full/empty, active/inactive. Also, channel and equipment status (e.g., ready, inoperative, end of file) may be examined by instructions in the PPUs.

The PPUs in the CYBER–70 models have interlock registers of 64- or 128-bits. These are accessible by all PPUs for communication between themselves and greatly reduce the number of memory accesses required for this function.

Summary of peripheral processor characteristics:

- 10, 14, 17, or 20 peripheral processor configurations available.
- 4096-word magnetic core memory (12-bit).
    All channels common to all processors.
    Maximum transfer rate per channel of 1 word/μsec.
    All channels can be active simultaneously.
    All channels 12-bit bidirectional.
- Real-time clock period of 4096 msec.
- Computation in fixed-point.
- Time-shared access to central memory.
- Inter-processor communication through the interlock register (not available on 6500).
- Central memory access priority.
- Addressing capability up to 131K words via direct, indirect, and indexed modes.

Central Memory

Central memory is composed of banks of 4096 60-bit words of core storage. The complete cycle time for one bank is 1 μsec. The banks are phased so that successive addresses are in different banks, to permit operation of central memory at rates higher than the basic cycle time. The maximum transfer rate is one 60-bit word/100 nsec.

There are five access paths to central memory available:

- Two central processor/central memory.
- Extended core storage/central memory.
- One or two groups of peripheral processors/central memory.

Central memory includes a control section that provides service to each of these access paths on a priority basis, queues access requests as necessary, and resolves any access conflicts.

The central memory access priority feature permits a designated peripheral processor preference over nonpriority peripheral processing units for central memory reads and writes. This feature also ensures that central memory/extended core storage transfers are maintained at the maximum rate for the given configuration.

Memory protection is based on upper and lower limits defined for each operational program and included as part of each program. All CP references to CM for new instructions, or to read and store data, are made relative to a reference address which defines the lower limit of a CM program. Changes to the reference address permit easy relocation of programs in CM.

Summary of central memory characteristics:

- Memory organized in logically independent banks of 4096 words with corresponding multiphasing of banks (maximum memory size of 32 banks).
- Transfer rate of up to 1 word/100 nsec in phased operation.
- Configurations of 65K (18 modules), 98K (24 modules), or 131K (32 modules) possible.
- Hardware capability of accepting addresses from 12 processors at 100 nsec-intervals, resolving central memory conflicts and performing instruction look-ahead during access.

Input/Output

All peripheral processors communicate with external equipment and each other via the independent, bidirectional I/O channels. The number of channels depends on the number of peripheral processors in the system. All channels are 12-bit (plus control), and each can be connected to one or more external devices. Only one external equipment can utilize a channel at one time, but all channels can be simultaneously active. Data are transferred into or out of the system in 12-bit words at a maximum rate of 1 word/μsec. As many as eight different types of external equipment can be connected to an I/O channel (magnetic tape controllers, card read/punch controllers, etc.).

Extended Core Storage

The optional extended core storage subsystem is comprised of the extended core storage, its controller, and, for the CYBER–70 models only, one or more distributive data paths which attach to I/O channels.

The extended core storage is composed of banks of 125,952 60-bit words of core storage. Eight 60-bit words are contained in a 488-bit physical extended core storage word. Each 60-bit word has an associated parity bit in the extended core storage word. The complete cycle time for one bank of extended core storage is 3.2 μsec/488-bit extended core storage word.

The multiple bank extended core storage subsystems, banks are phased such that consecutive eight-word records come from different banks. This phasing, combined with the wide (eight-word) access span enables very fast transfers to or from extended core storage. After an initial access of 3.2 μsecs, extended core storage can transfer at a rate of one 60-bit word/100 nsecs. This gives a minimum rate of 600 million bits/sec.

Extended core storage is available in sizes ranging from 125,952 words (one bank) to 2,015,232 words (16 banks). The very fast transfer rates and short access time of extended core storage makes it ideal for use as a buffer between central memory and rotating mass storage devices, such as high-speed program swapping devices and for storage of large data arrays, and for storage of frequently used programs and system routines.

There are two access paths to extended core storage:

- Central memory to extended core storage.
- Input/output channel(s) to extended core storage via the distributive data paths (in the CYBER–70 models only).

The distributive data path provides a direct path of data flow between extended core storage and the peripheral processors in the CYBER–70 models. It allows fast peripheral processor access to data in extended core storage via an I/O channel, and greatly reduces the data traffic through the central memory. This reduces central memory conflicts and also reduces the overhead of the operating system.

Mass Storage or Secondary Storage

In addition to extended core storage described above, several types of disk and drum storage devices are available. These devices range in capacity from 8 million to 167 million characters per spindle and in average access time from 17 to 75 msec.

SYSTEM SOFTWARE

A schematic example of CYBER–70 communications and control paths appears in Figure D-3.

Components of the SCOPE operating system are distributed among the central memory, the peripheral memories, ECS, and the system disk unit. One peripheral processor, containing the monitor, is in permanent control of the system.* A second peripheral processor, under control of the monitor, is permanently assigned to the console keyboard and displays; the remaining processors are available for assignment as required.

The monitor distributes work among the peripheral processors, communicating with them through an area in central memory reserved for this purpose. The peripheral processors contain routines that examine continually this communication area for requests. When a request appears, a peripheral processor carries it out. When the task is complete, the peripheral processor informs the monitor and returns to the idling routine until another request is made. This use of the independent peripheral processors achieves a minimal use of central memory and the central processor, thus reducing overhead.

Job Control†

Up to 15 individual programs may reside in central memory at one time. Each is assigned a control point number and central memory field length. When a job is active (in central memory), the control point area in central memory resident contains information such as: job name, length, starting address in central memory, cumulative time used, I/O equipment assigned to the job, and its control statements. The control point area also contains an exchange package, a 16-word section consisting of the contents of all central processor registers used in executing a program. This information is needed to start or resume a program.

Jobs assigned to control points and waiting for execution are stacked by priority. At the top of the stack is the job using the central processor.

---

* Version 3.4 of the SCOPE operating system, which is the current version of the operating system and the base for subsequent revisions, provides for some of the functions to be performed by an additional CP-resident monitor. These include some of the memory allocation and management and job control functions. In the previous releases of SCOPE, all supervisory functions are controlled by the single PPU-resident monitor.
† Job control and CPU scheduling have been greatly changed in SCOPE 3.4. In general, the discussion presented here applies to earlier releases.

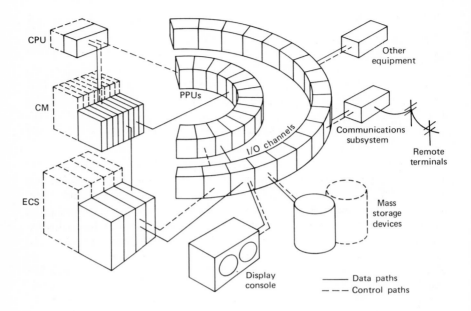

CPU

Other
equipment

PPUs

CM

I/O channels

Communications
subsystem

Remote
terminals

ECS

Mass
storage
devices

Display
console

——— Data paths
— — — Control paths

Figure D-3   Data and control flow.

When it is interrupted (e.g., to await completion of a peripheral processor function), the next job in the stack becomes the top, and the first job is removed from the stack temporarily. When it reenters the stack, the job using the central processor, and the jobs below are pushed down.

A job consists of one or more programs, preceded by control cards specifying job name, priority, time limits, operator instructions, and other pertinent information needed. SCOPE begins processing by reading the first control card. It copies the job file on disk storage and adds the name of the job to the list of input files. When a control point is available and the required amount of memory is free, the job is brought to the control point where memory is allocated and execution begins.

Blocks of central memory storage assigned to control points occupy positions in central memory relative to the control point number to which they are assigned. As jobs at control points request and release storage; storage assigned to control points is relocated up or down if necessary so that each job occupies a contiguous block of storage. Such relocation is possible because all references to central memory are made relative to the reference address.

All job scheduling and resource allocation is unified. Jobs from all sources—batch, remote batch, and interactive—are queued according to five classes. Each of the queues is managed according to installation parameters governing initial priority and aging rate, maximum priority, time quantum length given when a job is swapped into a control point, and quantum priority (priority of the job class when it is at a control point). (Applicable to SCOPE 3.4 only.)

Operator controls are provided for adjusting system scheduling to the current work flow.

Input/Output Control

SCOPE is a file-oriented system: all information in the system is considered to be either a file or part of a file. Active files—immediately available to the system at any moment—are any of the following:

- All jobs (each job is a file) waiting to be run; they comprise the job stack or input queue.
- Output files which are waiting to be disposed of by printing, punching, and so on.
- Jobs (files) presently in some state of execution.
- Local user files currently being used by the jobs in execution.

User files may be declared to be permanent. The file name, location, and owner-declared permission passwords are retained in a catalog. Permanent files may be accessed or updated by users who can provide the appropriate passwords. A copy of the original file may be retained if required.

Local or permanent user files may be defined as sequential or random access. Random access files are referenced through an index created by standard SCOPE routines or by a user routine. INTERCOM, the communications subsystem under SCOPE, provides the user with interactive remote access to the central site computer configuration through remote terminals. INTERCOM also allows users to submit jobs to the SCOPE batch queue and receive output from these jobs. INTERCOM controls the flow of data between remote terminals and the central site. It provides all the routines necessary for interface between the user and the SCOPE operating system.

APPENDIX E
DIGITAL EQUIPMENT
CORPORATION

DEC System 1055 AND 1077

INTRODUCTION TO SYSTEM ORGANIZATION

The DECsystem-10 can be a single-processor system or a dual-processor system, composed of a primary processor and a secondary processor. The two dual-processor systems are the modular 1055 and 1077. (See Figure E-1.)

Each processor in the dual-processor system runs user programs, schedules itself, and fields instruction traps. In addition to these tasks, the primary processor also has control of all the I/O devices and processes all requests to the operating system. The primary processor completes any job that the secondary processor could not finish because of a request to the operating system. The two processors are connected to the same memory and execute the same copy of the operating system, thereby saving core memory over a multiprocessing system in which each processor has its own copy. The primary objective in the DECsystem-10 dual-processor environment is to provide more processing power than that found in the single-processor DECsystem-10. This means that with the addition of the second processor, more users can run at the same time. Or, if more users are not allowed on the system, the addition of the second processor reduces the elapsed time required to complete the processing of most programs.

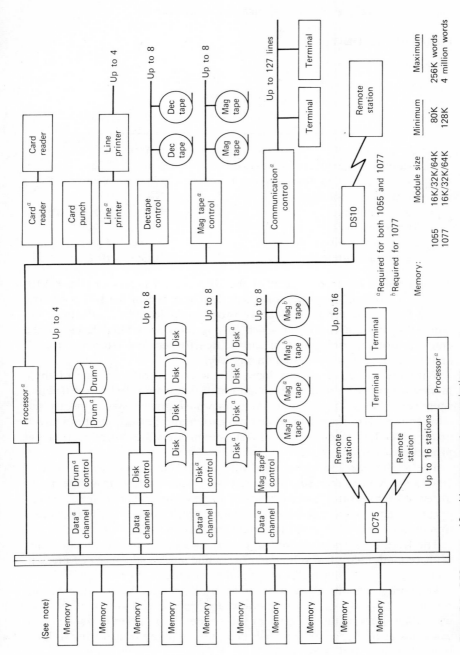

Figure E-1 DEC system—10 multiprocessor system organization.

	Module size	Minimum	Maximum
Memory:			
1055	16K/32K/64K	80K	256K words
1077	16K/32K/64K	128K	4 million words

[a]Required for both 1055 and 1077
[b]Required for 1077

FUNCTIONAL UNITS

Processor

SUMMARY

	1055	1077
Processor used	KA10	KI10
Number of hardware instructions	366	378
Double precision floating point hardware	No	Yes
Instruction lookahead	No	Yes
Accumulators	16	4 × 16
Index registers	15	4 × 15
Interrupt service time	6 μsec	3 μsec
Maximum interrupt delay	40 μsec	10 μsec

The priority interrupt system of the 1055 central processor (the KA10) has seven levels of interrupts for the devices attached to the I/O buss. The entire priority interrupt system is programmable. With software, any number of devices can be attached to any level, individual levels or the entire priority interrupt system can be deactivated and later reactivated, and interrupts can be requested on any level.

With the executive control logic, the KA10 operates in one of three modes: (a) executive mode, which allows all instructions to be executed and suppresses relocation; (b) user mode, in which some instructions are not allowed (i.e., I/O instructions) and relocation and protection are in effect; and (c) user I/O mode, where all instructions are valid but relocation and protection are still in effect.

The KI10 central processor used with the 1077 system is nearly twice as fast as the KA10 processor. This increase in speed results from the use of different architecture, faster circuits, a more complex adder, improved algorithms, and lookahead instruction logic, which obtains the next instruction during the execution of the current instruction.

The KI10 operates in one of two modes, user mode and exec mode. Each of these modes have two submodes: (a) public mode and concealed mode in user mode, and (b) supervisor mode and kernal mode in exec mode.

User programs operate in user mode. In this mode, the program can access up to 256K words. All instructions are legal except those that interfere with other users or the integrity of the system. A program in public mode can transfer to a program in concealed mode only by transferring to locations that have ENTRY instructions. A program in concealed mode can read, write (if allowed), execute, and transfer to any location designated as public. Concealed mode allows the loading of proprietary software with a user program and data, but prevents the user program from changing or copying the software. This provides direct interaction between the user and the proprietary software with virtually no overhead.

An interrupt on the KI10 causes the processor and the interrupting device to initiate immediately one of several possible actions. In response to the "interrupt grant" signal from the processor, the device may supply a 36-bit word which is decoded as 18-bit address, 12-bit data, 3-bit interrupt level and 3-bit function. The processor then does one of the following:

- Execute the instruction found at the supplied 18-bit address.
- Transfer a word into or out of the addressed location.
- Add a signed 12-bit value to the addressed location.

Peripheral devices which are not equipped with the decoding logic perform an interrupt and transfer of control as on the KA10, to one of the standard interrupt trap locations.

Central Memory

Memory for both the 1055 and 1077 has a cycle time of 1 μsec/36-bit word. The 1055 can have half-word or full-word operands; in addition, the 1077 can use double-word operands.

The memories for either system can have two- or four-way address interleaving. The 1077 also has memory overlap control and paging capabilities. The 1055 does not support virtual memory paging but does have relocation and protection registers.

In the 1077, core memory is managed by the paging system of the KI10. This system allows the user program to access an effective address space of up to 256K words. This space is segmented into 512 pages of 512 contiguous words each. These pages do not have to be contiguous in the physical core memory.

The KI10 processor also provides memory address mapping from a program's effective address space to the physical address space by substitution of the most significant bits of the effective address. This mapping provides access to the entire physical memory space, which is 16 times larger than the effective address space. [The program's effective address space is 256K (18 bits); the physical address is 4096K (22 bits).] Memory mapping takes place using a page table.

Input/Output

SUMMARY

	1055	1077
Low speed I/O rate (multiplexor)	222K words/sec 1,110K bytes/sec	370K words/sec 1,850K bytes/sec
High speed I/O rate (4 selector channels, 8 levels each)	4,000K words/sec 20,000K bytes/sec	4,000K words/sec 20,000K bytes/sec

SYSTEM SOFTWARE

The resident operating system is made up of a number of separate and somewhat independent parts, or routines. Some of these routines are cyclic in nature and are repeated at every system check interrupt (tick) to ensure that every user of the computing system is receiving his requested services. These cyclic routines are as follows:

1. The command processor, or decoder.
2. The scheduler.
3. The swapper.

The command decoder is responsible for interpreting commands typed by the user on his terminal and passing them to the appropriate system program or routine. The scheduler decides which user is to run in the interval between the clock interrupts, allocates sharable system resources, and saves and restores conditions needed to start a program interrupted by the clock. The swapper rotates user jobs between secondary memory (usually disk or drum) and core memory after deciding which jobs should be in core but are not. These routines constitute the part of the operating system that allows many jobs to be operating simultaneously.

The noncyclic routines of the operating system are invoked only by user programs and are responsible for providing these programs with the services available through the operating system. These routines are as follows:

1. The UUO handler.
2. The I/O routines.
3. The file handler.

The UUO handler is the means by which the user program communicates with the operating system in order to have a service performed. Communication is by way of programmed operators (also known as UUOs) contained in the user program, which, when executed, go to the operating system for processing. The I/O routines are the routines responsible for directing data transfers between peripheral devices and user programs in core memory. These routines are invoked through the UUO handler, thus saving the user the detailed programming needed to control peripheral devices. The file handler adds permanent user storage to the computing system by allowing users to store named programs and data as files.

DECSYSTEM-10 OPERATING CAPACITIES

Number of simultaneous jobs	127
Number of concurrent batch streams	14
Maximum user file size	No operating limit within the total file space available
Minimum file size	128 words (768 characters)
Maximum core-resident job size (less monitor size on 1055)	256 words (1028K bytes)

APPENDIX F

GOODYEAR AEROSPACE SYSTEMS
STARAN COMPUTER SYSTEM

SYSTEM ORGANIZATION

STARAN is a digital computer system that simultaneously performs arithmetic, search, or logical operations on either all or selected words of its memory. Four major features distinguish STARAN from the conventional computer:

- Multidimensional access array memory.
- Content addressable memory (associative memory).
- A simple processing unit at each word of memory.
- A unique permutation network for shifting and rearranging data in memory.

In STARAN, each multidimensional array consists of a square 256 bits by 256 words, a total of 65,536 bits per array. In each array module, data may be accessed in the bit direction or the word direction. In other words, either a bit slice (bit *n* of all 256 words) or an entire word (256 bits) is available to the processing units or I/O channels. In STARAN, the usual location-addressed memory is replaced by a content-addressed memory. To locate a particular item, STARAN initiates a search by calling for a match against an input data item. All words in memory that satisfy the search criterion are identified during a single memory cycle. Hence any data item can be located in one memory access.

In STARAN, the single processing unit of the conventional computer is replaced with a processing unit at each word. Each arithmetic processing unit operates serially by bit on data in the memory word to which it is attached. The arithmetic units simultaneously execute operations as designated by the control unit. Therefore, in one instruction execution, the data in all selected words of memory are processed simultaneously by the processing unit at each word. A permutation network is employed which permits shifting and rearranging of data so that parallel arithmetic and search operations can be performed between words of the array memory.

A substantial gain in processing speed can be realized when STARAN is used for applications having the following characteristics:

- An operational requirement for extremely rapid processing.
- Highly dynamic data.
- Simultaneous existence of large numbers of data items requiring similar processing.
- A requirement for an immediate response to a variety of queries.

The most appropriate use of STARAN is made in applications having a high degree of parallelism. The greater the parallelism, the more appropriate is the use of STARAN.

Studies at Goodyear Aerospace have shown that applications such as sensor processing, tracking, data management, weather prediction, and other matrix problems can use the parallel capabilities of STARAN effectively. In most applications studied to date, Goodyear Aerospace has found that the computer system required to solve a complex information-handling problem is a hybrid system composed of a parallel and a sequential processor. Each processor performs the tasks best suited to its capabilities.

FUNCTIONAL UNITS

The internal organization of STARAN is shown in Figure F-1, and a functional summary of the organization appears in Table F-1. The associative arrays and associative processor (AP) control are the key elements of the STARAN system. The AP control memory is used basically for program storage. The program pager, sequential controller, and external function logic are supporting elements used for various housekeeping functions.

Associative Array

The single most important element of STARAN is the associative array, which provides content addressability and parallel instruction execution capabilities. Most STARAN computing is done within a word of associative

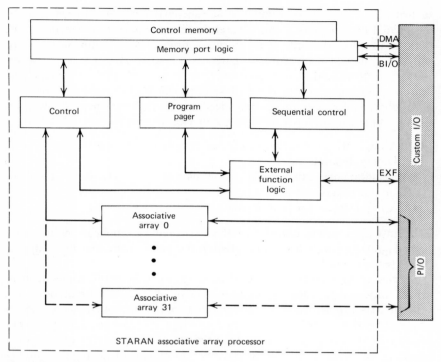

Figure F-1   STARAN block diagram.

array memory rather than between words of memory as in a sequential processor. An associative array word is normally divided into fields of varying lengths by the programmer to suit the requirements of specific programs. The values of these fields then can be added, subtracted, multiplied, and dividied within the word. In effect, STARAN can perform the same operations as a sequential processor—but with the added capability of performing these operations simultaneously on literally thousands of words in the associative processor arrays.

A basic STARAN configuration contains one associative array. However, up to 32 associative arrays can be included in a single STARAN system. Arrays can be selected and operated in parallel or one at a time. Also, an array, with the optional addition of a second control part, can be switched dynamically between two AP control units giving the STARAN a multiprogramming capability. As previously stated, each array contains 65,536 bits organized as a square, 256 words by 256 bits, of solid-state storage. Parallel access can be made in either the bit or word direction. An entire word of 256 bits or a bit slice, bit n of all 256 words, can be accessed. Each associative array contains 256 processing elements. Each element provides the means of operating on many sets of data simultaneously and also stores the results of search, arithmetic, and logical operations.

The processing element can be used for temporary storage of data read from the array or can contain the data to be written into the array. The processing element also is used to combine logically data from successive read operations and to generate the word address of the first responder to a search.

Associative Processor (AP) Control

AP control performs data manipulations within the multdimensional array memory as directed by instructions stored in AP control memory. AP control can perform parallel search operations to identify data by content and

TABLE F-I   STARAN ORGANIZATION SUMMARY

Element	Function
Associative array	Provides multidimensional-access, content-addressable memory with 65,536 (2^{16}) bits of storage and 256 processing elements; permits parallel arithmetic, search, and logical operations.
Control	Performs data manipulation within associative arrays as directed by program stored in AP control memory.
Control memory	Stores AP control instructions. Can also store data and act as buffer between AP control and other system elements.
Program pager	Moves program segments into high-speed page memories.
Sequential controller and memory	Performs maintenance and test functions, controls peripherals, maintains job control, and provides means for operator communication between various STARAN elements.
External function	Transfer control information among STARAN elements.

Page 0	Page 1	Page 2	High-speed data buffer	Bulk core memory	DMA memory
Subroutine library memory (512 words)	Instruction memory (512 words)	Instruction memory (512 words)	(512 words)	(16,384 words)	(30,720 words)

Figure F-2   AP control memory organization.

then execute logical and/or arithmetic operations upon these data items. Important capabilities of AP control are as follows:

- The selection of many operation subsets of the total memory contents.
- Performance of operations on these subsets without disturbing the contents of unselected words.

AP Control Memory

The organization of AP control memory provides the user with considerable operating efficiency. This is achieved by partitioning the memory into several sections as shown in Figure F-2. The word length of the AP control memory is 32 bits. Each word has a 16-bit address.

The three page memories uses solid-state elements and have cycle times of less than 200 nsec. Each page memory can be doubled to 1024 words on an optional basis. Page 0 is used to store a subroutine library. Pages 1 and 2 are used in ping-pong fashion with AP control reading instructions from one page while the other is loaded by the program pager. Each memory has a port switch to prevent premature use of a page before it is loaded.

The high-speed data buffer (HSDB) is a section of AP control memory that also uses solid-state elements. In the standard STARAN configuration, it contains 512 words. As an option, its size can be doubled to 1024 words.

The HSDB is a convenient place to store data and instruction items that need to be accessed quickly by different elements of STARAN.

The bulk core memory uses nonvolatile core storage with a cycle time of less than 1/μsec. In the standard configuration, it contains 16,384 words but is expendable to 32,768 words. The bulk core is used for program storage.

A block of AP control memory addresses is reserved for direct memory access (DMA) to external memory. In the standard configuration this block consists of 30,720 words.

The program pager loads words from the bulk memory, high-speed data buffer, or DMA channel into any of the three page memories. Operation of the program pager is under program control.

Sequential Controller

The sequential controller provides:

- Off-line capabilities for assembling and debugging STARAN programs.
- A means to initially load the AP control memory.
- A communication link between the operator and the STARAN for on-line control and monitoring.
- Control of STARAN error processing, diagnostic, and maintenance programs.
- Capabilities for sequential arithmetic and housekeeping.

The sequential controller of STARAN contains 8K of conventional memory, a keyboard printer, a perforated tape reader/punch unit, and interface logic to connect the sequential controller to other STARAN elements. The 8192 words of memory are used for storage of sequential control programs and data.

Input/Output

The STARAN I/O can be custom designed for integration with a variety of computer systems (and other external devices). Four interface options are available:

- Direct memory access (DMA).
- Buffered input/output (BI/O).
- External function logic (EXF).
- Parallel input/output (PI/O).

Direct access to a host computer memory enables the host computer memory to act as part of the STARAN control memory. Items in the host computer are equally accessible by both the host computer and STARAN; thus the need for buffered I/O transfers between the host computer and STARAN is reduced. Address translation may be required on the DMA interface to match the STARAN control addresses with the host computer addresses. This translation is accomplished in the custom I/O cabinet. The DMA block of addresses may be put to other uses besides access to a host computer memory. Possible uses include access to an external memory, which may or may not be accessible by other devices, and access to special I/O devices.

Buffered I/O is available for tying different types of peripherals into the STARAN control memory. Also BI/O can be used to transfer blocks of data and/or programs between the STARAN control memory and host memory. In general, a DMA interface to a host computer memory is preferable to the BI/O interface because BI/O cycle times are usually longer than DMA cycle times in the host computer. Also, BI/O forces the programmer to put the data in blocks while DMA can operate with scattered data. The basic width of the BI/O interface is 32 bits plus a parity bit. The custom I/O cabinet can include buffers that allow a wide variety of repacking to take place so that I/O channels of any width can be assembled.

The external function (EXF) logic facilitates coordination between the different elements of STARAN for special functions and simplifies housekeeping, maintenance, and test functions. By issuing external function codes to the EXF logic, elements of STARAN can control and interrogate the status of other elements. Function codes may be transmitted to EXF logic by AP control, the program pager, sequential controller, and the host computer. STARAN has function codes for page port switches, interlocks, program pager, error control, AP control interrupts, sequential control interrupts, miscellaneous, and spares.

The EXF channel is used extensively for direct communication with the devices connected to the custom I/O cabinet. Up to 19 bits of function code can be received simultaneously at the custom I/O, which handles each of the function codes one-by-one on a priority basis until all have been processed. The EXF channel can be used for:

- Interface with a host computer.
- Buffered I/O (BI/O) external functions.
- Parallel I/O (PI/O) external functions.

STARAN and the host computer can communicate via external interrupts. If the host computer has an external function output capability, it can exercise complete control of STARAN by generating any external function code. Buffered I/O can be initiated easily by means of EXF codes. Word counts, starting addresses, and other information are packed into the format necessary for communication. Parallel I/O is initiated with EXF codes in much the same manner as BI/O.

Each associative array can have up to 256 inputs and 256 outputs into the custom I/O cabinet. They can be used to:

- Increase speed of inter-array data communication.
- Allow STARAN to communicate with a high-bandwidth I/O device.
- Allow any device to communicate directly with the associative arrays.

For example, a multihead disk with heads operating simultaneously can be connected to STARAN efficiently via the PI/O. The rates (refer to Table F-II) obtained with this configuration are generally dependent upon the cycle time and the number of heads on the disk being used. In requesting data from the disk, for example, STARAN will send the disk one or more external functions specifying a starting sector address, the number of sectors, and the direction of transfer.

The disk system may interrupt STARAN when the disk reaches the requested sector to initate the transfer over PI/O lines. The STARAN control instructions that actually read or write the PI/O can be synchronized to the disk so that STARAN timing is slaved to the disc timing during the transfer.

TABLE F-II   STARAN INPUT/OUTPUT RATES

Function	Rate
Direct memory access (DMA)	200-nsec/32-bit word plus external memory access time
Buffered input/output (BI/O)	
High-speed data buffer to/from host	400-nsec/32-bit word
Core program memory to/from host	1-μsec/32-bit word
External function commands	
To accept interrupt and return sense to host	1 μsec
To generate interrupt to host	1 μsec
Parallel input/output (PI/O)	
STARAN memory to external device	200-nsec/bit slice or word slice
External device to STARAN memory	400-nsec/bit slice or word slice (slice = 256 bits/array)

SYSTEM SOFTWARE

A group of stand-alone system programs designed to enable the user to generate, load, and debug programs is furnished with the basic configuration of STARAN. The system software consists of the following programs:

- Assembler.
- Utility package.
- Debug package.
- Diagnostics.
- Subroutine library.

All of these programs are executed by the sequential controller except the subroutine library and some diagnostics, which are executed by AP control.

APPENDIX G

HONEYWELL INFORMATION SYSTEMS

6180 MULTICS SYSTEM AND 6000 SERIES

INTRODUCTION TO SYSTEM ORGANIZATION

The Honeywell Series 6000 and the 6180 Multics System are based upon similar architectures pioneered by the 635 and 645 systems.

The general system architecture is a fully modular, asynchronous, interrupt-driven, memory-oriented, multiport, distributed control system. The term "memory-oriented" means that each memory controller module functions as a passive coordinating element allocating memory accesses on a hardware priority basis (tie-breaker). Each demand driven memory contains 32 interrupt cells which are accessed via data lines, thereby eliminating direct connections between processors and I/O control modules. Interrupt priorities may be altered dynamically under program control by means of interrupt mask registers. Another feature is that processor interrupt control logic is extendable indefinitely by the use of supplemental memory location multiplexing, with each memory bit functioning as a mask register.

The general system organization illustrating data paths and the "central" role of the system (memory) controller is shown in Figure G-1. A summary of the Series 6000 and 6180 characteristics is given in Table G-1.

FUNCTIONAL UNITS

An overriding consideration in the design of the 6180 system was that each major module in the system differ as little as possible from the standard

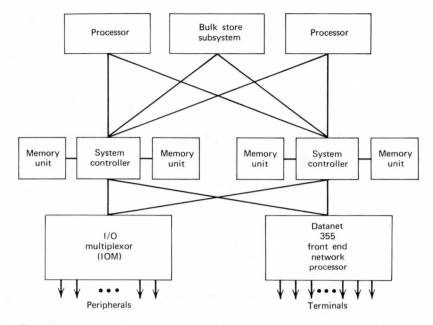

Figure G-1   Honeywell multiprocessor system organization.

series 6000 product line. The major notable exception is the processor; in this case the goal was that the processor should differ logically from the current 645 processor only in ways which will enhance significantly the total cost/performance of MULTICS or retain compatibility with series 6000 software.

Consequently, the system specification is an incremental specification to the series 6000 system, except for the processor proper, which is an incremental modification to the current 645 processor specification.

Processor

Most of the special capabilities of the 6180 which are seen by its users are provided by the processor. The processor module has full program execution capability and conducts all actual computational processing within the 6180 system. The processor performs instruction fetching, address preparation, memory protection, data fetching, and data storing. These functions are overlapped to provide the highest rate of instruction execution.

TABLE G-1 SUMMARY OF SERIES 6000 AND 6180 CHARACTERISTICS

	Model 6050/6060	Model 6070/6080	Model 6180
Maximum number of processors	4	4	6
Maximum number of DATANET front end network processors	3	3	3
Maximum memory size (in 36-bit words)	524,288	1,048,576	2,097,152
Maximum memory size (in 9-bit bytes)	2,097,152	4,194,304	8,388,608
Memory cycle time (8 bytes)	1.2	0.5	0.5
Maximum number of I/O multiplexors	4	4	4
Maximum transfer rate per IOM (bytes/sec)	2.3M	4.0M	4.0M
Maximum transfer rate per IOM (characters/sec)	3.7M	6.0M	6.0M
Number of data channels per IOM	24	24	24
Peripheral capacity (subsystems)	24	24	24
I/O compute simultaneity	24	24	24
Programmable registers	49/57	49/57	
Floating point	Yes	Yes	Yes
Memory protect	Yes	Yes	Yes
Hardware radix conversion	Yes	Yes	Yes
Interleaving	Yes	Yes	Yes
Instruction overlapping	Yes	Yes	Yes
Instructions per second (maximum)	550,000	1,400,000	1,400,000

The 6180 central processor contains all the general features of the Series 6000 processor plus the following additional features:

- Hardware for handling segments and pages.
- Hardware to generate 24-bit memory addresses.
- Two associative memories to speed up address generation (one for segments and one for pages).
- Program addressable registers used in segment and page address.
- More extensive address modification capability.
- Instructions to handle the segmentation and paging hardware and the system clock.
- Several levels of memory access permission.
- Several new processor faults.

- A maximum of eight ports for connection to system controller modules.
- Hardware implemented ring protection mechanism.

The 6180 also incorporates a manual mode switch to allow it to function selectively as either a 6180 processor with the extended instruction set capability. (MULTICS MODE) or a Series 6000 processor (GCOS MODE). This switch causes the appending unit to be added or removed logically.

PROCESSOR ORGANIZATION

The processor is organized into four functional units:

- Control unit.
- Operations unit.
- Decimal unit (EIS).
- Appending unit.

The first three units constitute a Series 6000 processor and perform all the functions they normally provide in a Series 6000 processor. In the 6180 processor, they operate as a processor and provide interfaces and control signals to the appending unit which performs the system requirements for segmentation and paging of memory.

APPENDING UNIT

The registers and functions provided by the appending unit are as follows:

- Provide 24-bit addressing.
- Contain up to 16 segment descriptor words and 16-page table words on a most recently used basis.
- Provides a descriptor segment base register.
- Provides 8 segment pointer registers.
- Provides ring protection hardware.

CONTROL UNIT

The control unit of the 6180 processor functions as a standard series 6000 control unit which provides the interface between the processor operations unit and the system controller. It also performs instruction fetching, address preparation, memory protection, data fetching and storing, and overall timing. In addition, the following apply to the control unit of the 6180:

- *Modes of operation.* The control unit of the 6180 processor uses the normal-absolute or append word addressing modes and the privileged or unprivileged instruction execution modes (identical to the processor). As a Series 6000 processor, the 6180 processor is limited to the combination of Series 6000 master and slave modes.
- *Operation decoding.* In either of the two processor modes (6180 or 6000), all instruction operation codes (10 bits) not defined as legal *in that mode* cause an illegal procedure fault if execution is attempted.
- *Fault and fault control logic.* As a 6180 processor, the control unit recognizes up to 27 faults. As a series 6000 processor, the processor recognizes only the first 16 of these faults.

OPERATIONS UNIT

The operators unit contains the logic to execute arithmetic and logical operations.

DECIMAL UNIT (EXTENDED INSTRUCTION SET)

The extended instruction set hardware adds to the processor's standard repertoire of instructions, capabilities for processing bytes, BCD characters, packed decimal data, and bit strings. The EIS hardware also affords a second level of address indexing for all of the standard instruction as well as the EIS instructions.

MODES OF OPERATION

The processor has two modes of operation in GCOS: master and slave. For MULTICS operation there are four operational modes: MULTICS absolute, MULTICS privileged, MULTICS nonprivileged, and MULTICS base address register. All instructions are available in absolute and master modes. Most, but not all, of the instructions are available in slave and unprivileged modes. General users are restricted to the unprivileged mode and hence are prevented from executing any instructions that could damage other programs or MULTICS. Privileged instructions such as those which operate upon the descriptor base register, the system clock, and I/O devices are available only in absolute and privileged modes.

The full segmentation and paging capability of the processor is used in the privileged and unprivileged modes for fetching instructions and operands. The addressing in the absolute mode does not use any of the seg-mentation and paging capability.

Memory

The 6180 system is memory-oriented. Memory serves as a coordinating passive system component that provides both interim information storage and system communication control. For this reason the controller associated with the memory is not merely a memory controller but is, in fact, the system controller.

SYSTEM CONTROLLER

The system controller modules serve as the centers for communications between the other modules in the 6180 system by providing the following functions:

- Core memory for storage of instructions, control words, and data.
- Control point for forwarding control signals from one active module to another.
- System Clock (52 bit) for providing data and time of day in-formation.

Each system controller has up to eight ports for connection to processors, IOM's and bulk store subsystems.

A System Controller may contain 32K, 64K, 128K, or 256K of 36-bit words (plus parity) and has a cycle time of either 1.2 μsec or 500 nsec/word. Either one or two words can be read or written in one memory access. It is also possible to store a 6 or 9-bit character in a word without disturbing the other characters in the same word.

STORAGE FUNCTION

To store or retrieve information, an active module (processor, IOM, or bulk store) sends a command, an address, and the necessary data to the appro-priate system controller. The system controller executes the command and either stores the data received or sends the desired data to the requesting module.

Six commands are used by active modules in communicating with system controllers:

- Read restore, single precision.
- Read restore, double precision.

- Clear write, single precision.
- Clear write, double precision.
- STAC (store conditional, used for lock words).
- Read and clear, MULTICS BAR mode.

The STAC command makes it possible for an active module to read and alter the contents of a location without permitting another active module access to that location while it is being altered. This is a very useful characteristic of the 6180 in a multiprocessor environment.

A typical 6180 system has more than one system controller. Memory access requests are distributed among the various system controllers by a memory interlace technique. This equalizes the load among the system controllers and increases system performance by decreasing the competition and queuing of requests for the same physical system controller. There can be two-way interlace, four-way interlace, or no interlace. The choice is a basic parameter of the system configuration.

SYSTEM CLOCK

The system clock consists of a calendar clock which is a 52-bit binary counter which counts at 1-μsec intervals, providing a capacity greater than 142 years without overflowing. The program can read the contents of the calendar clock with a precision of 1 μsec. The 142-year capacity of the clock makes it possible for the software to operate on universal time. To accomplish this, the Honeywell Field Engineer must set the clock to the number of microseconds since midnight, January 1, 1901, Greenwich Mean Time. Although a process can read the calendar clock at any time, provision for setting it under program control is deliberately omitted so that programming errors or hardware malfunctions outside the clock cannot destroy the current time.

Input/Output Multiplexer

The Input/Output Multiplexer (IOM) interfaces peripheral units and the DATANET 355 communication preprocessor with the memory of the 6180 system and is capable of operating a large number of devices of almost arbitrary variety and speed. The IOM is controlled by information stored in memory, with access to the memory being shared with the other active modules in the system. Data transfers between I/O devices and memory are accomplished by the IOM while processors continue to run programs. Input/Output control words prepared by MULTICS are stored in memory. When an I/O transaction has been completed, or when specific conditions are detected, the IOM informs MULTICS by causing a program interrupt.

Bulk Core

- *Capacity.* A single bulk storage controller has a capacity range of from 1 million to 8 million 36-bit words increments.
- *Speed.* The device is capable of transferring a 1K word block to or from main storage in 382 μsec excluding software overhead.
- *Ports.* The device will interface directly to the system controllers. It is capable of accommodating eight ports, the same number of memory ports as found on the IOM and the 6180 processor.

SYSTEM SOFTWARE

Supervisor

The MULTICS supervisor acts in response to any information in the MULTICS system that affects the status of a process and/or processor. A process can exist in several states: running, ready, or blocked. A running process is one currently executing on a processor. A ready process is one that is not running but is held up awaiting availability of a processor. A blocked process is one awaiting an event (not necessarily eminent) in another process or in the external world, such as receipt of input from a device. The supervisor must not only keep track of what process is in what state and when to switch the state of a process, but it must also provide a method of communicating to a process the occurrence of significant events in other processes.

Traffic Control

Processors are shared (multiplexed) among the processes from an "anonymous pool" of processors. The traffic controller makes the multiplexed system appear to the user as if his process were the only one executing on a processor at any given time. This technique shields the user from details of hardware management and handles the multiplexing of system resources among the users in such a way that the user need not be concerned with the problems of multiplexing processors. Protection included ensures that one user cannot affect another without prior agreement.

Since there are many processes and only a few processors, not all unblocked processes can be running. This is the reason for the existence of the ready state of a process. Intrinsic to the ready state is the "ready list" which lists all processes in the ready state as previously described.

The ready list contains the basic information to direct the dispatching of a processor when it is released by a process. A call to wake up a blocked process means "put it on the ready list." When a processor calls to block, it means that the process is abandoning temporarily the processor upon which it is executing and that the first process on the ready list should be given control of the processor.

Process exchange is the name applied to those procedures of the traffic controller that handle dispatching of processors among processes, scheduling of processes, and switching of processes. The process exchange is driven entirely by calls from other supervisor procedures, usually as a result of interrupts.

The basic hardware mechanism by which a processor switches from one process to another is the load descriptor segment base register instruction (LDBR). At the instant the descriptor segment base register (DBR) is reloaded, the processor sees the "memory image" of a new process. However, the contents of the processor registers temporarily remain the same.

The process exchange maintains a "ready list" of all processes in the ready state in the order in which they are to be run. The ready list consists conceptually of pairs of entries; a process identification and a running time limit imposed by the scheduler (time slicing).

The ready list is ordered and maintained by the scheduler procedure. In general, scheduler evaluates the process request for priority in execution, comparing the request with present status of the ready list. Scheduler establishes a time limit for the process and places it in the ready list at its appropriate point. After a process is put on the ready list, it is run in turn on a first come first served basis. However, if a process is known to have a high priority, it can be given a favorable position on the ready list in accordance with its priority in relation to the priorities of the other processes on the list. Scheduler has the option of using a preemption interrupt to force a process to relinquish a processor to a process with a higher priority. When a process has exhausted its allotted time but has not completed execution, it is demoted to its proper level in the ready list.

To permit parallel processing, each user procedure and many MULTICS system modules execute as collections of separate processes, called process groups. Communication between processes is the function of interprocesses communications.

The sending process places message information in a segment accessible to both itself and another process (the target process). The message may be either data, control information, or procedure. The target process reads the message information from the common segment. It is possible for the target process to suspend operation while awaiting a message. The sending process causes the target process to resume running when a message is in the common segment by calling wakeup.

The notion of an event is fundamental to interprocess communication. An event is anything recognized during the execution of one process that is of interest to another process. For example, the completion of the task of collecting the characters of an input line from a typewriter is an event which might be recognized by a device manager process and be of interest to a working process. An event is a unique occurrence that happens exactly once. If the device manager process of the example recognizes several successive line completions, each completion would be a separate event. The interprocess message is a signal from one process to another that an event has occurred.

Distributed Operating System

In executing a user program, MULTICS combines the needed portions of the operating system—selected segments—with the user program segments in such a manner as to perform the task requested by the user. Thus a process in execution is neither a user program nor a collection of MULTICS System Segments but a combination of both. This concept is called a distributed operating system, since system functions are distributed as needed within the process. A sophisticated MULTICS user can substitute his own system coding for MULTICS code in much of the system if he wishes. Furthermore, the programs the user writes for execution become indistinguishable from system coding in MULTICS.

Dynamic Linking

Since segments are brought into core memory from secondary storage only when needed in executing a process, the linkage of each *sympolic reference* between segments occurs the first time that the reference is encountered at execution time. Each segment of a program includes a linkage section which contains word pairs, called link pairs, representing the references to external segments from this segment. Before linking is performed for the first time, each link pair contains a modifier that causes a linkage fault when the external reference is made initially.

APPENDIX H

HUGHES AIRCRAFT COMPANY

H4400 COMPUTER SYSTEM

INTRODUCTION TO SYSTEM ORGANIZATION

The H4400 is a modular multiprocessor with automatic reconfiguration, provided with software (SHOC Control System) designed for directing the reallocation of resources. The system is composed of independent modules interconnected by a memory/processor switch (MPS). The types of modules include arithmetic and control processor (ACP), input/output processors (IOP), special-purpose processor (SPP), and memory modules. The functional relationship of these modules is shown in Figure H-1, which also indicates the configuration expandability.

While in the multiprocessor configuration each ACP or SSP operates with equal system stature, with two-way interleaved access to up to 16 memory modules. The SSP facility provides for operation of "customized" communication, display, or other processors that can be dedicated to functions not normally provided by the more general arithmetic and control processor. The centralized memory/processor switch (MPS) provides, in addition to memory-to-processor interconnections, central system functions, including from two to eight independent real, elapsed time clocks diagnostic control, executive assignment, and interrupt direction.

These last three functions are implemented through 16 system switch registers, each configured within a standard 32-bit word. Probability of a complete system failure due to a failure in the MPS is minimized through functional logic partitioning and provisions for a redundant power supply. The MPS is central to automatic reconfiguration and diagnostic actions—the system diagnostic sequencer is housed in the MPS; logical addresses of memory modules can be reassigned; faulty processors or memories can be

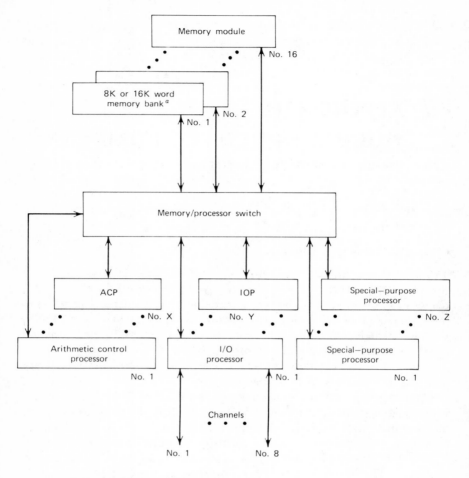

- From one to seven ACPs
- From one to seven IOPs
- Up to six special purpose processors
- Up to eight total processors per system
- One to 16 memory banks for up to 262,144 words (1,048,576 bytes)

^{a}Up to 4 memory banks may be packaged in a single module.

Figure H-1   H4400 configuration.

locked out; and automatic redesignation of executive processor or executive memory occurs if the previously assigned unit fails.

The MPS controls priority for processor access to up to 16 memory ports (Ports 0 and 1 have highest priority for memory module access; others are serviced on a rotating basis). Hardware contained within the MPS implementing executive functions ensures that only one processor is in the executive mode and services requests to relinquish or assume executive status; directs system interrupts to the processor designated as the "interrupt director;" and contains system status indication.

Five classes of interrupts are provided, allowing up to 83 recognizable interrupts in a maximum I/O configuration (includes 56 channel interrupts). The classes of interrupts, in the order of their priority, are (1) hardware fault, (2) local programmable (interprocessor communication), (3) external (clocks, signals), (4) input/output, and (5) local nonprogrammable (internal program faults).

The first four classes of interrupts are processed by the MPS prior to their acceptance by the receiving processor. The MPS provides buffering for all interrupts and establishes a priority structure for interrupts destined for an "interrupt director" ACP. All local nonprogrammable interrupts are handled by the ACP in which they occur, and the MPS is not made aware of their occurrence. Unlike the first four classes, the interrupts of this class (except arithmetic faults) may not be locked out.

An H4400 prototype system has been in operation at a Hughes Data Center since the latter part of the fourth quarter of 1970. The prototype includes two ACPs, two IOPs, 65K of memory, three magnetic tapes, card reader, line printer, disk, paper tape reader and punch, and a console I/O writer system. The software includes an operating system, a JOVIAL (J-6) compiler, meta assembler, two separate debugging systems, and a full set of general utilities.

FUNCTIONAL UNITS

Processor

The H4400 ACP contains 35 registers (16 general registers, 16 interrupt return registers, two program status word registers and an interrupt flag register), all of which are 32 bits in length and are program accessible. A single ACP can execute up to 600,000 instructions per second using an "instruction look-ahead" feature that overlaps the fetching of an additional 32-bit instruction word with execution of a prior instruction. Control of the ACP is effected via an LSI read only memory (ROM) microprogrammed with 2048 bits per configured processor. Up to 24 hardware implemented macros can be specified using this ROM as a "modular option" within a single ACP module. This feature allows the system designer the ability to specify and implement his own subinstruction set, in addition to the standard set of 108 half-word and full-word instructions. The other modular options are the addition of 18 instructions for single and double precision hexadecimal floating point operations, and the addition of nine instructions which operate on any contiguous group of bits within a 32-bit word performing all basic operations.

Addressing capability is provided for up to 524,287 half-words through 19-bit effective addresses generated for direct, multilevel indirect, indexed or base-plus-displacement addressing modes. In addition, direct addressing of 8-bit bytes within a word is provided for load byte, store byte and compare byte instructions, where the least significant byte of one of the 16 multiuse registers (MURs) is involved in the operation.

Each ACP is equipped with a 64-bit program status word (PSW), which functions approximately in the same manner as the IBM S/360 PSW, containing among its fields arithmetic condition codes, fault codes for arithmetic exception conditions, processor activity status, processor number indicating MPS/ACP port connection, memory protect key and program instruction counter. Unlike the System 360, however, each ACP is equipped with 16 interrupt return registers (IRRs) each 32 bits wide, which are organized into five groups of three registers each and one spare register. The five groups correspond to the five classes of interrupts described earlier, so that when an ACP acknowledges an interrupt, its then-current PSW is stored into two of the IRR's which correspond to the class of interrupt; this is the "old PSW," which in the IBM 360 must be stored in a reserved double word in lower main memory. Otherwise, the interrupt procedure is essentially the same, with the "new PSW" coming from a predetermined memory location just as in the 360, so that an old and new PSW replacement scheme is executed for all interrupts.

PROCESSOR SUMMARY

- Microprogrammed read-only memory allowing up to 27 additional instructions, or "hardware macros" to be implemented.
- Sixteen general registers, seven of which are usable as base address registers and all as index registers.
- A special Repeat instruction for automatic repetition of up to seven sequential instructions up to 524,287 times.
- Addressing capability up to 512K half-words (256K words is the cur-

rently implemented maximum) via direct, multilevel indirect, indexed, or base-plus-displacement modes.

- Two-way interleaving with instruction look-ahead, giving a maximum execution rate of 600,000 instructions per second per processor.
- A bit string modularity option, providing nine instructions for partial word bit manipulation.

Primary Storage

The H4400 main memory utilizes wide temperature ferrite cores organized as a destructive readout memory with a cycle time of 1.4 μsec. Access time is 0.48 μsec. Word length is 36 bits (32 data + 4 parity). Up to 16K words constitute a bank and up to four banks can be contained in a single module. A configuration is expandable to a maximum of 16 memory banks or 256K words. System throughput is maximized by allowing any ACP or IOP to access two or more memory modules concurrently, under control of the MPS.

The memory module also includes a facility for an internal memory test. This mechanism cycles through all words in memory and compares their contents with the expected values set at a maintenance panel. From this panel an operator can also store or display any word within the memory.

The following capabilities are available as modular options within a single memory module:

- Either 8K or 16K words per module, with a parity bit for each 8-bit byte in each 32-bit word.
- A memory privacy protect subunit, which provides a 5-bit Privacy Key, 4 bits of which is the Privacy Key code for matching against the memory Protect Key for access to 1024 word blocks, and 1 bit is used for specify whether read-only or read/write access is permissible for the block.

All memory references are controlled by two system switch registers (SSRs) in the MPS. The two registers contain sixteen 4-bit fields, each field corresponding to a particular memory port. Each field contains the logical designation of that physical memory module. When a processor (either ACP or IOP) requests a memory access, the 4 most significant digits of the address are compared with the contents of all 4-bit fields in the two SSRs. The access request is then directed to all memory modules having that logical designation. If the privacy situations for all modules referenced are not identical, or if the memory contents are not identical for a read request,

TABLE H-1   I/O TRANSFER RATES BASED ON 1.4 USEC MEMORY

	Words/sec	Bytes/sec	Bits/sec
Cumulative per IOP	1.4×10^6	5.6×10^6	4.5×10^7
Per channel			
Bit serial	38×10^3	1.4×10^5	1.1×10^6
Byte serial	250×10^3	1.0×10^6	8.0×10^6
Full word	350×10^3	1.4×10^6	1.1×10^7
External multiplexor	250×10^3	1.0×10^6	8.0×10^6
Computer-to-computer	350×10^3	1.4×10^6	1.1×10^7
Block transfer	250×10^3	1.0×10^6	8.0×10^6

then the results of the operation are unpredictable. If a port does not have a memory module attached to it, then its field in the two SSRs is effectively ignored during access requests. A "nonexistent address" interrupt will occur if no live port with a matching bank address is found.

Input/Output Control Module

The input/output processor (IOP) provides the communication link between the computer and external devices with self-sustained operation, independent of the arithmetic and control processor (ACP). Performance features include command and data chaining, memory data protection, and parity checking at all interfaces. The IOP can have from one to eight channels. Each channel, regardless of type, adopts a standard internal interface to the required system I/O interface. Any number and mix of the channel types is available without changing the back panel wiring. The six channel interface types (see below) are interchangeable within an IOP module. All channels operate independently of one another, and all are capable of concurrent operation. A fixed priority within the MPS resolves main memory conflicts. Each IOP is capable of directly addressing a maximum of 16 memory banks (262,144 words). With a main memory cycle time of 1.4 μsecs, the memory overlapped operation capability of the IOP provides a maximum data transfer rate of 1.4 million words/sec. I/O transfer rates for each of the standard channel types are given in Table H-1, and a description of the channel types follows. Each of the standard channel types except the bit serial channel communicates with external devices via an 8-bit byte interface.

Channel priorities are by type of request and by port position (physical location of the channel in the module). Requests for data transfer have highest priority, interrupt requests next priority, and command requests lowest. Among similar types of request, port zero has highest priority, with port seven having lowest. Because requests for new commands have lowest priority over all operations, the priority structure serves to act as a load-leveling scheme whereby new data operations are not initiated until an overload in data rate can be leveled out.

Secondary Storage

The H4400 prototype system used in the Hughes Data Center operation includes a magnetic disk with a maximum capacity of 58 million bits. The organization of the disk is 10 surfaces, with 203 tracks per surface. The average access time is 85 msec with a 135-msec maximum access time.

SOFTWARE EXECUTIVE FEATURES

Job Control

The H4400 control system, software/hardware operational control (SHOC), is described by Hughes as a generalized real-time software executive system designed for multiprocessing operations. The size of the core-resident executive software is 12K words.

Multiprogramming is treated in a very generalized manner by the executive, which views multiple programs in execution as a network of interconnected control points called "nodes." A node is defined as either a control console (an external node) or "a major unit of applications software" called an internal node or "cluster." All nodes have the following common features:

- *Each has a "communications control point" (CCP).* For internal nodes, the CCP is a special job of the cluster which performs a twofold activity: processing incoming and outgoing communications messages, and, on the basis of a user-selected priority-defining algorithm, scheduling the node's activities. For external nodes, the CCP is a hardware device that has a suitable input and output capability, such as provided by a typewriter, or a terminal (function keyboard and CRT). The CCP of an external node must be attention-driven, and must be recognized as an allowed type of device by the I/O management portions of SHOC.

- *Each can claim exclusive ownership of certain resources.* Ownership is typically expressed with reference to hardware devices, if not dismountable, or to volumes (disk packs, tape reels, etc.). Areas of core storage may also be "owned" by internal nodes.
- *Each can define the extent of its privacy in the network, in a communications sense.* The definition of any specific node to SHOC includes the node's name and, optionally, a list (called a "permission list" for "authorization") of other nodes with which communications is to be allowed. Additional privileges such as the sharing of certain (otherwise private) resources may also be stipulated. Nodes can be "grouped" to exemplify both privacy needs and resource-sharability considerations of applications.

In addition to the features described above, this "network of interconnected nodes" concept makes available the following job control characteristics managed by the SHOC executive:

1. Job steps can be executed in parallel by multiple processors as a user option.

2. New jobs may be formed as additional nodes in the network by any other node (job or external console).

3. Concurrently executing jobs can communicate internally with one another via the CCP.

4. Job steps of a node can synchronize their execution to termination of another job step within the node, to event flags and counters updated at user request, to the reception of a reply to a previously transmitted message, to the completion of an I/O operation, and to a time interval or real time through event reference control statements implemented in both macro and message form.

To provide these capabilities, two mechanisms are provided within SHOC for dynamic requesting and control of services. The first is the system communications port of SHOC which performs the routing and conveying of messages between nodes. The text of a message consists of any sequence of characters up to a maximum length of 240 characters. Each node has an identifier assigned to it which is specified as the destination for the message by the sending node. If the destination is an external node, routing the message consists of printing or displaying at the node (external CRT, line printer, etc.) as appropriate. If the destination is an internal node, the message is stacked in an input queue associated with the node, and a mechanism is activated for reception of the message by the node's control point. Provision exists for bypassing the input queue for higher priority messages (such as conventional input from an external node) and placing the message in a special buffer defined by the node's control point. In addition, any node can declare "communications streams" to be resident on devices it owns. This provides a sort of dynamic input stream allocation capability for nodes dealing with job streams and/or batched data from local or remote terminals.

The second mechanism for obtaining dynamic software services is the availability of SHOC routines that can be entered by applications programs to perform the desired service. These routines are usually entered via the monitor call (MON instruction) linkage mechanism, and behave as direct immediate extensions of the applications programs that call them. These system-service programs can be called by issuing macros with appropriate arguments defining the extent of the service required (such as the amount of core space desired in a request for additional space) or in some cases by entering messages to the node containing the SHOC nucleus in a control-card fashion.

I/O Control

SHOC I/O support is performed by a centralized input/output control systems (IOCS). Several file organizations are provided, as functions of the types of devices on which they can reside. SHOC I/O is totally file-oriented (as opposed to device-oriented).

There are seven macros within this category:

FILE—declare a file.
FREL—release a file.
OPEN—open (acquire access to) a file.
CLOSE—close (relinquish access to) a file.
FIN—input from a file.
FOUT—output a file.
FPOS—position within a file.

These operations have been designed to create the minimal level of logical I/O required for device-independence. It is also the minimal level that allows centralized I/O management within SHOC.

APPENDIX I
IBM
SYSTEM/360 MODEL 65 MULTIPROCESSOR

INTRODUCTION TO SYSTEM ORGANIZATION

IBM defines a multiprocessing system as "a computing system employing two or more interconnected processing units to execute programs simultaneously" and offers this capability on only one system of its 360 product line, the Model 65 MP. (The Model 67 is designed primarily for time-sharing applications and is usually controlled by a special purpose operating system, such as TSS/360, although it may be used as a model 65 with standard software by disabling its virtual memory address translation mechanism.) Multiprocessing on the Model 65 is offered as an option, called the multisystem feature, with the following characteristics:

- It uses a version of the OS/MVT operating system called M65MP.
- Two tasks can be executed simultaneously; to prevent access to critical supervisor data by both CPUs at the same time, a programming technique called *lockout* is used.
- Most devices are available from either CPU through the use of a two-channel switches; devices that do not have the two-channel switch capability (logically or physically connected to only one CPU) depend on CPU to CPU communication for the nonconnected CPU to have accessibility. (However, a device without the two-channel switch cannot be accessed from the nonconnected CPU).
- System reconfiguration is under operator control, so that in addition to peripheral devices, CPUs, channels, and storage elements can be removed and replaced without disruption of normal job processing.

The dual processor configuration is organized using a multibus, multiple-port configuration to provide interconnection for the sharing of system components, as illustrated in Figure I-1, depicting a typical multiprocessor configuration. The CPUs have single access ports but storage units have multiple ports for connection of CPUs and channels.

The approach taken by IBM allows the Model 65 multiprocessor to be configured as a single computer system with two CPUs sharing all storage units under control of a single operating system or as two separate, partitioned systems each with its own CPU, storage and peripherals, and controlled by two separate operating systems. Between these two extremes, devices and storage can be reserved for the exclusive use of either CPU under control of a single operating system. The major disadvantage of the multisystem feature is that it precludes the use of 2361 core storage (LCS), which provides 8-μsec cycle time, directly addressable bulk core of up to 8,388,608 bytes. However, primary processor storage is available in 256K-byte increments providing up to 2,097,152 bytes with a memory cycle time of 750 nsecs.

The major advantage found in adapting the Model 65 to multiprocessing is that field-proven hardware and software can be used with minimal modification. All object programs that can be processed with the standard OS/MVT operating system can be processed with the M65MP version without changing the code, the job control statements, or the data.

FUNCTIONAL UNITS

Processor

Each of the Model 2065 processing units contain the following standard 360 registers and functions:

1. Sixteen 32-bit general registers, program addressable as index registers, accumulators or base address registers.

2. Four 64-bit floating point registers for single and double precision arithmetic.

3. A 64-bit Program Status Word (PSW), addressable by supervisor state programs, used to control the status of the system in relation to the program currently being executed.

4. Execution of two and three address instructions of five formats and three lenghts from a universal instruction set containing 87 standard instructions, 44 floating point instructions, and 8 decimal instructions.

5. A priority interrupt system permitting recognition of five classes of interrupts.

The five instruction formats are register-to-register (RR), register-and-

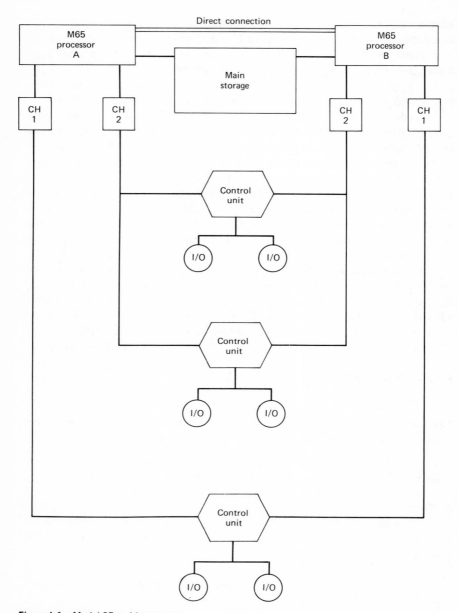

Figure I-1 Model 65 multiprocessor.

indexed-storage (RX), register-and-storage (RS), storage-and-immediate-operand (SI) and storage-to-storage (SS) operations. All references to memory are of the base-plus-displacement type, where the displacement fields are 12-bit positive integers to be added to the rightmost 24 bits of the general register designated the base register, providing a simple way of logically addressing up to 16,777,216 bytes of main storage.

Although the 8-bit byte is the basic unit of data storage, eight different data formats are recognized, such that every instruction operates on one and only one format. A storage boundary alignment constraint is imposed on these data types. The byte storage address for the data field must be a multiple of the length of the field in bytes. For example, if the processor references a full word, fixed-point operand whose address is not a multiple of four (a full word boundary), an address specification interrupt occurs.

The processor operates in one of two modes, the problem state, where all I/O instructions and a group of control instructions are invalid, and the supervisor state where all instructions are executable. The states of the processor, including whether it is running or in the wait state, are indicated by the contents of the Program Status Word (PSW), a 64-bit control word. The system mask, 8 bits of the PSW, is used to inhibit interrupts from the I/O channels (bits 0–6) and from the timer, the interrupt key, or an external signaling device. The 4-bit protection key is used to protect blocks of 2048 blocks of core against unauthorized reads, read/writes or writes as indicated by keys in storage (nonaddressable) associated with each block. Two privileged instructions, Set Storage Key and Insert Storage Key, are used by the system supervisor to change or inspect the protection assigned to a block.

Since each processor must respond separately to automatic transfers and PSW exchanges with fixed memory locations, two dedicated areas of storage must be provided, each addressable in the range 0-4095. The Model 65 multisystem feature provides direct address relocation which applies a 12-bit prefix to the preferential storage base address which always has the high order 12 bits set to zero, since addresses 0-4095 can be generated without a base address or index. Thus one processor refers to the actual low core preferential storage for items such as interrupt vectors (PSWs), channel status words, interval timer, and I/O control words while the other processor refers to a predefined 4K block at the top of memory.

The Model 2065 Model MP processor is used when configuring a Model 65 multiprocessor system, the Model MP processor must have direct control features for direct CPU-to-CPU communication and one processor requires the configuration control unit feature. The MP processor model conforms to the data flow diagram shown in Figure I-2, differing only in the

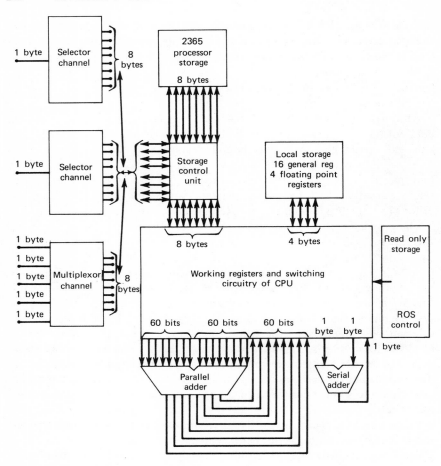

Figure I-2   Model 65 data flow diagram.

ability to access progressively larger main storage capacities. This figure illustrates the four major logical parts of the 2065 processing unit:

1. An arithmetic-logic unit, containing a 60-bit wide parallel binary, 8-bit decimal/binary adder with a 200-nsec logic cycle time.

2. A local store, containing processor working storage registers and addressable general and floating point registers having 200-nsec cycle time.

3. A read only storage (ROS) used to control data flow and instruction execution.

4. A storage control unit, effectively independent of the processor, servicing processor storage requests and resolving simultaneous access conflicts between the processor and data channels.

Note in Figure I-2 that the 2065 processor fetches 8 bytes/instruction cycle, at a 200-nsec basic cycle rate. In addition, an instruction buffer permits high-speed instruction preparation and overlap of most of the instruction fetch time.

Three operating modes are selectable at the multisystem configuration control panel: Multisystem, Mod 65, and Partitioned. The Multisystem mode provides direct CPU-to-CPU communications via the basic direct control interface for conventional multiprocessing with a single executive program. The Mod 65 is used for those cases where the direct control interface must operate identically with all other Model 65s. In Partitioned mode, multisystem direct communication between CPUs is disabled so that each CPU is treated as a separate system having its own control program, main storage units, and I/O devices. A partitioned system could continue to run the MP operating system, however, with one CPU varied out of the system.

Primary Storage

From two to eight Model 2365-13 processor storage units can be configured in a Model 65 multiprocessing system, each providing 265K bytes of storage, so that up to 2,089,152 bytes are available in a maximum memory configuration. Each memory module has a basic 750 nanosecond storage cycle, with access to 8 bytes in parallel. A store function is possible on a byte basis (8 bits + parity) and any number of combinations of up to eight contiguous bytes can be stored in one storage cycle.

Each memory module contains two independent storage sections, each with its own address and storage buffer registers. Each section can access 8 bytes in parallel and has 131,072 bytes of storage organized into 16,384 doublewords. One section contains even-numbered doublewords while the other section contains odd-numbered doublewords accommodating two-way address interleaving.

The Model MP processor provides shared storage, shared I/O, and floating-storage addressing capabilities to the system. Each shared storage feature consists primarily of a dual buffer control unit-storage interface. A priority scheme determines which buffer control unit is to have access to the storage unit and ensures that neither unit is allowed two successive references to a particular storage unit if the other control unit is waiting for access.

Input/Output Control Module

The channel is the System/360 I/O control module, providing the data paths and direct control for I/O control units and the I/O devices attached to the control units. Channels are of two types: selector and multiplexor. Selector channels are for high-speed devices such as a tape, drum, or disk. These channels allow data to transfer to or from a single device at a time. Multiplexor channels are generally for slower devices such as a typewriter, card reader, or printer. Data may transfer to or from many of these devices at one time. Actually, the characters are transmitted interleaved in time, and it is the function of the multiplexor to keep those characters intended for the card punch separated from those intended for the line printer.

A maximum of seven channels can be attached to each 2065 processor in either of two combinations: one 2870 multiplexor channel and six selector channels in two 2860 Model 3 selector channel configurations, or two 2870s and five selector channels in 2860 Model 2 and Model 3 channel configurations. Each selector channel has addressing capability for up to 256 I/O devices, one at a time in an overlapped, burst mode. The basic multiplexor channel can address up to 16 I/O devices each. However, using model MP processors, the second 2870 multiplexor channel on each processor cannot have selector subchannels configured. Each selector subchannel can operate one I/O device concurrently with the basic multiplexor channel. Each selector subchannel permits attachment of eight control units for devices having a data rate not exceeding 180,000 bits/sec. Regardless of the number of control units attached, a maximum aggregate data rate for the multiplexor channel ranges from 110 to 670 kbits depending on the number of selector subchannels installed. Each selector subchannel in operation diminishes the basic multiplexor channel's maximum data rate of 110 kbits, while the first three selector subchannels operate at 180 kbits each and the fourth subchannel has a maximum data rate for 100 kbits, providing the 670-kbits aggregate data rate.

A channel-to-channel adaptor feature is optionally available, providing a path for data transfers between two channels. The channels may be either within the same system or on separate systems. The two-channel switch feature of the control units and the channel-to-channel adaptor feature of the 2860 selector channels may interconnect two CPUs for shared I/O units. The total number of shared I/O units in a multiprocessor configuration cannot exceed the total number of units attachable in a basic Model 65 system.

Secondary Storage

Mass storage on the basic 360/65 is provided by large capacity bulk core storage, drums, and disks. However, bulk core cannot be utilized on the Model 65 Multiprocessor.

Two drum storage units are available, each with an 8.6-msec average rotational delay. The 2301 drum storage unit provides access to approximately 4.1 million bytes and four drum units can be attached to a single 2820 storage control for a total capacity of some 16.4 million bytes. In addition, the 2820 can be switched between two channels with an optional two channel switch. The data transfer rate to or from the CPU is 1,2000,000 bytes per second. A smaller, slower drum, the 2303, is available, providing direct access in units of 3.91 million bytes and a data transfer rate of 312,500 bytes/sec. Two units can be controlled by a 2840 storage control, for a total of 7.82 million bytes/2841.

Disk storage is available in either fixed disk or removable disk pack form. The fixed disk is the 2302 disk storage Models 3 and 4, consisting of one and two modules, respectively, of 112.79 million bytes each. Up to four 2302s can be attached to a single 2841 storage control, providing approximately 902 million bytes of direct access mass storage having up to eight access mechanisms. Removable disk pack storage is offered in the Models 2311 and 2314 disk storage drive configurations. The 2311 provides direct access storage for 7.25 million bytes in a single pack. Eight disk drives can be attached to a 2841 storage control providing 58 million bytes total storage with an average seek time of 75 msecs. The 2314 Model 1 contains eight independent disk storage drives and their control unit. A ninth drive is provided as a maintenance spare. Another 2314 configuration, the A-series, provides a variable number of drives up to nine.

SYSTEM SOFTWARE

Job Control

Multiprocessing on the Model 65 is provided under the MVT option of the System/360 operating system (OS). MVT provides Multitasking with a Variable number of Tasks for 15 concurrent jobs. The term "task" is defined by IBM to denote a program subdivision which is treated as a basic unit of work by the supervisor.

Jobs are placed on a separate input queue for each job class and the position of a job on a queue is determined by the job priority. A maximum number of 15 jobs can be active concurrently.

Program-initiated scheduling is available under MVT. A program executes a request to the supervisor to attach another task. The supervisor then creates a new task and schedules its execution. The new task is a subtask of the originating task. A different priority may be specified for the subtask than that of the originating task. All tasks within a job step can execute asynchronously.

Certain system resources, such as core storage and CPU control, are assigned only to tasks. This assignment takes place on a priority basis. The system supervises allocation, keeps track of all assignments, and frees resources upon task completion.

In a multitasking environment, more than one task may be contending for the same resource at the same time. Requests are queued, and, when the resource becomes available, it is given to the ranking member of the queue. To keep track of assignments, the supervisor maintains queues that represent unsatisfied requests for resources and tables that identify available resources.

The amount of core required for a job may be specified for each step or for the job as a whole. Although a fixed amount of core is allocated to a job or job step, under MVT additional storage can also be allocated through the roll-out/roll-in feature. This feature allows a job to temporarily expand dynamically beyond the amount of core originally allocated. If no unassigned storage is available, another job is rolled-out onto disk and its core area is used by the first job for as long as necessary.

The supervisor controls and allocates storage space dynamically, and permits problem program requests for dynamic allocation. Areas of storage can be passed or shared between tasks, under MVT. The system provides for the creation of subpools (2K blocks of main storage allocated for a particular task under one label). Subpools are made available to a task when it is attached. The subpools may be released at the termination of the task or be retained by the attaching task. Core cannot be shared by succeeding steps of the same job.

I/O devices are allocated at the beginning of the job and jobs are not scheduled until all devices are available. Devices may be allocated by physical device ID, by device type (e.g., card reader, and tape) or by device category (e.g., sequential and direct access).

The system provides access control facilities for three types of routines: nonreusable, serially resuable, and reentrant. The reentrant routines may be used by more than one task simultaneously. Serially reusable routines may not be used simultaneously; however, the requests are placed in a queue until the routine becomes available, at which time the first request receives control of the routine. Nonreusable routines are loaded from disk for each access request.

Time is allocated on a contention basis, with the highest priority program in a ready state receiving use of the CPU. A program releases control of the CPU when it must wait for the completion of some event, such as an I/O operation. At this point a lower priority task is granted use of the CPU. When a higher priority task is ready to resume processing, a lower priority task is suspended and the CPU is given to the higher priority task.

A time-slicing capability is also available. All tasks with a certain priority may be allocated CPU time for an equal, predetermined interval. The time-slice group competes for CPU time on a contention basis and the tasks within the group are time-sliced only as long as the group has control of the CPU.

Task execution may be suspended until some specified event or events occur. The supervisor will notify the program that the event has occurred, and schedule the program for execution. Events recognized are specified I/O conditions, timer interrupts, and external interrupts. A task may also be suspended until an attached subtask reaches a certain stage of execution. Coordination of the activities of two CPUs is achieved using a lockout function to prevent access to critical data by both CPUs at the same time, and a technique IBM calls "shoulder tap" which uses the write direct instruction for communication between the two CPUs. In the multiprocessing mode, when interruptions are disabled on one CPU, they are not disabled on the other, making it necessary to "lock out" partially manipulated tables and queues from being used or altered by the CPU which is not interruptible. To achieve lockout, a programmed switch called a lock byte is tested and set wherever interruptions are disabled and released where interruptions are again enabled, such as in the system dispatcher. When the lock byte is on, the affected routines may be executed only on the CPU which executed instructions that turned on the lock byte.

I/O Control

Two or more simultaneous requests for use of a channel or control unit cause one of the requests to be entered on an I/O queue. I/O queues are normally serviced according to the dispatching priority of the task requesting the service, but in some cases the supervisor considers hardware optimization over priority when selecting an entry from the queue. For example, requests for access to a disk may be serviced in a fashion that minimizes disk seek time.

The following file organizations are supported: sequential, indexed sequential,partitioned, direct access, and teleprocessing.

Two general techniques are provided for handling data: the queued technique and the basic technique. The queued technique deals with individual records and may only be used to retrieve records in sequential order. Records are brought into main storage before they are actually requested, thus eliminating unnecessary waiting for programmed I/O operations. The basic technique deals with blocks. A block is brought into core at the time of the request, not in advance of it.

Simple, exchange, and chained segment buffering techniques are available. In addition, a dynamic buffering technique (used only for the queued access technique) takes a buffer from a system buffer pool and assigns it to an input record. The buffer is returned automatically to the pool once the input record has been processed. The supervisor provides automatic blocking and deblocking facilities as part of its buffering activity. The data may be accessed in a work area independent of the input or output buffer or via a pointer to a specific record location within one of the buffer areas.

Teleprocessing access routines provide the following functions: polling terminals sharing the same line, analyzing message headers to determine where input and output messages are to be routed, queueing and checking the sequence numbers of incoming messages, translating between external transmission code and internal processing code, and checking for transmission errors.

Diagnostic Error Control

The machine-check handler analyzes the malfunction to determine the level at which recovery is feasible. If recovery is not possible at the functional level (by repairing the failure and/or retrying the interrupted instruction), it then attempts, at the system level, to associate the failure with a specific task to allow the selective termination of the affected job.

Recovery may also be attempted at the system-supported restart level by reinitializing the system using system, job, and data queues that have been preserved by system restart facilities.

The Channel-Check Handler receives control when a channel failure is detected. The analysis performed by this routine aids error recovery routines in setting up for a entry of the failing operation. The channel-check handler also generates an error record containing the environment of the channel failure.

The user may provide his own routines to process program check errors. The user may specify the types of program interruptions his routines will handle and the types the supervisor is to handle. The supervisor normally acts on uncorrectable program errors such as execution of privileged instructions and violation of storage protection.

For abnormal conditions that can possibly be corrected, control if returned to the processing program with an indication of the probable source of the error. If conditions indicate that further processing would result in destruction of data or possible degradation of the system, an abnormal termination routine receives control.

APPENDIX J

IBM

SYSTEM/370 MODELS 158 AND
168 MULTIPROCESSORS

INTRODUCTION TO SYSTEM ORGANIZATION

IBM defines two types of "multiprocessors"—loosely coupled with separate main memories and separate copies of the operating system as contrasted to tightly coupled systems with a shared main memory and a single copy of the operating system. It is the latter class, tightly coupled systems, that coincide with the definition of a multiprocessor as presented in this text. The basic system organizations are shown in Figures J-1 and J-2.

Tightly coupled multiprocessing on the S/370 Models 158 MP and 168 MP is offered as an option, called the multisystem feature with the following characteristics.

- Uses a major revision of the S/370 operating system called Operating System/Virtual Storage 2 (OS/VS2).
- Each system user (or job) has a private 16 million byte virtual address space for user programs, system programs, and shared data and program areas.
- Multiple program locks are used for each of 13 types of serially reusable resources. In this way, a lock held by one CPU on a resource does not prevent the other CPU from using a different resource. (In MVT/360 M65MP only a single lock was used.)
- The Multisystem Communication Unit provides the hardware necessary for interconnection of two 158's or two 168's. In addition, the unit contains the Configuration Control Panel which is used to affect manual reconfiguration.

250

- The two processors in a 158 MP system share from one to 8 million bytes of main storage with each processor having a separate 8K byte cache with 230-nsec access to 8 bytes.
- The two processor in a 168 MP system share from 2 to 16 million bytes of main storage with each processor having a separate 8K (or 16K optional) byte cache with 80-nsec access to 8 bytes.
- When a CPU in a MP environment can no longer function, a signal is emitted before the CPU enters a permanent wait or stopped state. The alternate CPU recovery function of the operating system (OS/VS2) attempts to transfer work which was in progress on the failing CPU to the nonfailing CPU.

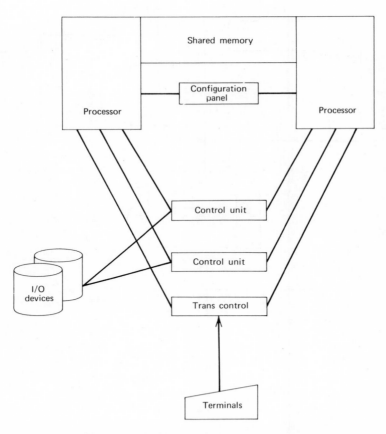

Figure J-1 IBM configuration tighly coupled mulitprocessing system.

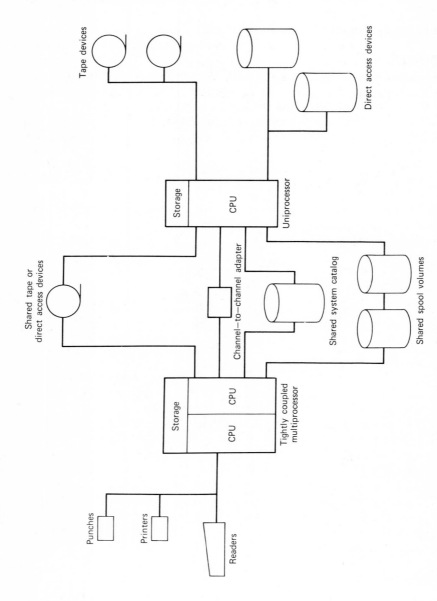

Figure J-2 IBM configuration. A tightly coupled multiprocessor in a loosely coupled configuration.

FUNCTIONAL UNITS

Processors

The S/370 processors are upward compatible with System/360 processors. New S/370 facilities include:

- *Dynamic address translation*, a CPU facility that provides hardware support to the virtual storage operating systems. Dynamic address translation allows the use of up to 16,777,216 bytes of virtual storage.
- *Timing facilities* include a time-of-day clock, a clock comparator, and a CPU timer, along with an interval timer that is also available in S/360.
- *The block multiplexor channel,* which\ permits concurrent processing of multiple channel programs for high-speed devices.
- *Error checking and correction* in main storage, instruction retry, and I/O command retry to reduce number of system failures.

370 MP INSTRUCTIONS

In addition to instructions that are unique to the S/370 as contrasted to for functions such as dynamic address translation, there are the S/360 three additional classes of instructions included for multiprocessing.

- *Prefixing.*   Each CPU uses low end storage (0-4096) to contain key status and control data. Prefixing provides the ability to logically reassign this block for each CPU to a different physical block in main storage.
- *The time of day (TOD) clock synchronization* provides the facility to synchronize the clocks of two CPUs in a MP configuration.
- *CPU signaling and response.*   Facility provides for communications among CPUs by means of the signal processor instruction. It provides for transmitting and receiving the signal, decoding a set of assigned order codes, and responding to the signaling CPU. Twelve orders are provided for communications among CPUs in a MP system. These include such orders as: External Call, Emergency Signal, Start, Stop, IPL, and CPU Reset.

SHARED MAIN STORAGE

The Model 158MP System consists of two processors, both MP models having equal storage. Total shared storage is available with 1, 2, 3, 4, 6, and 8 million bytes. On the Model 168MP shared storage varies from 2 to 16 million bytes in 1MB increments. The processors can operate in an MP mode or as uniprocessors each with its own dedicated portion of storage. The storage available to the uniprocessors is assigned via the configuration control panel with all storage assigned to one processor or divided between the two.

Input/Output Control Module

The System/370 channels operate in one of three modes: selector and multiplexor mode (as in System/360) plus block multiplexor mode.

In block multiplexor operation, the channel controller disconnects from the device during certain nondata-transfer operations and becomes available for an I/O operation on another device so that data transfer operations are interleaved. A block multiplexor can also operate in selector channel mode—compatible with system/360 selector channels.

A 158 MP system can have up to 10 block-multiplexor channels and up to 4 byte-multiplexor channels (with a maximum of 12 channels). The aggregate data rate of the 158 MP System is 7.5 million bytes/sec.

A 168 MP system can have up to 22 block multiplexor channels with a total of 24 channels including byte multiplexor channels. The aggregate data rate of the 168 MP system is 28 million bytes/sec.

Secondary Storage

The 3330 disk storage subsystem provides large capacity, high-speed direct access storage utilizing 100 million byte disk packs with a maximum of 800 million bytes per subsystems. A 3330 facility may be attached to a block-multiplexor channel via the 3830 control unit or 3330 type modules may be attached to the channel via the Integrated Storage Control (ISC). Four 3330 subsystems may be attached to the ISC for a maximum of 32 attached drives, 3330 subsystems using the 3830 control unit may be shared between eight CPUs in a loosely coupled multiprocessing environment.

SYSTEM SOFTWARE

System 370 multiprocessing system is supported by OS/VS2; a virtual storage system with time-sharing and multiprocessing support integrated into the control program. OS/VS2 will support both loosely coupled multiprocessing and tightly coupled multiprocessing.

Job Control

The job control language (JCL) of OS/VS2 remains basically unchanged from OS/MVT for compatibility. Many S/360 installations have used HASP or ASP as a front-end scheduling/spooling systems. OS/VS2 uses a job entry subsystem which can be either HASP or ASP like in nature. The user has a choice of either standard feature of the operating system. The front-end scheduling/spooling system performs the following functions:

- Readings jobs into the system.
- Scheduling jobs.
- Maintaining data submitted with jobs.
- Supporting the system management facilities.
- Handling all output from batch jobs and time sharing users.

In OS/VS2 the systems resource manager provides the facilities to manage the system workload according to installation specified performance objectives and manage the use of system resources. Performance objectives are distinct rates, called service rates, at which CPU, I/O, and real storage resources are provided to users in a performance group at a certain workload level in the system.

- CPU execution: one unit is the execution of 10,000 instructions.
- I/O measure: the I/O event count.
- Real storage occupancy: one frame occupied for some multiple of CPU execution units.

Coefficients can be supplied which multiply each of these factors to form a linear combination which will yield the service rate desired. By defining workload levels, the installation can express the varying service relationships between groups of users at different system workload levels. The systems track the service rates provided to users and the average workload level of the system, adjusting service rates to maintain the relationships between the performance objectives.

Time sharing, which is an option (TSO) in S/360 OS/MVT, is a standard feature of the OS/VS2 control programs. All the facilities available with TSO are standard facilities with time sharing in OS/VS2, with the exception of the command language, which remains optional.

The control program creates private virtual address spaces (16, 777, 216 bytes) for the following users and system components:

- Each batch job scheduled by an initiator.
- Each logged-on time-sharing job.
- The master scheduler.

- The job entry subsystem.
- The virtual telecommunication access method.
- The auxiliary storage manager.

Although each user job is given its own private address space, it does not have control over all of it. Each address space is divided into the system area, the user area, and the common area. The pages utilized in the virtual system each contain 4K bytes. Real storage is divided into 4K-byte page frames. The virtual storage management system makes use of segments which can contain up to 16 pages (64K-bytes). A maximum user virtual storage (16, 777, 216 bytes), therefore, contains 256 segments.

I/O Control

In S/370, the I/O Supervisor divides I/O operations into two distinct areas. Basic IOS manages the I/O devices, control units, and channels. IOS drivers function as interface routines which provide the validity checking, page fixing, virtual to real translation, and related request queuing that is unique to a particular type of I/O request.

Dynamic allocation of auxiliary storage, which was previously available only through time sharing, can now be invoked by both background and foreground jobs. Data sets may now be closed and unallocated prior to ending of the job or job step.

Diagnostic Error Control

Alternate CPU recovery is provided when a CPU fails and cannot continue functioning. I/O is reset on the failing CPU, and for symmetrically connected I/O, attempts are made to restart it through channels to the working CPU. When one channel path fails an attempt will be made to process the I/O on a alternate channel path. New instructions and software allow devices to be dynamically reconfigured on the system, bypassing permanent I/O errors, without restarting (re-IPL) the system or abnormally terminating the affected job.

APPENDIX K
RCA CORPORATION
MODEL 215 MILITARY COMPUTER

INTRODUCTION TO SYSTEM ORGANIZATION

The RCA 215 is a multiprocessor, general purpose, stored program, digital computer functionally compatible with the SPECTRA 70 series with ten additional instructions for multiprocessor control and error recovery. It was designed to meet specific military needs for the 1970s and therefore is designed to meet normally specified military standards.

The basic configuration of the 215 consists of two to four central processors, two to four I/O units, and from one to eight main memory units. A Signal Distribution Unit interconnects the processors and the memories and is divided into partitions, each of which is powered from the corresponding active unit (each unit of the system has its own power supply). Any active unit, including its partition of the signal distribution unit, can be automatically configured out of the system and can be shut down while the remainder of the system continues in normal operation.

Each unit of the computer is self-contained, including that portion, partition, of the Signal Distribution Unit (SDU) through which it interfaces with the system. The system is designed so that units can be added without modification to other units; units can be interchanged; unit failure does not affect the proper operation of other units of the system.

As can be seen from Figure K-1, the SDU is the heart of the system, since all communication passes through and is handled by the SDU. The SDU is essentially a network of exclusive OR circuits interconnected as shown in Figure K-2 to enable, for example, four-way simultaneous access, between the two I/O units and the two central processors and any four out of the eight main memory units. In the event of simultaneous requests for

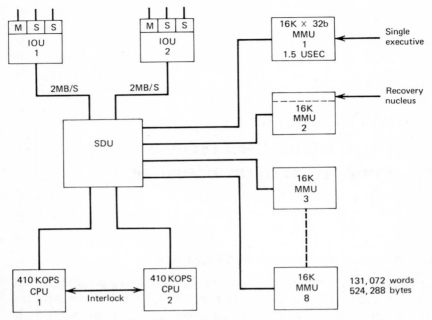

Figure K-1 Basic RCA 215 multiprocessor configuration.

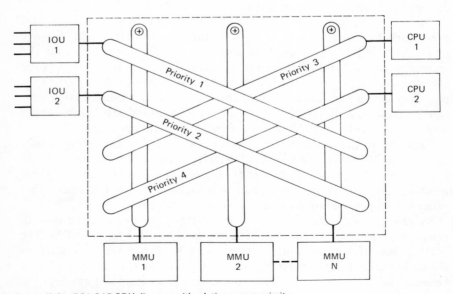

Figure K-2 RCA 215 SDU diagram with relative access priority.

service by the two I/O units for any one main memory unit, the priority will be resolved as shown in Figure K-2 with I/O unit 1 having higher priority than I/O unit 2. Similarly, if the two CPUs vie for service for one main memory unit at precisely the same time, then CPU 1 will have a higher level of priority than CPU 2. In the event of conflict between an I/O unit and a CPU, the I/O unit will have higher priority than the CPU. The circuits in SDU (largely line-drivers and receivers) are partitioned and powered from the active units. Each of the four processor units, the two I/O (IOU) and the two central processors (CPU), may have simultaneous access to any four different main units (MMU) at the same time. This simultaneity allows the system to handle the throughput of 4 million byte/sec combined I/O rate and a double 410K operation/sec CPU rate. The system can be expanded from a minimum of one CPU, one 16K MMU and one IOU module to a maximum configuration consisting of four CPUs, eight 32K MMUs, and four IOUs.

All commands, control words, data acknowledgements, interrupt signals, and error signals transmitted among CPUs, IOUs, and MMUs pass through the SDU. The SDU is subdivided into eight main memory partitions, four processor partitions, and one O&M Panel partition. Each MMU is associated with a main memory partition of the SDU and each IOU or CPU is associated with a processor partition of the SDU. All MMU partitions of the SDU are identical except for the physical address. The physical address of an MMU is determined by the partition of the SDU to which the MMU is connected and corresponds to the highest order three bits of the 19-bit address which defines the location of a byte in main memory. All processor partitions are identical in regard to signals transmitted between an IOU or a CPU and an MMU, except for priority. IOU partitions are identical except for the routing of interrupt signals and commands. CPU partitions are identical except for priority when commanding an IOU.

A unique feature of the 215 system is the recovery nucleus. This alleviates the problem of a failure in the main memory unit containing the single executive. (Note, that in Figure K-1, MMU 1 stores a single executive which manages all of the resources in the entire system. There is no master/slave relationship between the CPUs. Each operates independent on the highest priority program to be run). The recovery nucleus consists of two parts, one being a bootstrap program which enables another copy of the single executive to be called in from off line, the other part of the recovery nucleus is a copy of the current operating status of all programs operational when the memory failed. This status table contains the information to enable the system to restart at the point the memory failed.

An optional feature with the system is an elapsed time clock which will provide interrupt on elapsed time intervals. The 215 system has extensive error recognition capabilities, recognizing prime power failure, power failure of any CPU, IOU, or MMU, parity errors in data instructions, and failures in processing and control hardware. Each CPU is capable of accepting signals indicating failures in other elements of the system, including prime power failure.

FUNCTIONAL UNITS

Processor

The CPU within the 215 system consists of arithmetic and control sections capable of addressing main memory, executing instructions, initiating I/O operations, performing machine checks, and monitoring the computer operation. General registers, floating point registers, status/control bits, and status/control information transfer registers are implemented through a 300-nsec, 64 word by 36-bit scratch pad memory. The CPU utilizes a 1.5 μsec main memory cycle providing each CPU with a throughput speed of 410,000 operations/sec. The data format handled by the system is 16 or 32 bits fixed point and 32 or 64 bits floating point. Each access by the CPU fetches a 36-bit word of four 8 bytes plus 4 parity bits.

The 215 has an instruction repertoire totaling 153 instructions. The instructions include fixed point instructions, branch instructions, logical instructions, floating point instructions, decimal arithmetic instructions, privileged instructions, logical instructions, floating point instructions, decimal arithmetic instructions, privileged instructions, and multiprocessing and error recovery instructions.

Each CPU is entirely independent, having its own power supply and capable of executing instructions, having access to main memory and of commanding IOUs independently of the activity of another CPU. Neither failure of a CPU nor the maintenance actions required to repair the failure interfere with proper operation of any other portion of the 215 system.

There are thirty-two levels of interrupt in the 215. Priority 1, machine condition, is for power failures and machine checks. Priority 2, CPU alert, is for CPU to CPU signal handling and priorities 9 to 24 are for processing I/O operation. Priority 25 is reserved for the elapsed time clock feature and 26 is for manual interruption from the operator panel. Priority 27 is for a set of eight program depenent interrupts; priorities 28 to 31 are a set of individually maskable program dependent interrupts, and priority 32 is for a test mode of operation of the CPU for program testing.

Primary Storage

The main memory of the 215 system is coincident current core composed of 16,384 words (36 bit/word, four 8-bit bytes, and four parity bits). Each module has its own set of controls, buffer registers, and address registers. In addition, each memory module has its own power supply. Memory is expandable in modular increments of 16K or 32K and can be expanded up to 8 modules. Main memory cycle time is 1.5 μsecs. Each memory module provides both write protect and read/write protect features implemented through a 2,048 byte key memory, each key consisting of five bits (1-bit, type; 4-bit, key). In addition, hardware keys are associated with each CPU and IOU. Each memory module operates independently with neither failure of a memory module nor the maintenance actions required to repair the failure interferring with the proper operation of any other portion of the system.

Input/Output Control Module

Transfer of data from external sources to the 215 system is via the input/output unit (IOU). Normally data transfers are initiated by a CPU and flow to or from the IOU through the SDU from or to a designated MMU. There are two types of channels supported by the IOU, multiplexor and selector. Each IOU has a high-speed scratch pad memory for channel control information and channel registers are used for receiving data transfers and for transferring control and status information to the CPU. The I/O multiplexor channel transfer rate is 400,000 bytes/sec and the selector channel rate is 800,000 bytes/sec. The 215 system can service a 64 to 128 device multiplexor channel and two 256 device selector channels on each IOU to yield a combined rate of 4 million bytes/sec.

Mass Storage or Secondary Storage

Standard equipment offered by RCA consists of:

- Disc storage unit providing 7.25 million bytes of storage on an interchangeable disk pack, with the capability of up to eight of these units attached to one controller. Data can be transferred between the processor and the disc pack at the rate of 156,000 bytes/sec. The average seek time is 75 msec with a maximum of 135 msec.
- Drum memory unit providing either 4.12 or 8.25 million bytes of

storage. The average access time is 17 msec and data are transferred at approximately 325,000 bytes/sec.

- Disk memory unit providing either 0.5 or 1.0 million bytes of storage. The average access time is 20 msec and data are transferred at approximately 280,000 bytes/sec.

SOFTWARE EXECUTIVE FEATURES

Job Control

The software system of the RCA 215 is basically the same as the SPECTRA 70 TDOS. This system provides for the concurrent execution of up to six programs in variable sized partitions. Programs may be scheduled for execution either by a monitor or by the operator. Any program may be executed as a part of a chain of programs which are executed sequentially. This mode of operation is accomplished either by having a program call another program internally after having completed execution, or through control statements entered on the job stream.

Main storage is assigned to each job based upon the requirements of the job and the available memory at initiation time.

Allocation is controlled by a free memory table. This table defines the areas in memory that are currently not assigned. Actual I/O devices may be assigned by means of control statements entered through the job stream at program initiation or by operator commands from the console. A program may dynamically assign a device during execution.

I/O Control

Input/output routines initiate all I/O operations on all devices except the console typewriter. Queuing and subsequent initiation are accomplished on a first-in, first-out basis provided communications devices are not being supported. If telecommunications is supported, this I/O receives the highest priority.

The system has a file controller which at the logical level allows the user to not be concerned with physical record reading or writing. This logical level provides buffering services, makes logical records available for processing (blocking and deblocking), and makes files available for processing. A file control processor provides for processing files recorded serially on devices such as magnetic tape and also provides for processing sequential or random files recorded on direct access devices.

A communications program provides for the execution of one user communication program concurrently with five other noncommunication programs. This program monitors all telecommunication activities.

Routines for checking and/or writing standard labels on a tape file are provided within the file controller program.

APPENDIX L
SANDERS ASSOCIATES
OMEN-60 ORTHOGONAL COMPUTERS

INTRODUCTION

The Sanders OMEN-60 computers are a family of upward compatible mini-orthogonal array processors (mini-OAPs). They are real-time devices designed for processing high rate data. Compared with other systems and architectures, these processors emphasize rapid communication between external devices and a large orthogonal memory (OM)—a memory with two modes of access: conventional (by word) and vetical (by bit-slice of 64 words at a time).

There are two central processors in each OMEN-60 computer, both of which reference one memory. The system is not a collection of separate pieces with complex intercommunication problems. One processor is a conventional serial processor, a Digital Equipment Corporation PDP-11; the other is a vertical arithmetic unit (VAU). The VAU of the OMEN-61 and -62 is designed primarily for associative and data manipulative operations. The VAU of the "upper 60s," however, is ideal for arithmetic processing and is extremely efficient for floating-point as well as integer calculations.

The OMEN computers are programmed using high-level languages (e.g., extended FORTRAN-IV) and the system operates under control of a disk operating system (DOS). Digital Equipment Corporation's software is the basis for the OMEN's compilers and operating system since an OMEN-60 includes an embedded PDP-11.

SYSTEM ORGANIZATION

The basis for the OMEN family of orthogonal computers is a specially designed memory system—an orthogonal memory (OM)—that can be accessed in two distinct modes. With reference to Figure L-1, this memory supplies the PDP-11, the horizontal arithmetic unit (HAU), with all bits of a single word in response to the HAU's fetch request. The combination of the HAU and OM is, therefore, a Von Neumann machine. The power of the OMEN processor results from the second mode of access. In response to an access request from the VAU, the memory supplies a slice of nth order bits from 64 words. In this manner a series of vertical registers can be loaded for parallel processing of 64 data words. The bit slice access is used by the vertical arithmetic unit (VAU), the collection of parallel processing elements (PEs). These levels of logic in the VAU are identical and, with only a few exceptions controlled by masks, all perform the same operations at the same time.

One thing to note in particular in Figure L-2 is that despite the physical boundary between words 63 and 64 or between 127 and 128, there is no

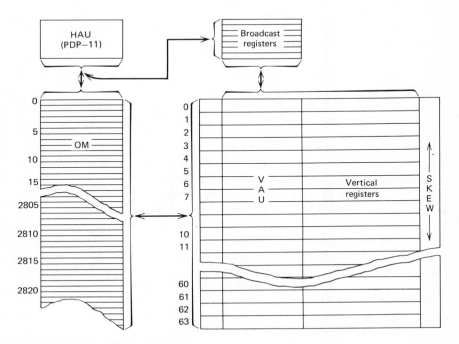

Figure L-1 OMEN-60 system organization.

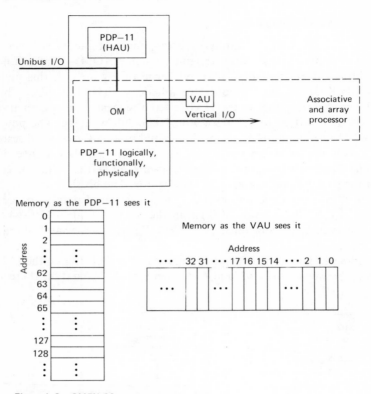

Figure L-2 OMEN-60 memory.

logical boundary from the PDP-11 viewpoint. The memory appears to be conventional memory. Similarly the VAU randomly addresses memory and does not see any boundary between bit slice numbers 15 and 16 even though there is a physical boundary there. Also, the VAU addresses to each byte so it can reference a block of words as bytes beginning at byte number 101 as fast as a vector of words or bytes starting at byte number 256. If one deletes the PDP-11 from the block diagram (as shown in the dashed box) the remaining processor is what is normally known as an associative processor or an associative array processor.

The speed of the OMEN-64 comes partly from the fact that there is a set of 64 processors, which are working in parallel and also from the fact that the instruction set is very powerful so that there are fewer instruction fetches and less instruction decoding. Algorithms such as many of those in linear algebra and signal analysis require but one instruction. Illustrative of the wide applicability of the OMEN-64 are the capabilities provided by complete floating point arithmetic in the VAU and the unified system design so that there is no separate control unit. A parallel processor with a separate control unit cannot as easily check for data dependency in the instructions as can an orthogonal computer, for example.

FUNCTIONAL UNITS

Processor Units

HORIZONTAL ARITHMETIC UNIT

The horizontal arithmetic unit is the digital equipment corporation PDP-11. This is a standard serial processor with 16-bit words. It has eight general-purpose registers and a repertoire of 400 instructions. All of the standard PDP-11 software will operate on the HAU.

VERTICAL ARITHMETIC UNITS

The VAU consists of 64 PEs, all of which are identical and operate in lock-step. Their complexity depends on the model number ranging from 1-bit add and logic with 8 bits of scratch pad to 16-bit adder and logic with eight 16-bit scratch pad registers.

In Figure L-3 more detail of the OMEN-60 is shown. Each level of logic in the VAU has skew logic which includes:

- *Invert.* Turns the data "upside down." Level 0 and 63 interchange positions as do 1 and 62, 2 and 61, and so on.

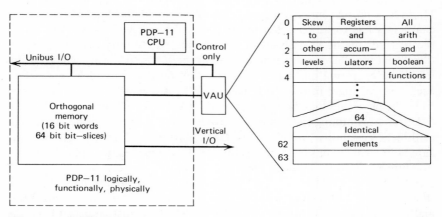

Figure L-3 OMEN-60 architecture.

- *Perfect shuffle.* Analogous to splitting a deck of cards in half then interleaving the two halves. level $0 \to 0$, $32 \to 1$, $31 \to 2$, $33 \to 3$, and so on.
- *Barrel shift.* Allows end-off or end-around vertical skews.

There are a number of registers at each level of VAU, actually 133 bits of storage in the OMEN-64—eight 16-bit registers and five mask registers. All the arithmetic and Boolean functions can be performed on these registers. In the bit by bit addition, the carry is initialized to 0, then at each clock cycle in the adding process the new carry bits replace the old carry bits in the carry register and the three inputs to the arithmetic logic unit that generates the sum, are the two operands and the carry register. Notice, that when one does an addition or a Boolean operation, which is performed the same way (but without the carry register), one starts with the low order of the operands and goes across the data field to higher order bits. At each successive clock cycle of the machine, the next bit slice (from the lowest order) is picked up and the operations are performed on it; thus when memory is accessed one knows in advance that the second access is going to be at the next lowest order bit-slice; the third access is the third lowest order, and so on. Thus interleaving the memory gives the full advantage— there are no statistical problems with trying to access the same physical memory twice during a memory cycle. This is exactly analogous to the situation of fetching a vector from an ordinary interleaved memory, where one knows that the succeeding elements of the vector are going to be located in physical separate memories. The memory addressing of the OMEN series is to the actual byte, both for the VAU and for the PDP-11. Just as there is no boundary between words number 63 and 64 to the PDP-11 there is no reason why access, fetching or storing a block of integers or characters has to be on a particular physical block boundary. Another of the features of the OMEN-64 is the distributed memory access. This optional feature allows each level of logic in the VAU to specify which datum it will be operating on. The only restriction on this type of access is that each level of logic in the VAU has to address a word which is displaced from the physical block boundaries by its VAU level number.

Differences among models in the OMEN-60 family are in the amount of arithmetic capability provided. The OMEN-61 and -62 have single-bit logic capability which makes them useful for data processing applications not involving multiply and divide (e.g., sorting, pattern matching, and retrieval). The OMEN-63 and -64 have full-word adders and hardware floating-point arithmetic, making them better suited for linear algebraic and other complex arithmetic calculations. The 61 is distinguished from the 62 only in the number of registers provided at each VAU level.

Orthogonal Memory

The orthogonal memory is constructed using MOS technology. It is interleaved for both vertical and conventional access, both of which are fully random. The transfer rate for horizontal access is 2 Mwords/sec; for vertical access it is 45 Mwords/sec. Memory sizes possible are 8K to 128K 16-bit wordsfor the OMEN-61 and -62 and 16K to 128K for the OMEN-63 and -64.

Input/Output

The I/O capabilities and the peripheral equipment for the OMEN–60 include that available for the PDP–11 since the primary OMEN I/O channel is a PDP–11 I/O channel.

Bulk storage devices can assume several forms. A conventional disk or tape drive can be connected to the UNIBUS and maintain a file system under direction of the OMEN's operating system. For environments where disk transfer speed is critical, the OMEN's optional 8,000,000 bit-slice/sec (equals 32,000,000 words/sec) vertical I/O channel can be connected to a special multiple-head or "solid-state" disk. In applications with such high data rates, a typical configuration might use an OMEN-61 as a buffer-formatter to convert data to their desired forms and to act as a buffer between the OMEN-64 and the high-speed I/O channel.

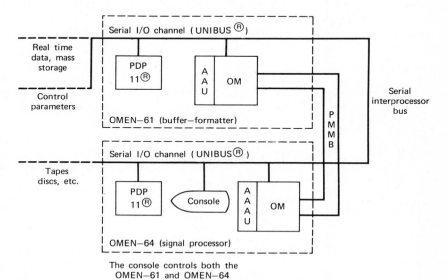

The console controls both the
OMEN–61 and OMEN–64

Figure L-4 Typical application for two processor system.

Figure L-4 shows a typical dual processor configuration where the small processor, an OMEN-61 in this case, acts as a buffer memory and data formatter between a very high speed realtime data channel and the main signal processor. For problems where there are data from cyclically sampled channels, the OMEN-61 deinterleaves the data as well as doing any other formatting that needs to be done to the data (such as shuffling into bit reversed order) so that the signal processor, the OMEN-64, is left free to do what it does best, namely the number crunching in such algorithms as Fourier transforming, beamforming, nulling out signals, searching for particular strong signals, signature analysis, and so on. The OMEN-61 would also be used to control the rest of the system, if this is necessary, as in a large system which is completely digitally controlled. The parallel memory to memory buss (PMMB) operates at more than 10 times the rate of the serial interprocessor buss so that very few cycles are stolen by the data transferring operation. This is due to two features: the buss is 64 bits wide and it operates at more than four times the clock rate of the UNIBUS.

SYSTEM SOFTWARE

Executives

The OMEN-60 utilizes either the PDP-11 disk operating system (DOS) or the PDP-11 real-time operating system (RTOS).

Languages

Higher level languages are utilized primarily. Supported are extended FORTRAN, BASIC and APL whose primitives are implemented in the OMEN-64 hardware.

Software generation for the OMEN has been simplified by use of existing PDP-11 software and by OMEN's microprogrammed instruction set. From a high-level language standpoint, a programmer doing an eight-by-eight matrix inversion might code in FORTRAN:

DIMENSION   ARRAY (8,8), VARRAY (8,8)

-
-
- (Statements defining ARRAY entries)
-
-

VARRAY = RMTINV (ARRAY)

- •
- •
- •

END

The PDP-11 FORTRAN interpreter recognizes RMTINV as a VAU operation and assembles a VAU machine instruction comprised of op-code for "matrix invert" and the starting address and size of ARRAY. This instruction word is then sent over the UNIBUS to the VAU where VAU's microprogram dictates the sequence of operations needed for matrix inversion. Additions to the PDP-11 FORTRAN interpreter consist only of appending the appropriate FORTRAN vector function names to the library function table and of supplementing the lsit of machine code generated by function references. A similar change reconciles the BASIC interpreter to parallel operations.

BASIC and FORTRAN, though widely used for general scientific programming, really do not support linear algebraic operations. While the OMEN's compilers permit activation of the VAU by use of special functions, a program so written for the OMEN must have a set of FUNCTION subprograms appended to run on a serial system. This is a cumbersome approach, but it is easily implemented in software. A more aesthetic programming system would use a matrix oriented language such as APL. The code generation portion of the OMEN's APL interpreter is quite simple since every APL primitive is expressable in *one* OMEN machine instruction.

As is true with any computing system, the OMEN's powers are exercised most precisely from assembly language. The high degree of microprogramming makes the OMEN's assembly language quite "high level." For instance, by coding:

$$VIJ;; \qquad 2 = ARRAY;$$

the programmer causes an eight-by-eight matrix stored beginning at location ARRAY to be transposed then inverted, and the result to be stored in vertical register 2. All the primitive instructions expanded from machine instructions are available to the assembler, so that no machine flexibility is curtailed by microprogramming. The user can specify his own special machine sequences, provided they are microprogrammed from available primitives. The OMEN assembler has a macro-language capability and produces relocatable code.

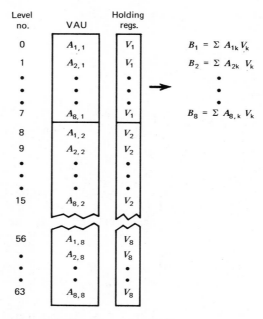

Figure L-5   Vector × matrix example.

The multiple broadcast registers (or holding registers) are very important for linear algebra instructions as illustrated in Figure L-5, which illustrates a vector × matrix operation. Here the vector (V1, V2, . . . , V8) is fetched into the holding registers and broadcast down.

Notice that V1 is replicated eight times, V2 is repeated eight times, and so on all the way down so that if A is in VAU and (V1, V2, . . . , V8) is broadcast, only one broadcast operation is necessary. The element-wise multiplication shown is the multiplication necessary for the vector times martix operation.

The summation necessary to perform the actual product is done by halving the array skewing up to bottom half and adding; repeating this operation twice more which leaves the vector result in the vector times matrix product in the first eight of the locations in the VAU, so that it can be stored directly into memory. In the case of a vector (or matrix) times constant operations the first holding register is used to broadcast its contents to all the levels of VAU. Also, the holding registers are connected to perform the vector times matrix operation for vectors and matrices which are stored in PL/I fashion (as well as in FORTRAN fashion as shown; for PL/I the vector is reproduced eight times: V1 → levels 0, 8, 16, and so on; V2 → levels 1, 9, 17, and so on).

Parallel (VAU) compare operations generate mask registers which give the order relations whether vector, matrix, or constant for the specified operands. These results frequently would be used with some type of Boolean operation to generate a mask in the storage mask register (SMR) or the arithmetic mask register (AMR). The SMR controls the flow of data into memory. If there is a 1 bit in the SMR at a particular level the store is successful, otherwise the contents of the referenced memory location is not altered. The AMR acts similarly for the VAU registers, effectively acting as an inhibit mask for each level of the VAU (each PE). There are fictitious masks of all 1's so that fewer operations moving masks are required than would be needed if there were only one of each type of mask.

APPENDIX M
TEXAS INSTRUMENTS
ADVANCED SCIENTIFIC COMPUTER SYSTEM

SYSTEM ORGANIZATION

Texas Instruments' Advanced Scientific Computer (ASC) is a very large general purpose multiprocessor. It provides multiprogrammed operation on job streams which include local batch, remote batch, and interactive terminal processing. The modularity and design concept of the ASC allows for processor expansion capability to meet expanding problem or volume requirements. The supporting software system accomodates any such expansion requirements with upward compatibility.

The ASC System incorporates several significant hardware and software features. Important hardware features include:

- High-speed, pipelining, or streaming central processor with both vector and scalar instructions.
- A peripheral processor system with eight independent virtual processors.
- Memory control unit with 640 million word/sec transfer capability, memory mapping without time penalty and memory protection.
- Interleaved, semiconductor active element, high-speed central memory with 400 million word/sec bandwidth.
- Optional multimillion word semiconductor active element central memory extension.
- Multiple high-speed data channels.
- Large, high-speed 25 million-word fixed head disks.

Important software features include:

- An operating system which executes exclusively in the peripheral processor.

- A FORTRAN compiler which produces object code optimized for both the vector and scalar capabilities of the central processor.
- A table-driven, multiprocessor, general-purpose operating system which is structured as a hierarchy of control components and system tasks executing entirely in the virtual processors.
- An extensive, tree-structured file management system incorporating a thorough file privacy feature.

The configuration in Figure M-1 illustrates the role of the memory control unit (MCU) as a control and "cross bar" switch between the memory and all of the processors and control units which are interfaced through the MCU ports. The high data transfer rate is accomplished by the MCU multiport design. Each of the ports on either side of the MCU can sustain a data transfer rate of 80 million 32-bit words/sec. When optional central memory extension is installed, an additional memory port is utilized, as shown in Figure M-1. The MUC ports are designed to operate on an asynchronous basis and will, therefore, support multiple data transfer rate requirements.

The design of the MCU is such that should faster memories become available, or a requirement develop for more processors, higher data transfer rates can be accommodated. The eight interleaved memory modules, each connected to its own MCU port, can maintain a total data transfer rate of 400M words/sec, which is considerably below the total capacity of the MCU. The 400M word transfer rate is twice that required in support of a central processor with four arithmetic units (four-pipeline CP) when processing vector instructions.

The MCU also contains the necessary hardware for controlling access to memory. This memory protection is accomplished by mapping and bounds registers. The mapping registers prevent different programs from interfering with each other's memory areas and allow the use of discontiguous memory pages without execution time penalty. The bounds registers permit or protect various classifications of access (e.g., read only) to mapped memory by an individual program.

The central processor (CP) consists of a pipelined instruction processing unit (IPU) which controls one, two, or four memory buffer units (MBUs) each with a corresponding pipelined arithmetic unit (AU). To ensure a continuous flow of instructions from memory, the IPU has two 8-word buffers. One buffer contains the current set of instructions and the other receives the next set of eight instructions from memory. All instruction processing except that part performed by the arithmetic unit is accomplished in the four-level IPU. Each MBU contains three pairs of 8-word buffer registers: one pair for each of two input operands and a third pair for an output operand. The buffers serve to allow overlapped, interleaved

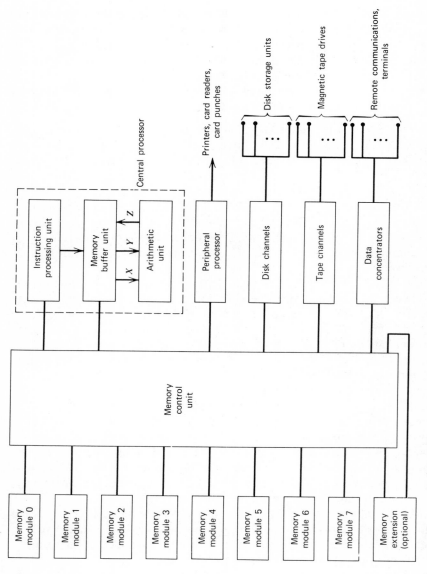

Figure M-1 A single-pipeline ASC system configuration.

memory access for each of the vector operands. Each AU consists of an eight-level arithmetic processing pipeline interfaced with its associated MBU.

The peripheral processor (PP) logical organization is shown in Figure M-2 with its eight virtual processors. The principle function of the PP is to serve as the processor for executing the operating system which provides the control facility for the entire ASC System—all peripheral devices, direct access storage, and the central processor.

Each virtual processor (VP) acts as a stand-alone computer having its own instruction and control capabilities. All VPs share a common arithmetic unit and a read-only-memory, used for frequently used OS instruction sequences. A buffer with associated control is utilized to allow overlapped memory access among VPs. A communication register (CR) file of 64 32-bit registers within the PP is utilized to transfer control and status information between the PP and other processors or control units. The CR file is accessible to all VPs and the devices requiring control information, e.g. disk channel controller.

The principal secondary storage for the ASC System is a disk storage system. Disk channel controllers, appropriately configured to support the system requirements, control the disk system.

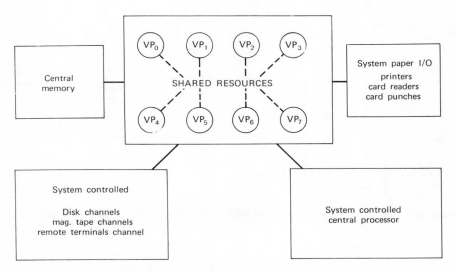

Figure M-2   Logical organization of the peripheral processor.

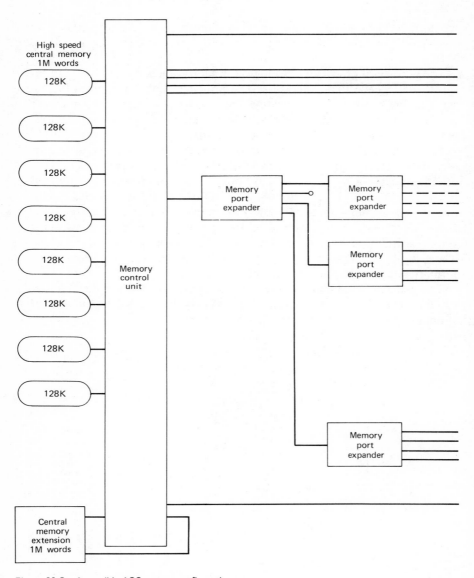

Figure M-3 A possible ASC system configuration.

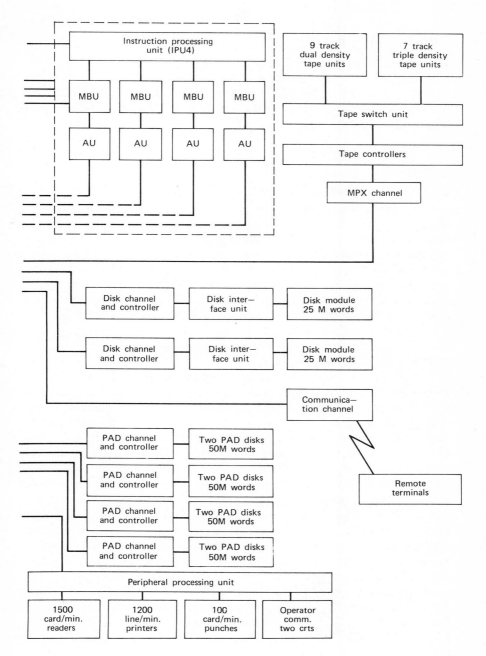

FUNCTIONAL UNITS

This section describes the characteristics of individual subsystems of the ASC configuration. The hardware configuration block diagram in Figure M-3 is used as a basis for this discussion. This configuration is considered reasonably typical for a general-purpose scientific environment having large computational requirements.

Central Processor

While the central processor (CP) shown in Figure M-3 is a four-pipeline CP, one- or two-pipeline CPs are available when computational requirements do not warrant the capacity of the four parallel arithmetic units. The basic structure of the CP, shown in Figure M-4 has three major components: the instruction processing unit (IPU) for nonarithmetic stages of instruction processing for the CP instruction stream, the memory buffer unit (MBU) to provide operand interfacing with the central memory, and an arithmetic unit (AU) to perform the specified arithmetic or logical operations. Figure M-4 shows diagrams for two- and four-pipeline CPs, each with a corresponding number of MBU-AU pairs. Note that a memory port is required for the IPU and, in addition, one memory port for each pipeline (MBU-AU pair) in a CP.

The pipeline or streaming concept, which allows many mutually exclusive instructions to be processed in an overlapped sequential manner, is applied throughout the CP. The CP utilizes an instruction pipeline for decoding and processing the classical scalar instructions. In addition, the vector instruction capability makes full use of the pipeline technique within each arithmetic unit, as do certain sequences of scalar instructions. The primary clock cycle of the CP is 60 nsecs; therefore, when the pipeline concept is most effectively employed, an arithmetic result is available every 60 nsec cycle time from each AU.

The CP is a vector as well as scalar processor. The scalar capabilities include an extensive set of Load and Store instructions: halfword, fullword, and doubleword instructions, with immediate, magnitude, and negative operand capabilities. Ability to load and store register files and to load effective addresses is also available. Arithmetic scalars include various adds, subtract, multiply, and divide for halfword (16-bit) and fullword (32-bit) fixed point numbers and fullword and doubleword (64-bit) floating point numbers. Scalar logical instructions include variations of AND, OR, and EXCLUSIVE OR. Shift capabilities for arithmetic and logical operands are provided together with circular shifts. Various comparison instructions and combination comparison-logical instructions are provided for halfword, fullword, and doublewords. Many combinations of test and branching instructions with incrementing or decrementing capability are also available. Stacking and modifying arithmetic registers can be done with single instructions. Subroutine linkage is accomplished through Branch and Load instructions. Format conversion for single and doublewords, as well as normalize instructions, are available.

The vector capabilities of the CP are made available through the use of VECTL (vector after loading vector parameter file) and VECT (assumes parameter file is already loaded) instructions. The vector repertoire includes such arithmetic operations as add, subtract, multiply, divide, vector dot product martix multiplication, and others for both fixed point and floating point representation. Vector instructions are also available for shifting, logical operations, comparisons, format conversions, normalization, and special operations such as merge, order, search, peak pick, select, and replace, among others.

One important characteristic of the vector instruction capability is the ability to encompass *three* dimensions of addressability within a single vector instruction. This is equivalent to a nest of three indexing loops in a conventional machine. An 8-word addressable register group (vector

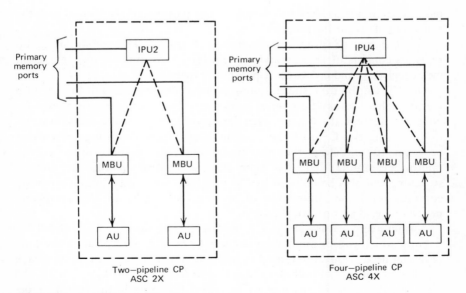

Two—pipeline CP
ASC 2X

Four—pipeline CP
ASC 4X

Figure M-4   Basic structure of the CP.

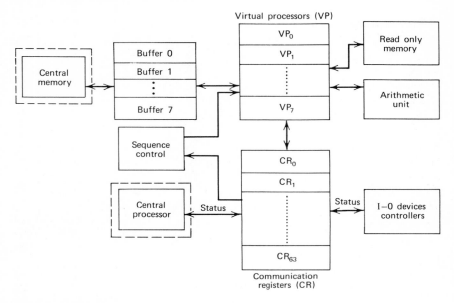

Figure M-5 Peripheral processor.

parameter file) is utilized for storage of the parameters associated with the execution of vector instructions.

The CP has 48 program-addressable registers. This group of 32-bit registers consists of 16 base address registers, 16 arithmetic registers, eight index registers, and eight vector parameter registers.

The CP can be time sliced among many programs through the use of a feature called automatic context switching. The operating system can invoke an interrupt at any time, even during the execution of a vector instruction, causing the CP to switch automatically from executing the current program to executing the next program. This feature supports both multiprogramming and real time process control. Automatic context switching can also be invoked by CP programs when they cannot correctly continue until the completion of services performed by the peripheral processor resident operating system.

A significant feature of the CP hardware is an operand look-ahead capability which causes memory references to be requested prior to the time of actual need. Double buffering in multiple 8-word (octet) buffers for each pipeline provides a smooth data flow to and from each arithmetic unit. The pipelined AU achieves its highest sustained flow rate in the vector mode, typically, a result each 60 nsec/AU.

The Peripheral Processor

The peripheral processor (PP) is a multiprocessor designed to perform the control and data management functions of the ASC. Several aspects of the implementation of the peripheral processor concept contribute to the effectiveness of the ASC System. Figure M-5 shows the logical organization of the PP.

The PP is a collection of eight individual processors called virtual processors (VPs). Each VP has its own program counter along with arithmetic, index, base and instruction registers. The eight VPs share a read only memory, an arithmetic unit, an instruction processing unit, and a central memory buffer. Use of the common units is distributed among the VPs using 16 single 85 nsec cycles. When an equally distributed sequence of time units is used, each of the eight VPs receives two 85 nsec cycles/1.4 μsec. The typical PP instruction requires two 85 nsec cycles for completion. The distribution of available time units can be varied to suit particular processing requirements.

The read only memory within the PP is utilized for program storage and execution of those short routines which are highly utilized by the VPs, such as polling loops. The ROM consists of 4K 32-bit words of nonvolatile memory elements with a cycle time of less than 85 nsec.

Because the PP is intended to perform control functions rather than execute mathematical algorithms, the instruction set is oriented toward control operations and does not require multiplication, division, or floating point operations. The instruction format is similar to that of the central processor, using a 32-bit word for each instruction. Instructions are provided for bit (1-bit), byte (8-bits), halfword (16-bits), and fullword (32-bits) operations.

Each VP has direct access to the entire central memory for program execution and data storage. Therefore, a single copy of reentrant code can be executed simultaneously by more than one VP.

The communication register (CR) file contains 64 32-bit word registers which are program addressable by the VPs. The CR file serves as the principal storage media for control information necessary for the coordination of all parts of the ASC System. Synchronization of communications is achieved between all processors (CP, VPs, channel controllers, and peripheral unit controllers) from interpretation of status bits received from all devices into the CR file.

Central Memory System

The CM of the ASC System consists of a MCU and appropriately sized modules of high-speed central memory and central memory extension.

The MCU is organized as a two-way 256-bit/channel (8-word) parallel access traffic net between eight independent processor ports and nine memory busses, with each processor port having full accessibility to all memories. The nine memory busses are organized to provide eight-way interleaving for the first eight busses with the ninth buss used for central memory extension. The MCU provides the facilities for controlling access from the eight processor ports to a CM having a 24-bit address space (16 million words). A memory port expander is utilized to expand the number of processor ports.

The MCU is designed to operate asynchronously, independent of cable delays, processor clock rates, and memory unit access and cycle times. This capability allows for flexibility to accommodate improvements in memory or processor technologies which may occur in the future. The MCU is capable of handling a maximum data transfer rate of 80 million words/sec/port, giving a total transfer capacity of 640M words/sec. Therefore, a capacity significantly beyond today's memory and processor speeds is available in the MCU.

The high-speed central memory is an active element memory having a cycle time of 160 nsec. Additionally, all transfers are 256 bits (eight words) with a Hamming Code such that single bit errors in each transfer block are detected and corrected, while double bit errors are detected but not corrected. High-speed central memory is typically divided into eight equal sized modules which allow for eight-way interleaving. However, a patch board within the MCU controls the memory address decoding and less than eight-way interleaving is allowable should circumstances warrant.

Central memory extension (CME), available as an option, provides for large amounts of medium speed low-cost memory to be utilized in support of high-speed central memory. This type of memory is an active element memory with a cycle time of 1 μsec. The CME is also accessed in 8-word increments, utilizing a hamming code for detection of bit errors with the automatic correction of single bit errors. CME is a part of the directly addressable memory and, therefore, may be addressed by any processor or channel controller for instructions or operands. It is also possible to effect block transfers of information between high-speed CM and CME. This is made possible because CME has both a normal memory buss and a memory access port to the MCU. The block transfer initiated by the PP specifies the two memory addresses and the number of words to be transferred. The CME transfers the data autonomously at 40M words/sec and informs the PP when the transfer is complete.

Central memory size is limited only by the 24-bit address (16 megawords). The proportions of fast CM and CME may be varied to balance memory capacities to suit the particular work load and problem solution requirements. High-speed CM in excess of 1 million words, in conjunction with several million words of CME, would be appropriate for many of the more recent applications.

Central memory management and access control by devices (processors and control units) on memory ports is achieved through the use of two facilities: map registers and protect registers. Each user program has its own unique page address map. Page addresses not required by the program are mapped into absolute page zero which is not accessible to the CP. When a program is loaded into memory, it will, in all probability, be loaded into discontiguous memory pages. During program execution, program developed page addresses are converted, without execution time penalty, to the actual page addresses by the map registers. Because a reference to page zero is denied and the relevant processor notified the map registers provide for interuser memory protection. Figure M-6 shows the schematic method of memory mapping. The ability to segment memory by pages among many programs in a discontiguous manner allows for very ef-

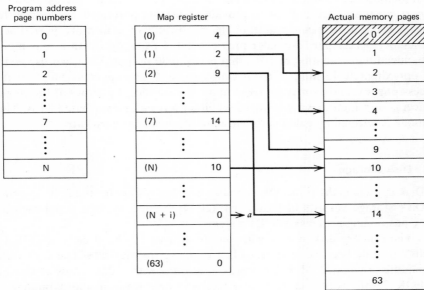

[a]A request for actual page 0 is referred to the operating system for resolution (invalid request, error, etc.)

Figure M-6 Memory mapping.

ficient memory utilization. Page size is a function of the size of central memory and the problem mix of a particular installation. Four different page sizes may be specified for an ASC system, varying from 4K 256K words. A program may utilize any one of the page sizes available.

The protect registers allow for intrauser protection. These registers consist of three pairs of bounds registers for defining the upper and lower addresses of access for read, write, or execute areas. The five combinations of protection presently used by the system software with the bounds register are as follows:

- Execute only.
- Read only.
- Execute, read, no write.
- Read, write, no execute.
- Read, write, execute.

An attempt to reference an area out of bounds for a particular control state is denied and the processor notified of the attempted violation.

In large ASC Systems, more processors and control units require access to memory than there are individual memory ports. In these cases, memory port expanders are utilized to provide additional ports and are utilized to service the devices not requiring the bandwidth of a memory port. Each memory access port expander provides a 1–4 expansion with a maximum bandwidth degradation of 10%, that is, from 80 million 32-bit words/sec to approximately 72 million 32-bit words/sec with an expander. Memory access port expanders may be treed upon one another. Priorities at the single access port interface are resolved on either a fixed or distributed basis. The mode is selected by patch card wiring in the expander hardware.

Disk Storage

Disk storage is the principal secondary storage system for the ASC system. Disk storage consists of head-per-track (H/T) disk systems supplemented by positioning arm disk (PAD) systems.

The primary disk system will contain at least one head-per-track (H/T) disk module because of its very fast effective transfer rate. The H/T disk module provides 25M 32-bit words of storage with a data transfer rate of 490K 32-bit words/sec and an effective access time of approximately 5 μsec. Generally, two to four modules of H/T disk storage are considered necessary for a balanced configuration.

The secondary disk system may consist of a number of modules of positioning arm disk (PAD). PAD modules are available in a wide variety of storage capacities and different effective transfer rates. PAD systems have a lower effective transfer rate when compared to the H/T systems for randomly access data.

The H/T disk system is a high performance device whose effective performance is further enhanced because the operating system utilizes a shortest access time first (SATF) algorithm for data transfers. This combination of hardware and software provides a very high effective transfer rate. A typical ASC system will include two to four H/T disk modules plus an appropriate number of PAD modules.

The magnetic tape system is controlled by configuring multiplexer channels and control devices to match the data handling requirements of the system. Generally, simultaneously access to any four magnetic tape transports of the system is adequate. Either seven or nine-track transports with the standard recording densities are available. A wide range of data transfer rates, up to 180K bytes/sec, may be selected.

The remote terminal communication system is controlled by configuring a data concentrator controller approximately to service the necessary terminal network. Because this concentrator-controller is a programmable system (TI 980 computer), most types of terminal devices can be accommodated. Presently, a batch terminal with interactive capabilities (printer, card reader/punch, tape drives, display consoles, data tablet, and function keyboard) is supported.

Standard card readers/punches, line printers, and operator's console (two CRTs) with required capacity may be attached to the peripheral processor which acts as the control and channel for paper input/output equipment.

Channels

The ASC system employs several types of channel control devices which have been structured to service various storage or terminal devices attachable to the system. The channel devices provide the interface and control between the MCU Port and the controllers for the various storage or terminal devices. Each channel is dependent on a controller for transfer of data and, once initiated, operates independently of the central or peripheral processors. It is typical when configuring an ASC system to have data channels attached to a memory port expander.

A high-speed data channel is utilized to service those devices with high-speed data transfer capabilities, that is., disks. The channel also has the capability to read and write data to discontiguous memory locations.

The multiplexor channel provides the interface to service medium-speed devices. The multiplexor performs time division multiplexing between memory and from one to four controllers. The multiplexer consists of five octets of 32-bit word buffers, four sub-channel buffers (SCBs)—one for each controller—and a channel buffer. The channel buffer interfaces with the MCU, and the four SCBs interface with the controllers.

SYSTEM SOFTWARE

The ASC software consists of several language processors—Fortran, Job Specification Language, Linkage Editor, Meta-Assembler—in addition to a comprehensive operating system.

The ASC Fortran is a superset of the ANSI Standard including many extensions applicable to the CP vector instruction capability. The extensions are natural to the language and give the user greater programming capabilities in the notation used to define solutions to mathematical problems. The object code produced is optimized to exploit both the pipeland concept and hardware vector instructions within the CP. Scalar code is reordered to achieve optimal overlap of instruction execution in the pipelined instruction and arithmetic processing units. The compiler not only performs a diagnosis of source programs, issuing appropriate messages where applicable, but also issues informative messages defining where optimization could not be achieved due to source program structure.

The ASC general purpose operating system design is a highly modular structure of control components and system tasks which are executed entirely within the PP's VPs. Thus the powerful arithmetic capabilities of the CP are reserved for the user and not utilized for overhead type control functions normally associated with operating system activities.

Modularity is achieved by defining fundamental operating system work units (tasks) in very small increments. Many of these work units are then gathered together in different combinations to accomplish the system processing requirements. Standardized and common interface methods are utilized by all modules. The result is an improvable and extendible software system—improvable because modules identified as using significant amounts of time, space, or both can be modified without impacting the remainder of the system, and extendible because the rigidly enforced common interface makes the addition of new modules performing new functions transparent.

System tasks are implemented as reentrant code modules designed to execute in any VP for very short time intervals, averaging approximately 1 msec. This time constraint eliminates the need for frequent interrupts and the resulting overhead required to save and restore processing states. Task-to-task linkage is performed at execution time by a control component. All tasks are scheduled for execution according to a simple priority, thereby achieving the results required in conventional interrupt driven systems by allowing each function to proceed without interruption at a rate determined by its relative priority among all active functions.

Tasks are aligned in logical groups called system commands. Many tasks are members of several commands, and one task code module can be simultaneously and asynchronously executing as two or more activations of the same command and/or of several different commands.

Commands are those elements of user and/or system programs which require accomplishment of a function. Some examples of such functions include: (1) opening a file, (2) reading a logical record from disk, and (3) loading a program. Most commands are elements of several such functions. All such functions are defined as command sequences in a CM resident system table. This table is interpreted by one of the control components and results in highly centralized control of the ASC. Existing functions can be modified and new functions added by modifying this table. Additional programming is required only if the necessary building blocks, in the form of commands and their tasks, are required. Such an addition is facilitated by the already mentioned modularity and rigidly enforced interfaces.

The Job Specification Language allows the user to program the job management and support activities required of the operating system in a user-oriented language structure and format. The ASC software includes a comprehensive file management system. A tree structure is used which allows cataloging of files at all nodes of the trees, not at the terminal branches alone. Therefore, many different files can be included in each path through the tree allowing for many user-defined file structures.

An elaborate file privacy feature allows owners of files to restrict either access to files at a node or traversal through the node. Therefore, users of a catalog of files may be restricted on an individual file basis or to certain parts of a catalog structure.

The meta assembler has an extensive macro capability and assembles code for both the CP and the PP. This type of assembler allows for definition of other object machine characteristics and, therefore, an assembler for any other object machine is readily definable. In addition, special requirements for CP or PP assembly language extensions are readily implemented.

The Linkage Editor provides the standard functions required for the creation of load modules from separate object code modules. In addition, this processor allows for load time binding of memory and provides an automatic overlay capability.

APPENDIX N
SPERRY RAND CORPORATION
UNIVAC 1108 COMPUTER SYSTEM

INTRODUCTION TO CONFIGURATION ORGANIZATION

The UNIVAC 1108 computer system is a general purpose uni- and multi-processor system whose modularity permits the selection of systems components to fulfill the speed and capacity requirements for applications ranging from a basic job-shop system to the comprehensive public utility computing complex. The responsibility for centralized control is borne by the software system designated "Exec-8 System." The "Exec-8 System" is designed to support various operational environments (e.g., batch, time-sharing, real-time, and multiprogramming) so that no penalties are imposed on any one of these activities by the support provided for the others. Also, an installation not required to support the full range of activities may specify capabilities to be eliminated at system generation.

In the minimum multiprocessing configuration this computer system consists of two central processor units (CPU), two banks of main storage (each with 65K words 36-bits), and one I/O controller. Modular expandability allows the addition to this configuration of one more CPU, two more 65K banks of memory, and one more I/O controller. The interconnection of the major units within the computer system is shown in Figure N-1.

The 1108 system is organized to allow multiple processors to perform a number of tasks simultaneously. Within the system, each functional unit has more than one access path and priority logic resolves possible access conflicts. The failure of any individual component within the system will not prevent continued operation of the system and system components are logically removable for servicing without disabling the system.

In the 1108 system each processor has the capability to perform all functions required for the execution of instructions including arithmetic, I/O, and executive control. Included in each processor is its own set of control registers providing accumulators, index registers, I/O access control registers, and special-use registers.

The I/O controller (IOC) is an independent processor used in the 1108 system to expand the I/O capabilities of the system. The IOC contains up to sixteen bi-directional (36-bit) high-speed I/O channels. The IOC provides independent access to main storage and data chaining capabilities and has its own high speed index memory for buffer control. Part of the hardware within the IOC consists of three groups of registers:

- Sixteen pointer registers used to point to the location in main storage of the function word which directs the IOC operation.

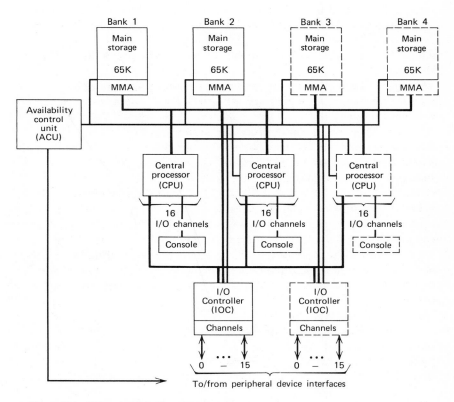

Figure N-1 UNIVAC 1108 multiprocessor system.

- Sixty-four external function and internally specified index (ISI) data access control registers.
- One hundred ninety-two communications externally specified index (ESI) access control registers (optionally expandable by 256 additional registers).

ISI registers are used for I/O channels connected to peripheral subsystems such as magnetic tape, magnetic drums, printers, and punched card equipment.

ESI registers are used for data transfers to and from communications subsystems. When operating in ESI mode, data flow for each communication line terminal is governed by its own data access control word in index memory.

Main storage of the 1108 system is expandable in 65K word increments up to a maximum of 262,144 36-bit words. Main storage read/restore cycle time is 750 nsec and up to four logical banks for instruction/data reference overlapping provide the capability for an effective cycle time of 375 nsec. Also, two-way interleaving (odd, even locations) of the two storage modules within each bank is possible to reduce the probability of access conflicts.

Auxiliary storage for the 1108 system consists primarily of up to eight magnetic drum devices which are attached to the system through one or two control units.

Characteristic of the multiprocessor systems is the sharing of all the main storage and all I/O subsystems by all processors. Access to main storage is provided by multiple module access units (MMA) and to I/O subsystems by shared peripheral interface (SPI).

Input/output subsystems within the 1108 system may be either single- or dual-channel with single-channel subsystems performing one I/O operation at a time and dual channel subsystems having the capability of executing two operations simultaneously using different peripheral units.

A programmable interval timer of 18 bits is provided within the system. The cycle time is 200 μsecs, and each time this period elapses the contents of the timer is decremented by 1. When the clock reaches zero an interrupt is generated.

An important unit within the 1108 system is the availability control unit (ACU). Because of system availability requirements, the multiprocessor system must provide a means for partitioning the system for specific jobs or maintenance. The ACU performs this and the other functions listed below.

- Partitions multiprocessor into independent systems.

- Takes units off-line for maintenance without disrupting system operation.
- Protects main storage in event of power failure in the CPUs or IOCs.
- Automatically initiates a recovery sequence after a failure.

The ACU partitions the hardware into specific configurations by disabling and enabling the interface between units. It can set up as many as three logically independent configurations which run concurrently under control of the executive system. The possible configurations can be prespecified for a given site. At the same time, the ACU can take units off-line for maintenance. The ACU is an independent unit with its own power supply logically situated between the peripheral subsystems, the central processors, I/O controllers, and main storage. It can interface with three central processors through one I/O channel of each, two IOCs, four banks of main storage, and six multiple-access peripheral subsystems. Additional peripheral subsystems, to a maximum of 24, can be added in groups of six. The ACU includes a control panel, physically located at the operator's console, that indicates all partitioning currently in effect and also shows which units are off-line. It also has manual controls to switch units on- or off-line. The automatic recovery sequence is based on a resettable system timer in the ACU. The period of this timer can be set to times varying from one to fifteen seconds. Unless the executive system resets this timer within its preset period, the ACU assumes that a catastrophic malfunction has occurred and it initiates an automatic recovery sequence. The processor can then interrogate the ACU to determine which units are on-line and available for use.

The 1108 system provides an operator console for each CPU within the system. This console consists of a keyboard and CRT display, pagewriter, and a day clock. The day clock on the console displays the time of day in hours, minutes, and hundredths of minutes. It furnishes the time of day to the CPU every 600 msec and sends a day clock interrupt to the CPU every 6 secs. This clock can be manually disabled from the operator's console and in a multiprocessor system any one day clock may be selected to be active either externally or by program.

FUNCTIONAL UNITS

Processor

The UNIVAC 1108 CPU is the principal component of the multiprocessor system. Each CPU within a multiprocessor configuration performs both arithmetic and logical operations; and can accommodate up to 16 I/O channels. Partial word addressability in 6, 9, 12, and 18-bit portions as well as full-word (36-bits) and double-word (72-bits) addressing is provided by the CPUs. Overlapping performed on instruction execution allows a processor to perform approximately 610,000 instructions/sec which includes floating point instructions.

Each CPU is logically divided into six interacting sections consisting of:

- Control registers, 128 program addressable registers used for arithmetic operations, indexing, and I/O buffer control.
- Arithmetic section.
- Control section.
- I/O section, controls and multiplexes data flow between main storage and the 16 I/O channels. This section includes an interrupt priority network and paths to peripheral subsystems for signals and data.
- Indexing section, contains parallel index adders and threshold test circuitry.
- Storage class control section, receives the final operand address from the index adder and establishes address and data paths to one of eight possible storage modules.

The instruction repertoire includes data transfer instructions, fixed point arithmetic (single precision 36-bit and double precision 72-bits) floating point arithmetic (single precision, range is from 10^{38} to 10^{-37} with eight-digit precision; double precision, range is from 10^{307} to 10^{-308} with 18-digit precision), split-word arithmetic, index register instructions, logical instructions, shift instructions, repeated search instructions, unconditional and conditional jump instructions, skip instructions, and I/O instructions.

The interrupt network is the means of affecting real-time, multiprogramming, and time-sharing operations on the system. Specific interrupt locations are assigned within the lower regions of main storage for each condition. These locations are used to provide transfers to programs that capture the interrupt address and enter response subroutines in the executive system. Input/output synchronization and response to real-time situations is accomplished through some of these interrupts, while other interrupts are provided for certain error conditions within the CPU.

Each CPU has an integral I/O control section which controls transmission of data between main storage and peripheral subsystems. Data are transmitted over one of 16 bidirectional I/O channels (each channel has 72 data lines, 36 input and 36 output), and, although most peripheral subsystems are both input and output lines, data flow in only one direction on a channel for a specific I/O instruction. I/O can be performed in either of two modes: ESI for multiplexed data communications devices (operates in either 36-bit, 18-bit, or 9-bit transfer modes), and ISI for other types of peripheral equipment. All I/O channels except channel 15 (operator console) can operate in either mode depending upon a mode switch setting associated with each channel.

The internally specified index (ISI) mode provides parallel transfer of 36-bit words to and from peripheral subsystems according to the contents of input and output access control registers (ACRs) associated with a given channel in the processor. Function words sent to the subsystem specify the operation to be performed by the subsystem, so that the word count and buffer address stored in the ACR by the processor in initiating an I/O operation are associated only with a channel, not with devices connected to the subsystem. If the mode switch is set to externally specified index (ESI) for a particular channel, the ACR registers become ESI identifier register associated with lists of access control words in main storage at addresses assigned to devices multiplexed to the channel. As a device transfers data, it presents the address of its own access control word to the processor so that the control word is transferred from main storage to the subsystem each time data is transferred under control of the subsystem. After the access control word is modified by the subsystem to indicate that data have been transferred, the control word is returned to main storage until the next data from the same source arrive. For each data transfer to or from main storage, three processor memory references are required, two for the access control word and one for the data, which either an 18-bit halfword or a 9-bit byte. Chaining of data buffers for scatter read/gather write operations is not available in the processor ISI mode. The two modes of processor I/O can be summarized by noting that in the ISI mode the processor associates a single buffer control register internally with a particular channel, while in the ESI mode, one of many buffer control registers is associated externally with, or specified by, one of the many devices multiplexed to a channel.

Input/output operations are arranged in sequence by a priority control network and although all sixteen I/O channels may be available for data transmission at the same time, only one channel can communicate with the CPU at any given instant.

Primary Storage

The basic storage module of the 1108 System includes 32K words of ferrite core array. Each word is 36 bits, and carries two additional parity bits, one bit for each half word. Parity is checked on reading or calculated on writing for each storage access. When a parity error is detected, the storage bank sends a parity error interrupt to the processor that it is serving and rewrites the word in its incorrect form to ensure subsequent data errors and thereby facilitate fault isolation.

The minimum core configuration for a multiprocessor 1108 system consists of two banks of 65K core, each bank composed of two 32K modules. This configuration is expandable in 65K increments up to 262K words of memory. Main storage (MS) provides a 750-nsec read/restore cycle time with access by up to three processors and two IOCs to each 32K module.

This access feature is implemented by a multiple module access unit (MMA). This unit furnishes five priority ordered paths to each 32K module within a bank. If access conflicts occur, the MMA grants storage access to the request having the highest priority, then the next, and so on. Communications between a processor and a single storage module can, therefore, be asynchronous. Since delays in honoring I/O transfer can result in undesirable lost drum cycles, rereading or rewriting on tape, or actual loss of data in the case of real-time input, IOCs are ordinarily attached to the higher priority inputs of the MMA, followed by CPUs.

Hardware storage protection is provided through lockout boundaries establishable in 512-word increments. The controlling element in this feature is the storage limits register (SLR). The SLR is loaded by the executive system to establish allowable operating areas for the program currently in execution. Before each main storage reference, the processor performs a limits check on either the instruction area or or the data area. An out-of-limits address generates a guard mode interrupt, allowing the executive to regain control and take appropriate action. Two different modes of control can be established by the 1108 System. One of the modes is privileged mode which protects against out-of-bounds writes by privileged programs (such as real-time programs, or executive-controlled subroutines) which may enter nonalterable subroutines, which are part of the executive. The other mode is user program mode in which read, write, and jump storage protection is in effect.

Relative addressing and dynamic program relocatability in main storage is provided through program base registers. Relative addressing allows storage assignments for one program to be changed dynamically to provide continuous storage for operation of another program, and it permits programs to dynamically request additional storage according to processing needs.

Two special techniques are provided for referencing the main storage modules to increase performance and to reduce the occurence of multiprocessor access conflicts. The first is called overlapping and enables the CPU to retrieve the current operand and the next instruction simultaneously; the second is called interleaving and enables two processors (CPUs, IOCs or CPU and IOC) to access a pair of modules with minimum access conflicts.

Within the main storage configuration, it is possible to remove a 65K bank of core from operation for on-line maintenance without stopping the entire system.

Input/Output Control Module

The input/output controller (IOC), Figure N-2, is an independent device that controls the operation of up to 16 peripheral subsystems under the direction of as many as three different CPUs. The IOC is functionally similar to the I/O section of the CPU discussed previously. Once an I/O request has been issued to it, the controller is in complete control of the operation, transferring data between main storage and the peripherals without further attention from the CPU that originated the request.

Both the ISI and ESI modes are provided by the IOC, but differ somewhat in their implementation from the I/O section of the CPU as described above. As shown in Figure N-2, the IOC is equipped with a 256-word index memory, expandable to 512 words, which contains the access control words for both ISI and ESI data transfer. These control words correspond to the ESI access control words held in main storage for use by the processor I/O section. Their use results in only a single memory reference for each ESI data transfer, as opposed to the three references for processor ESI data transfer. In addition, scatter/gather data chaining operations are possible in the ESI mode, unlike the processor ISI mode. The ESI mode effectively provides a multiplexed subchannel environment for channels operating in that mode, so that communications subsystems connected to the communication terminal module controller can be serviced through a single I/O channel without disturbing the program sequence of the processor.

The 1108 multiprocessor system includes one or two IOCs each of which controls its own group of peripheral subsystems with each IOC providing a direct path between main storage and 4, 8, 12, or 16 high-speed, bidirectional data channels. Each channel has a data transfer rate of 1,333,000 words/sec for all channels.

Data transfers proceed between peripheral devices and main storage, independent of the CPUs, allowing the CPUs more time for processing. No direct peripheral-to-peripheral transfers are possible and all transfers must be buffered in main storage.

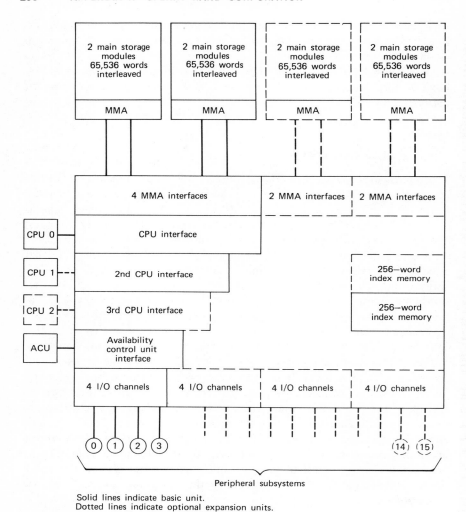

Figure N-2   The UNIVAC 1108 I/O controller

Reference should be made to the UNIVAC 1110 and the UNIVAC AN/UYK–7 discussions for descriptions of similar I/O buffering techniques. In particular, the 1110 system provides ESI and ISI data transfer modes only in the input/output access unit (IOAU), not within a CPU as in the 1108. However, the 1110 IOAU can accommodate up to 24 channels and provides data buffer chaining in both I/O modes, while the 1108 IOC services only 16 channels, with buffer chaining available only in the ISI mode. The AN/UYK–7 also does not provide CPUs with I/O capability, as in the 1108, but does provide a normal buffer mode and ESI mode similar to the 1108 ISI and ESI modes, respectively. In addition, the AN/UYK–7 input/output controller provides an externally specified address (ESA) mode and an intercomputer mode which offer additional means of data transfer control not found in either the 1108 or 1110 systems.

Mass Storage or Secondary Storage

Various mass storage options are available with the 1108 system. These options consist essentially of high speed large-capacity magnetic drums varying in access times from 4.3 to 17.0 msec and in storage capacity from 262K words (36-bits) to 22,000K words (36-bits). The characteristics of these mass storage devices are shown in Figure N-3.

Storage capacity	262,144 computer words of 36 data bits plus parity bits, or 1,572,864 alphanumeric characters per drum
Average access time	4.3 msec
Drum speed	7200 rpm
Number of read/write heads	432, one per track
Character transfer rates	1,440,000; 720,000; 360,000; 180,000; 90,000
Word transfer rates	240,000; 120,000; 60,000; 30,000; 15,000
I/O channels required	One per subsystem
Number of drums per subsystem	3 to 9 (14,155,776 characters maximum)
Storage capacity	2,097,152 computer words of 36 data bits plus parity bits, or 12,582,912 alphanumeric characters per drum
Average access time	17 msec
Drum speed	1800 rpm
Number of read/write heads	1782 (33 blocks with 54 heads per block)
Character transfer rates	1,440,000; 720,000; 360,000; 180,000; 90,000
Word transfer rates	240,000; 120,000; 60,000; 30,000; 15,000
I/O channels required	One of two per subsystem
Number of drums per subsystem (max.)	Eight (total of 100,663,296 characters)

Storage capacity (per unit)	220,020,096 words of 132,120,576 alphanumeric characters
Average access time	92 msec
Recording density	1000 bits/in.
Tracks per inch	106
Drum speed	870 rpm
Movable read/write heads	64
Character transfer rate	153,540 characters/sec
Word transfer rate	25,590 words/sec
Fastbands (fixed read/write heads)	24
Fastband average access time	35 msec
Fastband storage capacity (per unit)	258,048 characters
Write lockout protection	Yes
I/O channels	One or two per subsystem
Number of units per subsystem	8 (1,056,964,608 characters/subsystem)

Figure 3   Characteristics of drum subsystem.

SYSTEM SOFTWARE

Job Control

Dispatching and resource allocation is a component of Exec 8, the executive software system, and are designated as the supervisor. This component controls the sequencing, setup, and execution of all runs entering the 1108 system. It is designed to control the execution of a large number of programs without interaction among them.

There are three levels of scheduling within the supervisor; coarse scheduling, dynamic allocation of storage space, and CPU dispatching. Runs (the 1108 term for a complete job) entering the system are sorted into files which are used by the supervisor for run scheduling and processing. The coarse scheduling of each run depends upon run priority and facility requirements. The dynamic allocator takes runs set up by the coarse scheduler and allots storage space according to the needs of the run. When time-sharing of main storage is appropriate, the allocator initiates "storage swaps." This swapping function is performed between drum and main storage and is used only to provide reasonable response time to demand-processing terminals. Storage compaction is performed by the executive system but only if a large enough contiguous area of core is not available.

The dispatching routine is a third level of scheduling; it determines which task in main storage should receive CPU time and performs a switching function from one task to another. Usually a batch program will be allowed to use CPU time until it becomes interlocked against some event or a higher priority program(s) require CPU time.

The disposition of available facilities are indicated to the system at system generation time; the executive system assigns these facilities as needed and as available. This is done by maintaining current inventory tables indicating facilities available for assignment and the runs currently using the unavailable facilities.

Operator communication with the system is through a display keyboard and CRT. The executive system displays information such as current system load and operator requests associated with I/O setup and I/O interlocks. Also, the operator can request information such as backlog status.

I/O Control

Input/output operations are controlled by means of a central I/O routine, which accepts and queues requests and interrupts and gives control to the I/O device handler when appropriate. References to I/O control result in a transfer to the handler routine controlling the device referenced. The handler, in turn, considers the request and queues it for the particular I/O subsystem. When the subsystem becomes free, an entry is removed from the subsystem queue and the handler is entered at the appropriate point. Queuing is by-passed if the subsystem is initially free.

The executive system classifies an I/O request into one of three catagories depending on the activity which submitted the I/O request. The three categories are assigned priorities and all requests in one category are completed before any request is honored from the next lower category. The order of priority is real-time, executive, and demand/batch. Look ahead techniques are used within a category whenever appropriate so that the average execution time for I/O requests may be reduced.

The executive system classifies an I/O request into one of three interface the unit record equipment of the 1108 (all standard terminals, card readers, card punches, printers, paper tape readers, and paper tape punches) with the user program. Data to and from these devices are thus buffered on mass storage to provide an effective linkage to the asynchronous and relative slow devices.

For magnetic tape, mass storage, and communication devices, the system provides both single buffer and buffer pool capabilities. The pool can contain any desired number of buffers. The single buffer mode of execution is the most efficient, as there is little supervisor overhead involved. The single buffer mode will also use slightly less core storage per buffer, because the pool mode requires additional storage areas for pool control information. Separate buffer pools are maintained for data files and for communication devices. For each cataloged file assigned to a job, there must be an associated buffer pool. A buffer pool may be assigned to one particular file or it may be assigned to many files. The size of each buffer must be equal to the maximum block size specified for the file plus three extra words for control purposes. A buffer pool for use with the communication handler may be established in any portion of the core storage area which the user may elect to set aside as an I/O area.

The data handling routines are designed to process a wide variety of file formats. Few restrictions are placed on formats acceptable to the system. Files may be processed at the item, record, or block levels, with general disregard for the physical characteristics of the I/O device assigned. File access may be either random or sequential. Each file is defined by file format and item definitions. The item control table enables the user to access any item of a record on request.

A teleprocessing subsystem is available within the resident executive to handle all communications processing for a large number of independent terminals. The communications handler supports two other modes of operation. The first level consists of a buffer handling mode in which the handler supervises transmitting and receiving messages on a buffer by buffer basis with no assumption concerning the content of each buffer. The second level of support assumes a system defined format on devices capable of acknowledging transmission.

Demand mode processing is initiated and controlled by the executive control language. Commands are input via the user's remote console on a conversational basis. Provisions are also made for: (1) dialed communication connections in addition to leased lines and remote consoles on site; (2) paper tape input allowing pretyped command programs for high transmission efficiency; and (3) user communications with the computer center, other consoles, and the executive system itself.

Input symbionts operating in the demand mode normally accept data input from a remote terminal. Thus the rate of input to the system is subject to the descretion of the remote operator. Command input from the terminal is buffered in main storage in the same manner as the input stream from an on-site card subsystem.

The file supervisor controls the creation and maintenance of all program and data files. It also maintains an up-to-date master directory of files cataloged in the system and of the status of mass storage availability. For each file known to the system other than temporary files, an entry containing the identification and characteristics of the file is maintained by the system in a master directory of files.

File security is maintained by two keys which must be specified on an assignment statement to gain access to a cataloged file. The keys are initially obtained from the assignment statement which caused the file to be cataloged. The master directory also contains a count of the number of times the file is accessed and the time of last access. These fields along with the system log are available to the user to monitor file usage and to detect any encroachment on individual privacy.

Diagnostic Error Processing

Executive 8 maintains a standard error recovery procedure for each possible I/O malfunction which may occur. When an abnormal status is returned from an I/O operation and the user has not supressed error recovery, EXECUTIVE 8 will initiate the standard recovery procedure. In the event recovery is not successful, an error message is displayed on the console and the operator may issue specific error control instructions.

Computer/core malfunctions consist of I/O control memory parity errors, I/O data parity errors, core storage parity errors, and power failures. For I/O control memory parity errors, the executive determines whether the error is transient or permanent. If the error is transient, the I/O operation is reinitiated and control is returned to the interruption address. If the error is not transient and equipment on another channel cannot assume the responsibility of this channel, the program assigned to this channel will be terminated and the channel declared down. If a transient error exists in certain registers and the recovery routine does not use the faulty register, automatic recovery is attempted.

System processing is identical for I/O data parity errors and core storage parity errors. When a transient error occurs, the user program is given control at a restart point if one was provided. If a restart point was not provided, the program is terminated. If the error occurred within the executive and restart is impossible, the system will stop. If the error is not transient, the program interrupted is terminated and the block of memory involved is declared down. If the damaged coding was critical, the system will stop.

When a power failure occurs, the system initiates the following shutdown sequence: (1) upon occurence of the interrupt, the interrupt address and control memory are saved; channels containing I/O action are flagged; (2) if the computer is restarted without clearing, the I/O action restart flags are cleared, control memory is restored and a return is made to the interrupted address; and (3) if the computer is restarted after clearing, the flagged I/O actions are requeued on the I/O request list, control memory is restored, and control is given to the interrupted program.

A program contingency is a condition within a running program which causes a computer interrupt or psuedo interrupt. The user program may initially specify that it wishes to process such interrupts rather than accept the standard action provided by the system. The types of program contingencies recognized are illegal operation codes, privileged instructions, core storage violations, floating point overflow and underflow, divide overflow, and test and set interrupts. The test and set interrupt occurs when a user program seeks access to common data that is currently protected by another executing program.

APPENDIX O

SPERRY RAND CORPORATION
UNIVAC 1110 SYSTEM

INTRODUCTION TO CONFIGURATION ORGANIZATION

The 1110 system is composed of three basic groups of components: processors, storage, and peripheral subsystems. Each component is functionally independent and has the following properties:

- Has two or more access paths.
- Resolves access conflicts by priority logic.
- Does not prevent continued system operation if any individual component fails.
- Can be logically removed for servicing without disabling the entire system.

In the basic configuration this computer system consists of three functionally and physically independent units: two command/arithmetic units (CAU) and one input/output access unit (IOAU). The processor organization is designed for operation in a multiprogramming and multiprocessing environment. This basic processor may be expanded by adding CAUs and/or IOAUs up to a total of 4 CAUs and 4 IOAUs. The basic configuration is shown in Figure O-1.

Within the 1110 system all control and arithmetic functions are executed by the two CAUs. Each CAU is a multitask instruction-stacking device capable of controlling up to four instructions at various stages of execution. Each CAU can interface with up to four main storage units by means of either an instruction path or an operand path. Dual data paths connect each unit with extended storage through a maximum of eight multiple ac-

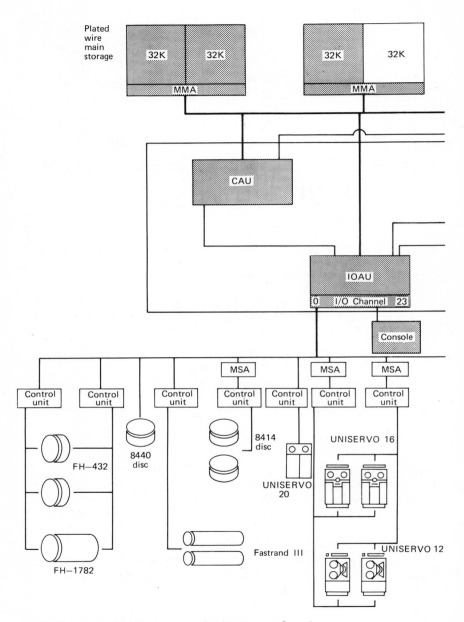

Figure 0-1 UNIVAC 1110 processor and main storage configuration.

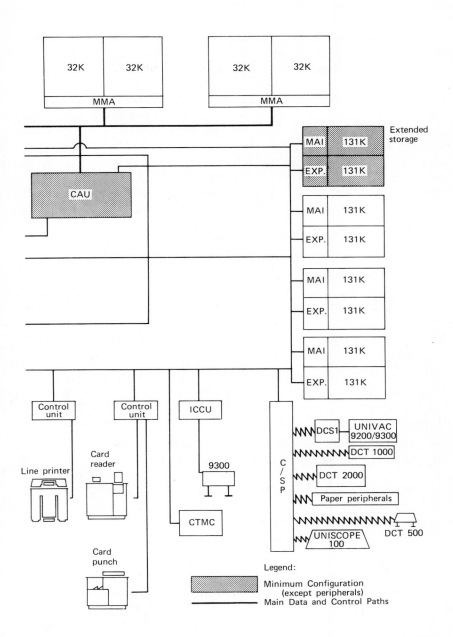

Legend:

Minimum Configuration
(except peripherals)
Main Data and Control Paths

cess interface (MAI) units. The data paths to both main and extended storage have overlapping and interleaving capabilities.

Each CAU has the capability of executing 1.8 million instructions/sec and has a basic instruction time of 300-nsec. The CAUs also provide character manipulation by means of byte oriented instructions.

The IOAU controls all transfers of data between peripheral devices and main and extended storage, transfers being initiated by a CAU under program control. The IOAU includes two concurrent data transfer paths, one for main storage and one for extended storage. The IOAU consists of two sections: a control section that includes all logic associated with the transfer of functions, data and status words between main or extended storage and the subsystems; and a section containing from 8 to 24 I/O channels.

The system console provides the means for communicating with the executive system and consists of the following major components:

- CRT/keyboard and incremental printer.
- Real-time maintenance communication system which provides the capability to perform diagnostic maintenance from a remote site via a telephone line.
- Fault indicator, a visual indication of a fault condition in a major system component.

The system partitioning unit (SPU), which is optional to the system, permits offline maintenance of units, enables the operator to logically divide the system into two or three independent systems, and initiates a recovery sequence in event of failure. With the SPU, the operator can:

- Partition the system into two or three smaller systems.
- Isolate units and take them off-line without disrupting the rest of the system.
- Function as a system monitor by observing the status of major components.
- Perform initial load into the primary system.
- Allow automatic recovery procedures if an interrupt is not received.

Under software control, the SPU presents status information to the I/O access units (IOAU).

In the 1110 system main storage consists of directly addressable high-speed, nondestructive readout (NDRO) plated wire storage units. The basic 32K-word (36-bits) storage unit consists of four 8K modules, and may be expanded in 32K increments to a maximum storage capacity of 264K words. The minimum amount of storage required for operation by an 1110 system is 96K words.

A second level of directly addressable storage in the 1110 system is the extended storage system. The minimum extended-storage configuration consists of two units, each with 131K 36-bit words. Extended storage may be expanded to 1048K 36-bit words in 131K increments. Extended storage is connected to the system by multiple access interface (MAI) units which provide up to ten channels to each storage unit.

A programmable interval timer of 18 bits is provided within the system. The cycle time is 200 μsec and each time this period elapses the contents of the time if decremented by 1. When the clock reaches zero an interrupt is generated to the system.

FUNCTIONAL UNITS

Processor

The command/arithmetic unit (CAU) is a multitask instruction stacking processor. The basic configuration of the CAU and interface equipment is shown in Figure O-2.

The CAU is capable of controlling one or two IOAUs and is divided into five interacting components:

- *Address formation section.* The relative and absolute operand and absolute instruction addresses are formed in this section. During the operand address generation cycle, storage conflicts are checked, the base address is formed, program limits are checked, and index incrementation is performed.
- *General register stack (GRS).* The general register stack (GRS) consists of 112 integrated circuit control registers, program-addressable, each with a capacity of 36 bits. The GRS includes indexing registers (18), accumulators, repeat counters, a mask register, a real-time clock register, and temporary storage locations for the processor state register. The stack is divided into an odd/even structure to allow simultaneous referencing when double-precision 72-bitword instructions are used.
- *Conditional jump section.* The conditional jump section minimizes execution time through the CAU when a conditional jump instruction is encountered. This section tests whether the jump conditions are satisfied before control passes to the arithmetic section.
- *Store operation section.* The store operation section, a subdivision of the control section of the CAU, handles all writing into storage. This section performs operations necessary for full-word and partial-word transfers into storage.

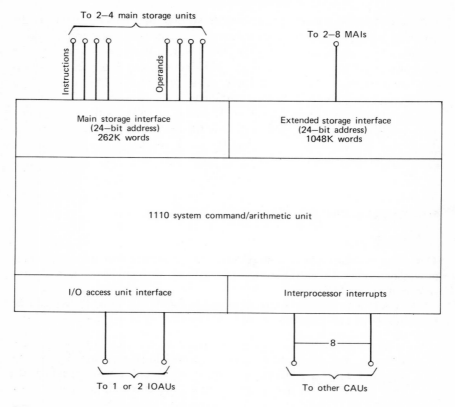

Figure 0-2 Command/arithmetic unit configuration.

- *Arithmetic section.* The manipulation of data (addition, sub-traction, multiplication, division, shifting) takes place in the arithmetic section of the CAU.

Each CAU within an 1110 system has the capability of executing 1.8 million instructions/sec and the effective basic instruction time is 300 nsec. The instruction repertoire includes partial-word or split-word transfers, split-word arithmetic, shifting, double precision fixed and floating point, load and store instructions, repeated search instructions, skip instructions, shift instructions, executive system control instructions, jump instructions, logical instructions, I/O instructions, byte instructions, byte/binary conversion instructions, and decimal arithmetic instructions.

Primary Storage

The 1110 system incorporates a two-level hierarchy of directly addressable, executable storage. Within the system, this two-level storage hierarchy is treated as a set of system components in the same manner as peripheral devices. The first level, main storage (MS), has nominal 320-nsec read and 520-nsec write cycles and is composed of NDRO plated wire storage modules and built-in multi-module access (MMA) units. The MS provides 8K-word modularity for simultaneous access and parity checking on addresses and data. Access to MS is provided, through the MMAs, for up to four CAUs and four IOAUs. MS is expendable in 32K increments up to a maximum of 262K words and MS is partitionable in 32K increments. Interleaved access is provided (odd-even addressing to two adjacent 8K modules) and access conflicts are resolved in 8K boundaries.

Each MS unit (32K-words) has its own power supplies, MMA, and maintenance panel. Each word is 36 data bits, two parity bits, and two spare bits. A 32K MS unit is capable of simultaneously servicing four requests, one per 8K module, while a fully expanded 65K MS unit can service up to eight simultaneous requests.

THE MMA unit is physically contained in the MS unit cabinet and is functionally located between the MS unit and the CAUs and IOAUs. The MMA furnishes eight (expandable to 16) priority-ordered paths to each of the MS modules. Should an access conflict occur among requestors, the MMA unit grants main storage access to the processor having the highest priority. Delays in honoring I/O transfers are minimized as the IOAUs are attached to the higher priority paths of the MMA.

The second level of directly addressable storage is called extended storage. This storage has a 131K-word modularity, and is expendable in 131K increments to a maximum of 1048K words. This storage has a read/write cycle of 1.5 μsec and parity checking is performed on addresses and data. Access to extended storage is through multiple access interfaces (MAI). The MAI performs the same function as the previously discussed MMAs and can interface with up to four CAUs and four IOAUs.

The featured characteristics of storage are as follows:

- Independently accessible modules.
- Continuous addressing structure.

To prevent inadvertent program reference to out of range storage addresses, the 1110 system includes a hardware storage protection feature. This function is performed by the storage limits register which is loaded by the executive system for the program currently in execution. These limits consists of both instruction and data boundaries.

Input/Output Control Module

The input/output access unit (IOAU) has exclusive control over all I/O operations. The basic IOAU section has eight channels and may be expanded to 24 channels. The IOAU has an aggregate transfer rate of 4 million 26-bit words/sec (24 million characters). Any channel can be operated in either the internally specified index (ISI) or externally specified index (ESI) mode. Data chaining is provided for operation in either the ESI or ISI mode to provide the IOAU with the capabilities for scatter/read, gather/write operations. External interrupt and monitor interrupt tabling in the ESI mode are provided with a table pointer for each channel.

The externally specified index (ESI) mode, in conjunction with data communications equipment, allows multiplexed remote communications devices to communicate with main storage over a single I/O channel on a self-controlled basis without disturbing the main program. Each such remote device communicates with its own area of main storage. Any I/O channel can be set to ESI mode by means of a switch and a patch card. Furthermore, by means of a patch card, an ESI channel can be set to operate in either half-word (18-bit) or quarter-word (9-bit) modes. Because an I/O channel can be used by many devices in ESI mode, data flow must be governed by an access control word (ACW) unique to the device currently in operation rather than to the channel as in ISI. These access control words are stored in storage at relative addresses assigned to the devices. As a device transfers data, it presents the address of its own access control word; thus, no complicated program monitoring is necessary to control data flow.

Mass Storage or Secondary Storage

The standard options for mass storage devices for the 1110 system are basically the same as for the 1108 system and are included within the 1108 system description.

Two disc subsystems are presented as options with the 1110 system. One disc offers a storage capacity up to 39.44 million 36-bit words with a data transfer rate of 69,444 words per second and an average access time of 60 msec. Each disk pack provides 5.0 million 36-bit words.

The other disc offers a storage capacity of up to 152 million 36-bit words with a data transfer rate of 138,888 words/sec and an average access time of 35 msec.

SOFTWARE EXECUTION FEATURES

Job Control

The supervisor is the UNIVAC 1110 executive system component that controls the sequencing, setup, and execution of all runs. It is designed to control the execution of a large number of programs without any interaction among them. The supervisor contains three levels of scheduling: coarse scheduling, dynamic allocation of storage space, and CAU dispatching. Runs entering the UNIVAC 1110 system are sorted into information files and these files are used by the supervisor for run scheduling and processing. Control statements for each run are retrieved and scanned by the control command interpreter in the supervisor to facilitate the selection of runs for setup by the coarse scheduler. The coarse scheduling of each run primarily depends on two factors: the priority of the run, and its facility requirements.

The dynamic allocator takes runs set up by the coarse scheduler and allots storage space according to the needs of the individual tasks of a run. Each run may be thought of as being made up of tasks, where a task is a single operation of a system processor or the execution of a user program. All tasks for a given run are processed serially but not necesarily consecutively; if there are several runs, the tasks of separate runs are interleaved.

When time-sharing of storage is appropriate, the dynamic allocator initiates storage swaps. This involves writing one program on drum storage and replacing it temporarily in storage with another program. Such action is taken only to provide reasonable response time to remote demand-processing terminals.

The CAU dispatching routine is a third level of scheduling; it selects among the various tasks currently occupying storage whenever it is appropriate to switch the commitment of one of the CAUs from one task to another. Under normal circumstances, a batch program is allowed to use a CAU either until it becomes interlocked against some event or until some higher priority program is freed of all of its interlocks.

Available facilities and their disposition are indicated to the system at system generation; thereafter, the executive system assigns these facilities, as needed and as available. The executive system maintains current inventory tables, that indicate what facilities are available for assignment, and which runs are using the currently unavailable facilities.

Operator communication with the system is through a display keyboard and CRT. The executive system displays information such as current system load and operator requests associated with I/O setup and I/O interlocks. Also, the operator can request information such as backlog status.

I/O Control

Same as that provided by EXEC 8 for the 1108 system.

Diagnostic Error Processing

Same as that provided for the 1108 system.

APPENDIX P

SPERRY RAND CORPORATION
UNIVAC AN/UYK-7

INTRODUCTION TO CONFIGURATION ORGANIZATION

The AN/UYK–7 computer is a ruggedized multiprocessor system designed for military applications. The system is designed to operate in a real-time environment with emphasis placed on packaging, reliability, ease of maintenance, and rapid removal/replacement of malfunctioning modules. The system is composed of functionally independent modules which slide into one or more AN/UYK–7 cabinets. The cabinet and module design permits rapid removal and replacement of plug-in modules.

The basic modules of the AN/UYK–7 system consist of central processors (CP), input/output controllers (IOC), input/output adapters (IOA), memory units, and power supply units (PSU). The functional relationship of these modules is shown in Figure P-1. A minimum system consists of one central processor, one I/O controller, one 4-channel I/O adapter, three memory modules of 16K words each, and one power supply in a single cabinet. Expansion from the minimum configuration to up to three central processors, four I/O controllers, four I/O adapters, and 256K of core is possible; however, each memory module has only 8 access paths to be shared as follows: two paths per central processor and one path per I/O output controller. Therefore, shared access to the total memory can be performed by a maximum of three processors and two I/O controllers or two central processors and four I/O output controllers. In a multiprocessor configuration each central processor has equal status and is capable of operating in either the task mode or interrupt mode. Interrupts are sent to all configured processors, except monitor interrupts which are sent only to

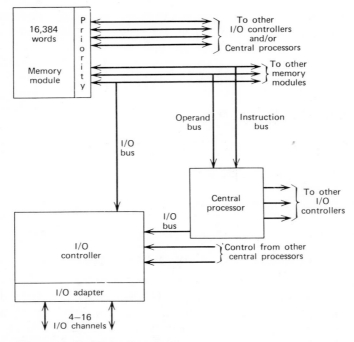

Figure P-1   AN/UYK-7 configuration.

those processors that allow monitor interrupts on the interrupting channel (processor-program controlled).

FUNCTIONAL UNITS

Processor

The central processor (CP) contains all the control, arithmetic, and timing circuitry required for processing alpha-numeric data and for executive functions. Each central processor can address up to 256K of memory via two busses: one for instructions and one for operands. With two or more memory modules, this permits overlapped instruction execution and access of the next instruction for each processor configured, ignoring memory access conflicts. In a two- or three-processor system, each processor may be connected to all memory modules and I/O controllers.

Central processors operate in two different modes or states—the interrupt state executes the executive-type functions, and the task state processes the application or worker programs. To facilitate the switching of modes, each processor contains two sets of seven index and eight base address registers, and two sets of eight addressable accumulators. This feature precludes the need for storing and restoring register resident data when leaving the task state and returning. Other control memory registers become functional for the interrupt state as assigned.

Hardware is provided for both fixed and floating-point operations using 8, 16, 32, or 64-bit operands. The instruction set consists of 130 basic whole and half-word instructions which include direct or indirect addressing, variable length character addressing, and a set of 18 privileged instructions. In addition, each processor is provided with a decrementing monitor clock which operates at 1024 counts/sec.

Each processor contains a 512-word assembly of magnetic core rope, nondestructive read-out memory (NDRO), containing the hardware interrupt analysis routine, two initial load or automatic recovery routines (bootstrap) and a diagnostic program. If desired, the routines in the NDRO memory may be other than those listed above, but the programs must be selected at the time of manufacture. The NDRO memory is separated from the total addressing continuum of main memory and the memory used (NDRO or main) depends upon the operating state and the operators panel switch positions. Hardware error interrupts, when enabled, force the processor into the hardware interrupt analysis routine for diagnosis and transfer to remedial action or stop. According to conditions causing the interrupt, an NDRO routine may exit to another routine or come to an orderly stop.

Eighty-two integrated-circuit random-access registers of appropriate size serve as control memory for each central processor. Access time for each stack varies according to the processor control and arithmetic section timing requirements. The contents of processor control memory are as follows:

	Task State	Interrupt State
Arithmetic accumulator registers	8	8
Index register	7	7
Base address registers	8	8
Breakpoint register	—	1
Active status register	—	1
Central processor monitor	—	1
Designator storage words	—	8
Initial condition words	—	8
Storage protection registers	—	8
Segment identification registers	—	8
Unassigned addressable register	—	1

A bit in the active status register determines whether the interrupt state or task state arithmetic and index register are set to be used. Although two sets of base address registers are provided, both sets are primarily addressable only in the interrupt state. The breakpoint register permits a comparison to be made between the contents of this register and the address and/or operand of each instruction executed, as designated by the control bits. A comparison match will cause a breakpoint interrupt or machine halt, if executed in the manual mode. The active status register (ASR) controls and indicates the status of various operations in a processor. The contents of the ASR provide central processor identification, the class of interrupt which has occurred, lower priority interrupt lockout masks, memory lockout enable/disable, task/interrupt state indicator, and base register, index, and arithmetic register set selection indicators. The designator storage words (DSW) and the initial condition words (ICW) are used by the processor in honoring interrupts.

Each processor is provided with a 20-bit program address register (PAR) within which 3 bits identify one of the eight base registers from the group with which the computer is operating and the lower 16 bits contain the relative address of the next instruction. In calculating an address, the instruction furnishes a displacement address that may be indexed by one of seven index registers to form a relative address. The final effective *operand* address is formed by adding the contents of a specified base address to this relative address. The final *instruction* address is formed by adding the contents of the base register defined by the 3 bits of the PAR to the relative address in the lower 16 bits in the PAR.

Worker programs may be prevented access to certain segments of main memory via the memory lockout feature. Any processor, in the interrupt state, can lock out from its own nonexecutive operating programs read and/or write operations in defined areas of any memory module. The lockout feature is disabled when the processor reverts to the interrupt state, and all memory locations become available to the executive program. Three groups of associated control memory registers govern memory lockout functions. For any block in memory, which may be any size up to 65K words, there are the following controls: a base register that holds the beginning address definition, an associated storage protection register (SPR) which defines the lockout function and the block size of displacement, and a segment identification register (SIR) which contains the relative address in main memory from which the lockout information is transferred. Memory protection applied to a segment of memory defined by a base register and its associated SPR governs the following operations in the task state:

1. Within the protected area.

    Prevent or allow reading operands.

    Prevent or allow storing operands.

    Prevent or allow executing instructions.

    Prevent or allow indirect addressing.

2. Outside the protected area:

    Prevent any operand references.

    Prevent executing instructions.

3. Prevent or allow the use of the Interrupt set of index or base registers for indirect addressing.

If memory protection integrity is to be maintained, each processor must be programmed in terms of the current status of the system, for a locked-out area for one processor can be utilized freely by another processor. In addition, an active I/O controller can communicate with a locked-out area defined by any processor.

Input and output transfers are controlled completely by the I/O controller module addressed by a central processor. I/O command chains are stored in a memory module accessible to the controller for execution. The central processor executes a privileged initiate I/O instruction which identifies the controller (one of four possible) and the address of the first command in the input/output program sequence. The addressed controller receives an absolute address on the memory-processor operand bus, which is also connected to the controller. Subsequent activity and details are directed by the program available to the controller.

The UYK–7 processes data from multiple sources in real-time, as events occur, or as scheduled. Interrupts may originate at some remote external device, or they may originate within the computer. Since more than one may occur at the same time, the processor has a priority network with decision-making qualities so that it can select the program routine for solving the problem requiring the most urgent attention. Under program control, the other interrupts may be honored in turn according to the next-highest priority, or they may be ignored. The interrupts in the UYK–7 are processed by an executive-type program when the central processor is in the Interrupt State. There are four classes of interrupts divided as follows, in order of highest priority:

Class I are fault and hardware interrupts, including the power tolerance interrupt which is never disabled.

Class II are program faults and error interrupts.

Class III are input and output program faults, program-imposed monitors on input and output transfers and the IOC monitor clock interrupt:

Class IV is a program-initiated entrance into the interrupt state, requesting executive service.

When an interrupt is honored in any class, entrance into the interrupt state disables all others of that class and also those classes having lower priority. Interrupt codes are generated by both IOC and the processor. Code words associated with a processor-detected interrupt are formed in the central processor, and those associated with an IOC-detected interrupt are formed in the central processor, and those associated with an IOC-detected interrupt are formed in the IOC. The IOC generates an 8-bit interrupt code for each interrupt request, the processor honoring the interrupt then assigns an additional 2-bit code that identifies the interrupting IOC.

Whenever an IOC generates a class I or class III illegal instruction, monitor clock, or central processor interrupt, it sends an interrupt request to all processors. Monitor interrupt (class III) requests are sent to the central processors that allow monitor interrupts on the interrupting channel (processor-program controlled). The processor which first responds to the interrupt request is sent the interrupt code having the highest priority within the initiating class presently not locked out. Because this could be other than the interrupt that generated the request, circuits in the IOC hold queued interrupts, pending timely response by a processor. A processor, responding to an IOC interrupt request that has already been acknowledged by another processor, will be sent a NO OPERATION signal. It then continues its operation without changing state.

When honoring an interrupt, the processor will store in the designator storage word (DSW) location the current contents of the program address register, the active status register, and the interrupt status code. The current active status register will be changed to reflect the new conditions. After the initialization process is completed, the program address is reset from the class-associated initial condition word in control memory to the address of the interrupt subroutine. The contents of the control memory ICW locations are initially set by the executive system. The interrupt routine is executed and terminated by executing the interrupt return instruction. Control is returned to the interrupted state by restoring from control memory the active status register and the program address register to the values existing at the moment of interrupt.

Interrupts occurring synchronously with central processor operations are not held pending if they are locked out. These include all class II interrupts except CP monitor clock and interprocessor interrupt; and all in class I, except IOC-memory resume and intercomputer time-out. All others, occurring asychronously with central processor operations, are held pending so the processor can detect them during an instruction priority scan sequence. An interrupt that has not been locked out may interrupt an operating program even if the program is itself processing an interrupt. Interrupts may therefore be cascaded from one class to another or within a class, by clearing the appropriate lockout designator in the active status register.

Of special interest for reliability and recovery/restart is the power tolerance interrupt. The power supply contains a feature that protects memory from transferring what may be defective data during primary power interruptions. However, if external sources are attempting data transfers to memory during this protected time, these data may be lost at the input interface. Conditions of both complete power failure, and of power decrease-and-recovery, are resolved without operator intervention if desired. An interrupt is generated when power falls below a tolerable level. At this time, the computer can still operate for $250 \mu sec$ on residual power stored in the power supply. The power tolerance interrupt routine contains a manual jump instruction to transfer to the restart routine, following the storing of volatile register data. Design characteristics of this specific jump instruction prevent its execution at below-voltage-tolerance level. Depending upon the length and severity of the power problem, two alternatives exist:

1. If power returns to normal before the failure level is readied, the jump is executed and an orderly restart is affected.

2. If the power falls to the failure level, an automatic computer MASTER CLEAR signal is generated by the power supply. Return to normal power, after the computer is cleared will cause automatic start from the last address in NDRO memory.

PROCESSOR SUMMARY

The following processor capabilities are of interest:

- Nondestructive Read Out memory of 512 words for initial load programs, fault analysis and recovery, and hardware diagnostic program.
- Eighty-two integrated-circuit random-access register for central processor control memory, including two sets of seven index and eight base registers, and two sets of eight addressable arithmetic accumulators.
- Addressing capability up to 256K ($K = 1024_{10}$) words of main memory via direct, indirect, index, or base-plus-displacement modes.
- Overlapped instruction execution when two or more memory modules are present.

Primary Storage

Main memory of the AN/UYK-7 is composed of modules (banks) of random access, coincident current, destructive-read-out magnetic core storage with a read-restore cycle of 1.5 μsec. Each memory module contains four 4K memory stocks, a power converter, address translation, and timing and control circuitry. A memory unit is interchangeable with any other memory unit and has a capacity of 16K 32-bit words.

Communication between a central processor, memory, and an I/O controller is via a bussed communication system consisting of three bussed channels: instruction, operand, and input/output. Each central processor interfaces with the memory units via both instruction and operand data busses and with an I/O controller via an operand data bus. Each I/O controller communicates with the memory units via an I/O bus. Eight interfacing paths (one bus and one port per path), allowing access to memory, are provided in a 16K-word module for communication with other modules. The memory bus serves as a bidirectional data path and address path between the requestor and memory. Control lines for both the requestor and memory are included in the memory bus. There are 32 data lines and 20 control lines per channel; however, only nine of the 20 control lines are used for any one memory unit. Each memory unit is capable of being addressed by any combination of central processors and I/O controllers with the restriction that the total combined number of two accesses per processor and one access per I/O controller does not exceed eight memory accesses to any one memory unit. Multiple requests addressed to a memory module at any time are retained and honored in a priority order by memory module priority circuits. The order of priority is fixed at the time the interconnecting bus harness is manufactured.

The ready and resume logic of the memory module permits asynchronous operation with the processors and I/O controllers. Each bus that connects a memory port to the I/O controller or central processor carries the service request and associated operand, or instuction address and the requested operands or instructions. For a specific memory reference the central processor or I/O controller presents a request signal and an address to memory on the interface bus. The memory module identified by the user, responds to the request (read, write, or read-and-write) when in the ready state and performs the function. Operands or instructions thus transferred are carried on the same bus as the respective addresses and requests. Sequencing and traffic direction on all busses connected to a memory module are controlled by the timing circuitry, the ready-resume logic, and the priority network. When the module is not in the ready state at a particular port, any request on that port is held in the priority network for its ordered turn. This asynchronous operating philosophy permits as many read, write, or read-and-write references to progress at any instant as there are memory modules in the system.

All memory modules with contiguous addressing contain addresses 00000–37777_8. Address translators interpret a 14-bit portion of an 18-bit address furnished by the requester to select a word within an addressed module. Each such module responds to requests when the value on the selection line corresponds to the number assigned to that module in the system. The memory system can be modified, an option, for interleaved addressing by module pairs (32K words of memory). In this configuration, the even-numbered addresses in the range 00000–77776_8 are accepted and translated by the even-numbered module of the pair, and the odd-numbered addresses in the range 00001–77777_8 are accepted and translated by the odd-numbered module of the pair.

Input/Output Controller (IOC)

The I/O controller of the AN/UYK-7 contains the necessary control and timing circuitry to conduct I/O transfers of data, external commands, and external interrupts between accessible memory modules and the external devices in 4, 8, 12, or 16 full-duplex channels and to update both the real-time clock register and an activated monitor clock register. Each I/O controller can perform direct-access data transfers to and from a maximum of 16 memory modules, under the control of one, two, and three central processors. Integrated-circuit control memory is provided within each I/O controller for buffer control words, command address pointers, function control fields, and clock storage. Control memory consists of 64 words of 56 bits each—one word is provided for each channel for each of the following operations: input data, output data, external function, and external interrupt.

Input/output controller functions are governed by a chain of commands (I/O programs) initiated by one or more controlling central processors. I/O programs define buffer area, channel numbers, and functions related to word or byte size, imposed monitors, and transfer types. Chains are formed, as required, from the 15 instructions in the IOC repertoire. The sequencing through chains and the transfers of information (data, interrupt codes, and commands to external devices) are controlled by the various fields in associated control words in the IOC control memory. These words are selected and loaded according to the commands executed by the I/O controller. Buffer control words define all operations for transferring information on an active channel, and when this process is finished, point to the address of the next instruction in the command chain.

Each channel, defined by changeable internal wiring, can communicate in the following modes: normal buffer, externally specified index (ESI), externally specified address (ESA), and intercomputer (IC). In the normal mode, an I/O adapter channel transfers or receives I/O data of 32 bits/word and performs the operations on the data as specified by the program. The transfer, receipt, and operation of data words is accomplished with the use of the normal control signals. Externally specified index (ESI) uses the lower 16 bits of the data on the input data lines for the address in main memory that contains the buffer control word. Bits 0–17 of the buffer control word contain the starting address of the data to be transferred and bits 18–28 of the buffer control word contains the final address of the buffer. The externally specified addressing mode (ESA) provides peripheral devices with a means of specifying an absolute memory location for storage or retrieval of data on a word-by-word basis. An active channel is required to respond to an externally specified addressing request. The intercomputer operation of an I/O adapter channel is an I/O-adapter-to-I/O-adapter communication. The computer does not wait for an acknowledge signal from the receiving computer; instead the source computer sets the data ready signal and sets the output data onto the output data lines at the same time. When a resume signal is received by the source computer the data ready and data are removed from the output lines and additional data are set onto the output lines or intercomputer operation is terminated. If the receiving computer had not received the data and returned a resume signal within the prescribed time (governed by the intercomputer time-out selection) a class I interrupt would have been generated. The mode select module contained in the I/O controller chassis contains the logic for determining intercomputer period of time-out, type of interface for each channel (normal, ESI, ESA, or IC), and governs the priority of each channel. Prior to manufacture of the mode select module, the time-out period must be selected and the type of interface for each channel must be selected.

Operations requested of the IOC are honored and executed according to priorities arranged in two groups. Buffered requests are those received on the I/O channels; nonbuffered requests are initiated by the processor, or via controls within the IOC such as the real-time clock and channel associated command chain. If requests from both groups exist at the same time, the IOC alternates execution between groups. After a request has been honored, the request priority sequence is reinitiated at its highest state.

A 16-bit monitor clock register in the IOC may be activated by loading it with a positive value. When it is activated, the count decreases at the rate of the clock employed (internal or external). As the count passes through zero, a class III IOC monitor clock interrupt is generated in an attempt to interrupt a central processor connected to the IOC. A zero value loaded into the monitor clock resister will generate a class III IOC-CP interrupt. Any negative value loaded will disable the monitor clock function. A 32-bit real-time clock register counts up, at a rate of 1024 counts/sec when the internal oscillator is used and at an external clock rate (up to 100kHz) when the external clock is implemented.

The interface adapter module associated with each IOC contains circuitry for 4, 8, 12, or 16 I/O channels. This interface comprises output registers, line drivers, input amplifiers, and acknowledge timing. The number and characteristics of channels are provided in groups of four input and four output. Incoming data or control lines terminate in input amplifiers and each outgoing control line is driven by one line driver. However, the four output channels in each group share the 32 data line drivers, but only one of these channels receives the associated control signal during the transfer. A serial interface is offered as an option on any group of four channels, for the normal and intercomputer communication modes. control line signals employed in parallel channels are replaced by coded control frames that precede the word transfer on serial channels. All control bits transmitted are generated by the serial interface hardware.

SYSTEM SOFTWARE

The operating system provided with the AN/UYK-7 is called the COMMON CONTROL PROGRAM and consists of four real-time functional components and one non-real-time component. The five software component—common control module, common peripheral module, debug module, and the ultility package—supply the control needed for multi-processing and multiprogramming.

The common control module's major functions are initialization, scheduling, I/O initialization, message handling, and interrupt handling. All modules, except the common control module and the user's error recovery routine, shall execute in the computer's task state. The common control module provides the basis for real-time operation via scheduling of the resources of the central processor, or processors. In addition, the common control module provides the capability for user intercommunications and functions which are privileged to an executive program by AN/UYK-7 central processor design. The common control module provides the applications program with distinct means of responding to external events and implementing the execution of time-critical, time-dependent, and nonreal time functions. These general purpose scheduling characteristics are controlled by the application program.

The common control module acknowledges scheduling requests based on a prescribed set of rules called the scheduling algorithm. The data designs and indexing structure of the common control module provide the facilities to schedule a maximum of 256 individual modules. A module may have one each of the following types of entrances: priority, message, periodic, deferred, I/O interrupt, and demand. Of these 256 modules, 63 modules may be registered simultaneously for a priority entrance. The system designer shall specify a time-out value for each entrance type. These time-out values are intended as a fail-soft feature to allow the common control module to regain processor control under abnormal conditions. The common control module does not allow a processor to enter any one module through the priority, message, periodic, or deferred entrances, if another processor is already executing in the module having entered through one of these entrances. However, the I/O interrupt and the demand entrances are not protected from reentrance.

All modules are provided with a name, priority number, and periodic time interval under the guidance of the system designer. The highest level of scheduling is provided for priority entrances. A module's priority number specifies which module shall be given preference if two or more modules are scheduled for priority entrance simultaneously. Every module must provide a message processor entrance that is capable of accepting at least the control messages. The periodic time interval, required by each module, establishes the desired time lapse between successive entries into the periodic entrance. Automatic time-slice scheduling is provided to all deferred entrance processors, with the common time slice defined by the system designer. The demand entrance is designed primarily for those functions that require very precise timing because of the overhead required to execute interrupt entrances. At request for demand servicing, the value of a real-time clock is specified and the demand entrance is initiated by an interrupt from a countdown of that clock.

All modules must register their I/O requirements with the common control module including the IOC number(s), channel number(s), and mode designation, that is, input only, output only, or both input and output. In addition, the module must specify the action to be taken for an input data monitor interrupt and external interrupt monitor interrupt when responsible for output. Because of the real-time aspect of the I/O interrupt entrance and the associated overhead, this entrance should be restricted to initiating functions that cannot be delayed until the module gains a priority entrance. The I/O interrupt entrance must be designed to allow two or more central processor units to execute simultaneously in the I/O interrupt entrance processor.

The common control module provides the software required for elements of the application program to indirectly communicate via messages. In addition, this module provides the implementation of memory protection, the centralized interrupt handling, and the execution of privileged instructions such as initiation of input/output functions. Program protection features are implemented making particular use of the privilege and memory lockout properties of the computer.

The common peripheral module provides a general purpose interface between the applications program(s), an operator, and the standard peripheral devices: magnetic tape read/record, paper tape reader/punch, keyboard/printer, character display/screen. The common peripheral module provides data recording and retrieval capabilities and permits the operator to monitor and control software activities. These functions can be requested by an application program via an intermodule message or by an operator request from a keyboard or punched paper tape. This module also provides functions for data format translations and conversions, magnetic tape management, CRT display management, and general error control and recovery.

The common system module provides a centralized location for the system defined error routines and allows the common program to provide functional tools which facilitate the maintenance of data placed in the common system module. The common program includes provisions for a common system data updating function, utilizing intermodule messages to insert data or update the common system data stores and receive control upon the completion of the change.

The Debug module provides the realtime tools used in program debugging, system testing and integration, and for general program maintenance. The Debug module provides on-line access to the memory or arithmetic registers for either immediate or realtime events. In addition, the Debug module provides the capabilities for the extraction of point-to-point and duty cycle timing information.

The utility package provides manual functions for the use and control of the AN/UYK-7 and the standard peripheral devices. It provides the capability to load and dump computer memory and non-real-time program execution for manual debugging. There is no interface between the utility package and the common control module.

APPENDIX Q
XEROX DATA SYSTEMS
SIGMA 9 COMPUTER SYSTEM

INTRODUCTION TO SYSTEM ORGANIZATION

The SIGMA 9 computer system is a high-speed general-purpose digital computer system. A basic system includes a CPU, a main memory subsystem, and an independent I/O subsystem with each major system element performing asynchronously with respect to other elements (Figure Q-1).

The SIGMA 9 is designed to function as a shared-memory multi-processor system. A total system can contain up to four CPUs and up to 11 I/O processors (the sum of both types of processors is restricted by the maximum memory port limitation of 12). All processors in the SIGMA 9 system address memory uniformly.

A memory map provides for dynamic program relocation into noncontiguous segments of memory. When the memory map is in effect, any program may be broken into 512 word pages and distributed throughout memory in whatever pages of space are available.

The main memory of the SIGMA 9 is expandable from a minimum of 131K words (32-bits plus parity) to a maximum of 524,288 words. The basic increment of expansion is 32,786 words. The SIGMA 9 core memory has a cycle time of 900 nsec.

In the SIGMA 9 system I/O operations are primarily under the control of one or more I/O processors (IOP). The IOPs require only an initializing sequence from the CPU; once initiated, each IOP performs independently of the CPU and without further intervention.

Two real-time clocks are provided as standard equipment with the system and two more can be added as an option. The clocks provide information such as elapsed time, time of day and each can have separate time bases and relative time priority.

The SIGMA 9 priority interrupt system is designed as a hierarchial structure. Up to 224 levels of interrupt are available with each level having a unique address in core, and a unique priority.

CONFIGURATION COMPONENTS

Processor

Basically, a SIGMA 9 CPU consists of a fast memory and an arithmetic and control unit. The CPU performs arithmetic and logical operations; sequences and monitors instruction execution; and controls the exchange of

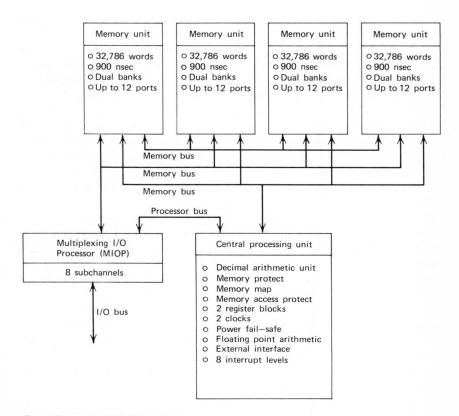

Figure Q-1   Basic SIGMA 9 system.

information between core memory and other parts of the system. The CPU provides general-purpose registers which can be used for a variety of purposes: as accumulators, index registers, or temporary registers. A CPU can contain up to 64 of these 32-bit registers, arranged in blocks of 16.

The CPU has three high-speed IC memories for storage of a memory map, memory access protection codes associated with the memory map, and memory write-protection codes.

The memory map feature provides for dynamic program relocation into noncontiguous segments of memory. When memory map is in effect, any program may be broken into 512-word pages and distributed throughout memory in whatever pages of space are available. Thus the memory map transforms virtual addresses, as seen by the individual program, into actual addresses, as seen by the memory system.

A CPU can operate in either a master, slave, or master-protected mode. The mode of operation is controlled by the setting of three bits in a control word. In the master mode, the CPU can perform all of its control functions and can modify any part of the system. The only restrictions placed upon CPU operation in this mode is that imposed by the memory write locks. The slave mode of operation is the problem-solving mode of the CPU. In this mode, access protection codes apply to the slave mode program if mapping is in effect, and all privileged operations are prohibited. Privileged operations are those related to I/O and to changes in the basic control state of the computer. The master-protected mode of operation is a modification of the master mode designed to provide additional protection for programs that operate in the master mode. The master-protected mode can only occur when the CPU is operating in the master mode with the memory map in effect.

In a multiprocessor configuration each CPU has the capability to gain exclusive control of a system resource (region of memory, peripheral device, and software process) through a special instruction which interlocks the resource until released. Due to the fact that all processors address memory uniformly, it is necessary that each CPU have a private area of memory. This private memory is used for information that is unique to each CPU such as: trap and interrupt locations and I/O communication locations. Private memory consists of 1024 words for each CPU. Faulty units can be isolated from the total system by selectively disabling it manually from the system busses.

A control function is provided with a multiprocessor configuration which provides three basic features:

1. Control of external I/O bus for controlling system maintenance and special purpose units.

2. Central control of system partitioning.

3. Interprocessor interrupt connection, allowing one processor to directly signal another processor that an action is to be taken.

Any CPU has the capability to direct I/O actions to any I/O processor; however, the end-action sequence of the I/O process is directed at one of the possible four CPUs. This means that I/O end-action tasks are dedicated to one CPU. The reason this is done is to avoid I/O conflict resolution problems.

The instruction set of the SIGMA 9 consists of over 100 major instructions. These instructions include load and store instructions with information fields of byte (8-bit), half-word, word, and double word lengths; analyze/interpret instructions; fixed-point arithmetic instructions using halfword, word, or double word fields; comparison instructions; conversion instructions; shift instructions; logical instructions; floating-point arithmetic instructions; decimal instructions; byte-string instructions; pushdown instructions; execute/branch instructions; call instructions; control instructions; and I/O instructions. Instruction times range from 730 nsec for a load instruction to 38 μsecs for a decimal multiply.

Primary Storage

The minimum operational memory of a SIGMA 9 is 131,172 words. This can be expanded up to 524,288 words in increments of 32K words. Memory is divided into banks (16K words), which are the smallest section of memory that can be independently accessed by a processor. Two banks of 16K words each, sharing common port logic, are called a memory unit. This provides for two-way address interleaving between 16K banks within a unit and four-way interleaving between the four 16K banks of two units. In two-way interleaving, even addresses are assigned to one bank and odd addresses to the other; in four-way interleaving, the assignment of every fourth address to its respective bank occurs between two adjacent units.

Memories consist of 33-bit words (four 8-bit bytes plus a parity bit) and all memory is directly addressable by both the CPUs and IOPs. The interchange of data between memory and the processors is asynchronous. The memory presently has a cycle time of 900 nsec providing each memory bank (16K) with the capability to process over 35 million bits/sec. Asynchronous operation is used within the SIGMA 9 system in which the individual functional elements operate on a proceed or continue-when-ready basis. This asynchronous memory design allows a memory cycle to be initiated at any time, yielding a maximum rate of over 1,110,000 Hz in each memory bank. Each core memory in a SIGMA 9 system contains two memory ports (expandable to 12) as standard, each port capable of connection to a separate memory bus. Since a memory module services only one requesting unit (CPU or IOP) during a single read/write cycle, one port has priority over the other in the event of simultaneous read/write requests; otherwise, the access requests are serviced on a first-come, first-serve basis. Parity is checked on all data and addresses communicated in either direction on busses between memory units and processors.

There are two methods available for controlling the use of main memory by a program; they are the memory map and the memory lock. In the memory map mode, the CPU performs a test to determine whether there are any inhibitions on using the virtual address by a slave or master-protected mode program. The four types of access protection are as follows:

- A slave or master-protected program can write into, read from, or access instructions from this page of virtual addresses.
- A slave or master-protected program cannot write into, but can read from or access instructions from this page of virtual addresses.
- A slave or master-protected program cannot write into or access instructions from, but can read from this page of virtual instructions.
- A slave or master-protected program is denied any access to this page of virtual addresses.

The memory lock mode is provided by a lock and key technique. A 2-bit write protect lock is provided for each 512-word page of the first 128K words of actual memory addresses. The write protect locks can only be changed by executing a priviledge instruction. The keys and locks control access for writing according to the following rules:

- A lock value of 00 means that the corresponding memory page is "unlocked;" write access to that page is permitted independent of the key value.
- A key value of 00 is a "skeleton" key that will open any lock; thus write access to any memory page is permitted independent of its lock value.
- A lock value other then 00 for a memory page permits write access to that page only if the key value is identical to the lock value.

Thus a program can write into a given memory page if the lock value is 00, if the key value is 00, or if the key value matches the lock value.

Input/Output Control Module

Input/output operations are primarily under the control of one or more IOPs. The IOP requires only an initialization sequence from the CPU; it then performs independently of the CPU.

Up to 11 IOPs can be incorporated into a SIGMA 9 system. These may be multiplexor IOPs (MIOPs), for use with standard-speed peripherals including medium-speed RADs; high-speed RAD IOPs (HSRIOPs), for use with high-speed RAD storage units; or special-purpose units. Interfaces between the CPU, core memories, and I/O units are generalized so that no redesign of existing interfaces is necessary to add new types of IOPs to the system.

The MIOP permits slow-to-moderately high-speed data rates to be handled, on a time-multiplexed basis, on two channels. The MIOP can service up to 32 subchannels with eight subchannels used in the basic configuration. The MIOP includes its own memory, registers, and arithmetic elements. A "move" option is available within the MIOP which provides the system with the capability to move large blocks of data from one area of memory to another area without assistance from the CPU once the move is started. Words are moved at the rate of 500,000 words/sec.

The I/O structure of the SIGMA 9 system provides for both command chaining (making possible multiple-record operations) and data chaining (making possible scatter-read and gather-write operations) without intervening CPU control.

Mass Storage or Secondary Storage

Mass storage for the SIGMA 9 system consists of rapid-access data (RAD) files providing storage capacities from 750K to 25 million bytes/sec with an average access time of 17 msecs; and up to four removable disk files, each providing a transfer rate of 312,500 bytes/sec with storage capacity ranging from 24 million to 49 million bytes per unit with an average access time of 87.5 msecs.

SYSTEM SOFTWARE

Job Control

The software systems for the SIGMA 9 system are designed as Xerox Operating System (XOS) and Universal Time-sharing System (UTS). Both systems support real-time processes concurrently with other modes of operation. XOS recognizes three major job classes: parallel jobs, production jobs, and serial jobs. Parallel jobs are cataloged jobs, each consisting of only one job step and are initiated by the operator from his console. The job scheduler in XOS activates jobs in a parallel job waiting queue on the basis of their respective priorities and resource needs. Jobs in the production job class normally contain several job steps. To allow for overlapping of processing for these job steps, the production job class is subdivided into five subclasses each having a relative priority. At any given time the user may have five production jobs in memory simultaneously. The serial job class contains only one class and one queue of waiting jobs. Jobs of the serial type are usually long-running batch jobs and only one serial job at a time is contained in memory.

In support of multiprogramming, the XOS can provide control of the following jobs in memory:

- Any number of parallel class jobs.
- Up to five production class jobs.
- One serial class job.

Symbionts are available for use by members of any of the job classes.

A job scheduler selects the jobs to be activated based upon the job class, availability of resources needed by a job, and the relative priority of the job (for serial jobs). The parallel job class has the highest priority, and, therefore, the scheduler first looks at the parallel job queue, then the production job queues, and finally the serial job queue.

Before the execution of any job, the scheduler conducts an inventory of resources to determine if the job can be activated; if it cannot, it is placed in a wait state. During operation it is possible for a user program to request/release pages of memory.

Through the operator console an operator can request the status of a job, the initiation of a parallel class job and the locking out or restoring of a failed peripheral device.

The system provides for memory parity error detection and recovery and automatic system recovery or restart.

I/O Control

The I/O supervisor services all requests for I/O operations. It initiates all I/O operations, recovers from errors, and keeps the system informed as to what user's I/O has completed. The I/O supervisor optimizes data flow through the peripherals using various techniques dependent upon the peripheral (e.g., taking into account the position of the fixed head disk, I/O requests are chained together in the order of their initial sector address and transfer length; optimizing arm movement for the movable arm disk, two waiting queues are maintained for each disk with requests placed in either queue according to the cylinder address and according to the queue then active).

The UTS supports up to 128 concurrent on-line time-sharing users, while performing local and remote batch well as real-time operations at the same time. This system allows users to initiate and access the on-line services via a variety of character-oriented communications systems.

The system provides for file creation, interrogation, modification, and deletion in a variety of user-oriented formats on a variety of secondary storage media. The formats include sequential, indexed sequential, direct access, and partitioned files. The media include magnetic tape, RAD, and removeable disk storage. Both standard labels are handled for both tape and disk. The user specifies the device, file, and operation, and the system proceeds on a concurrent basis, using buffering techniques for information transfer.

Diagnostic Error Processing

To isolate errors and failures caused by either the hardware or the software, the system provides such facilities as a watchdog timer (determines if a device does not respond in a specified time), power fail-safe interrupt, memory parity error detection and recovery, and an error reporting log.

The system provides for automatic system recovery or restart, snapshots of failed system for subsequent diagnosis, and diagnostic peripheral exercisers. Checkpoint capability is provided for displacing and restarting programs.

INDEX